Felt Making Wor

With
Jenny Barnett

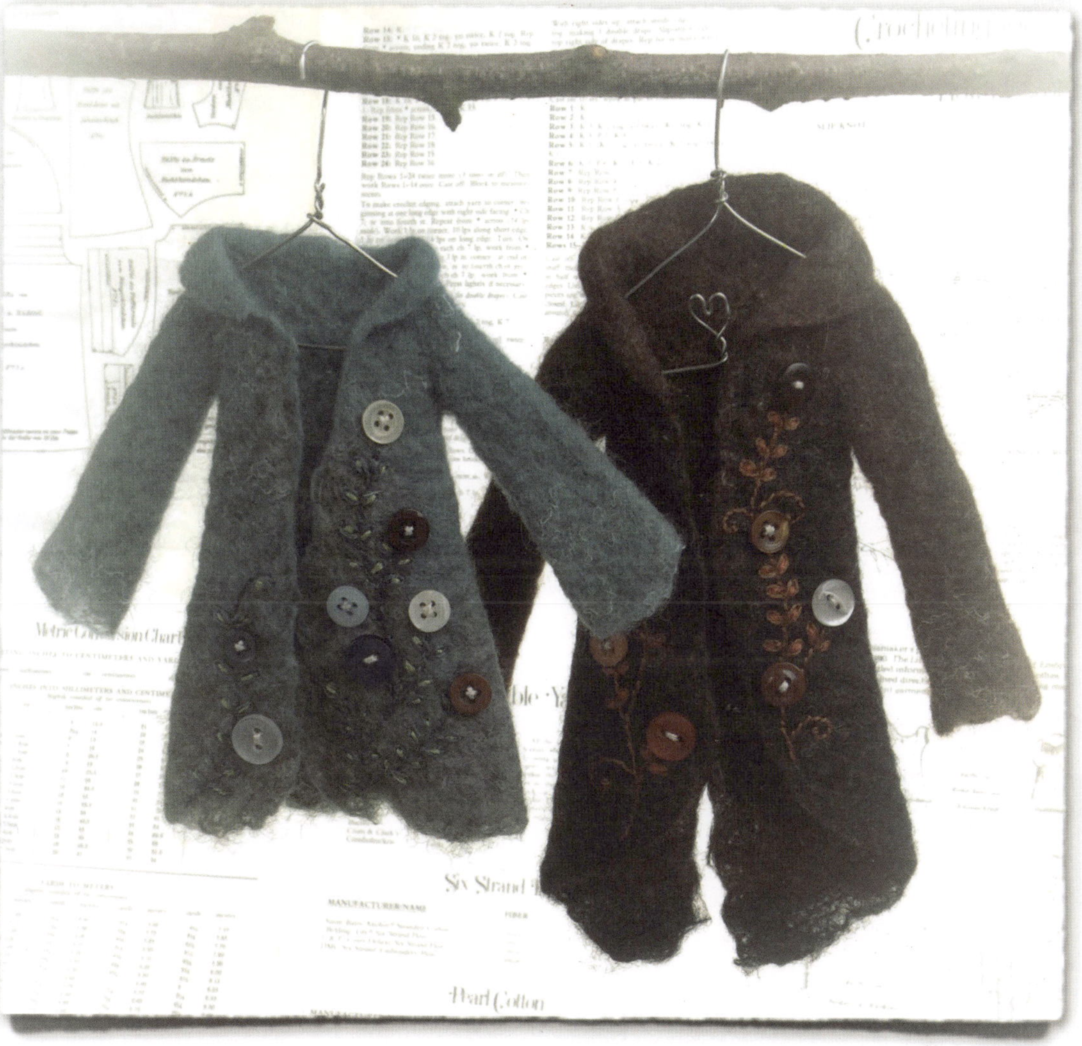

Wet felting techniques, patterns and inspiration to create a collection of miniature handmade felt treasures.

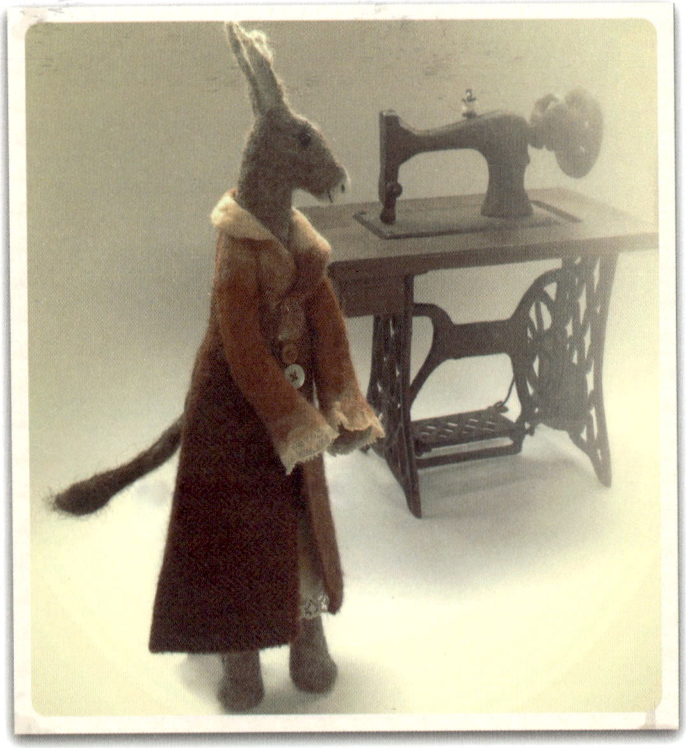

This book is a guide on wet felting. The items described are not recommended as toys.

First published in Great Britain in 2017 by Jenny Barnett
Printed in the United Kingdom by Design 2 Print Ltd

Design and text,
Illustration and photography
Jenny Barnett

Foreword

Carpe Cervisia

Foreword by Jenny's husband

It's been two years in the making but Jenny has somehow found the time to write yet another book on felty stuff, and apparently its absolutely necessary that I write yet another foreword.
Why she has picked on me again I really don't know, felt in all its glorious forms has practically reduced me to a mere husk of the almost adonis~like Fred Dibnah figure I used to be.
I know that there are many other men who too are suffering the same woolly injustices as myself. It is to you brave comrades that I now reach out as I offer some valuable tips on surviving with a woman who has developed a serious wool/fleece/soapy water/bubble wrap/soggy wool addiction.
Recognising the early symptoms of your loved one's felting obsession is the first step towards surviving woolly armageddon.

1.Does every room in your home smell of damp wool?
2.Do elvenesque gowns and dresses, along with miniature felt boots appear magically overnight on your kitchen table?
3.Does your better half secretly secrete enormous quantities of raw fleece about the home?
4.Do loved ones become sullen or irrational and threaten you with divorce, decapitation and/or castration when quizzed about bunting?
5.Do you have a copy of this book or any other book by Jenny Barnett in your home?

If the answer is yes to any of the above then without hesitation visit our self help facebook page **@Men who admire Fred Dibnah and like beer** for immediate advice and counselling.

K.R.Barnett

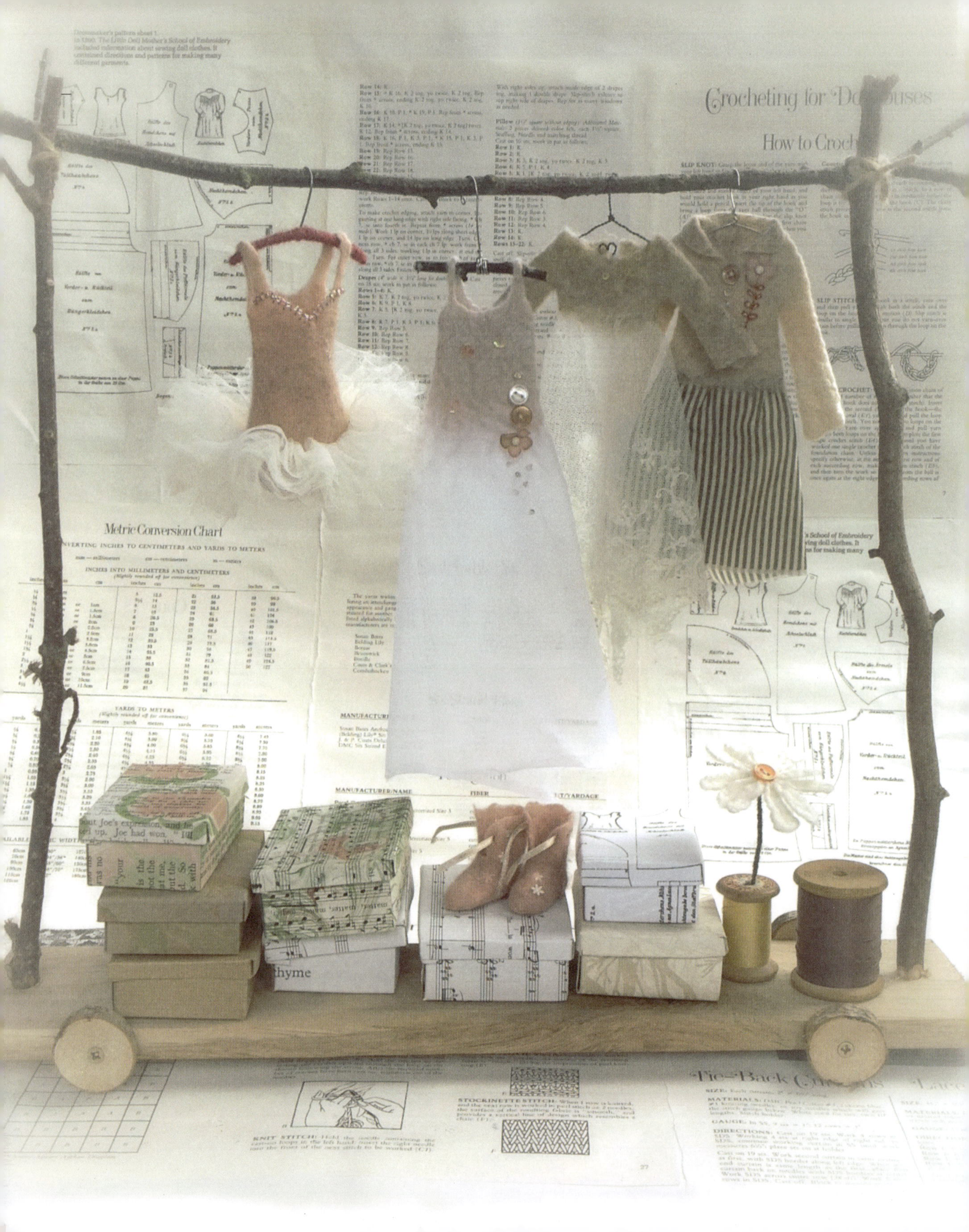

Contents

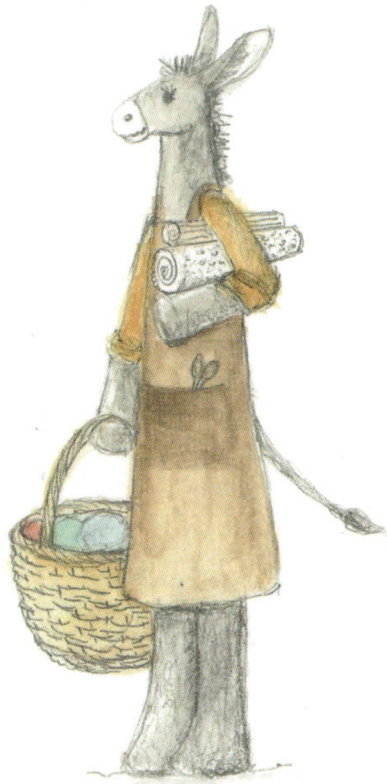

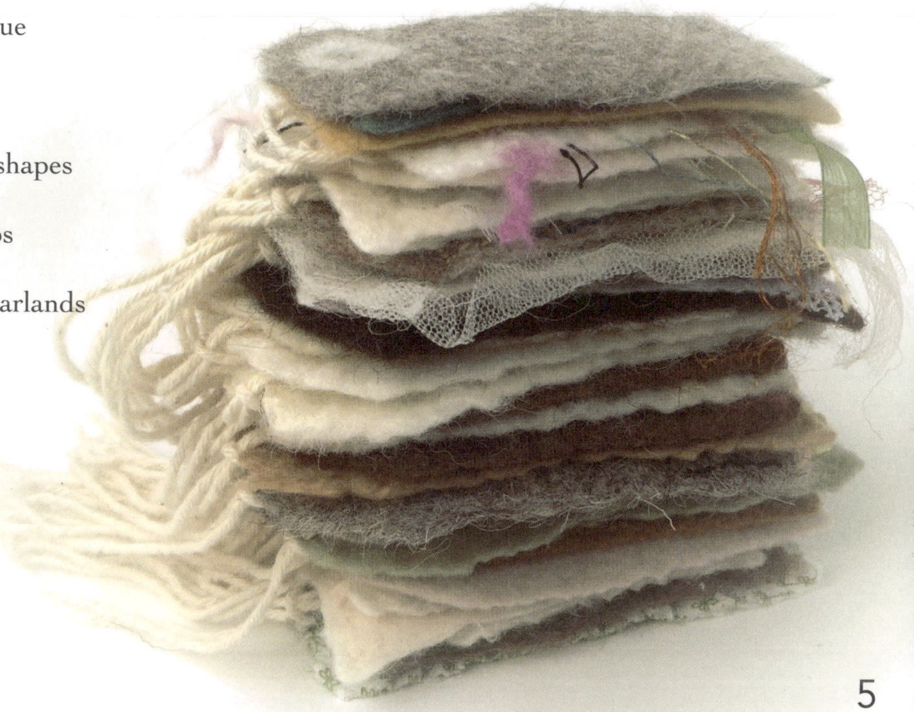

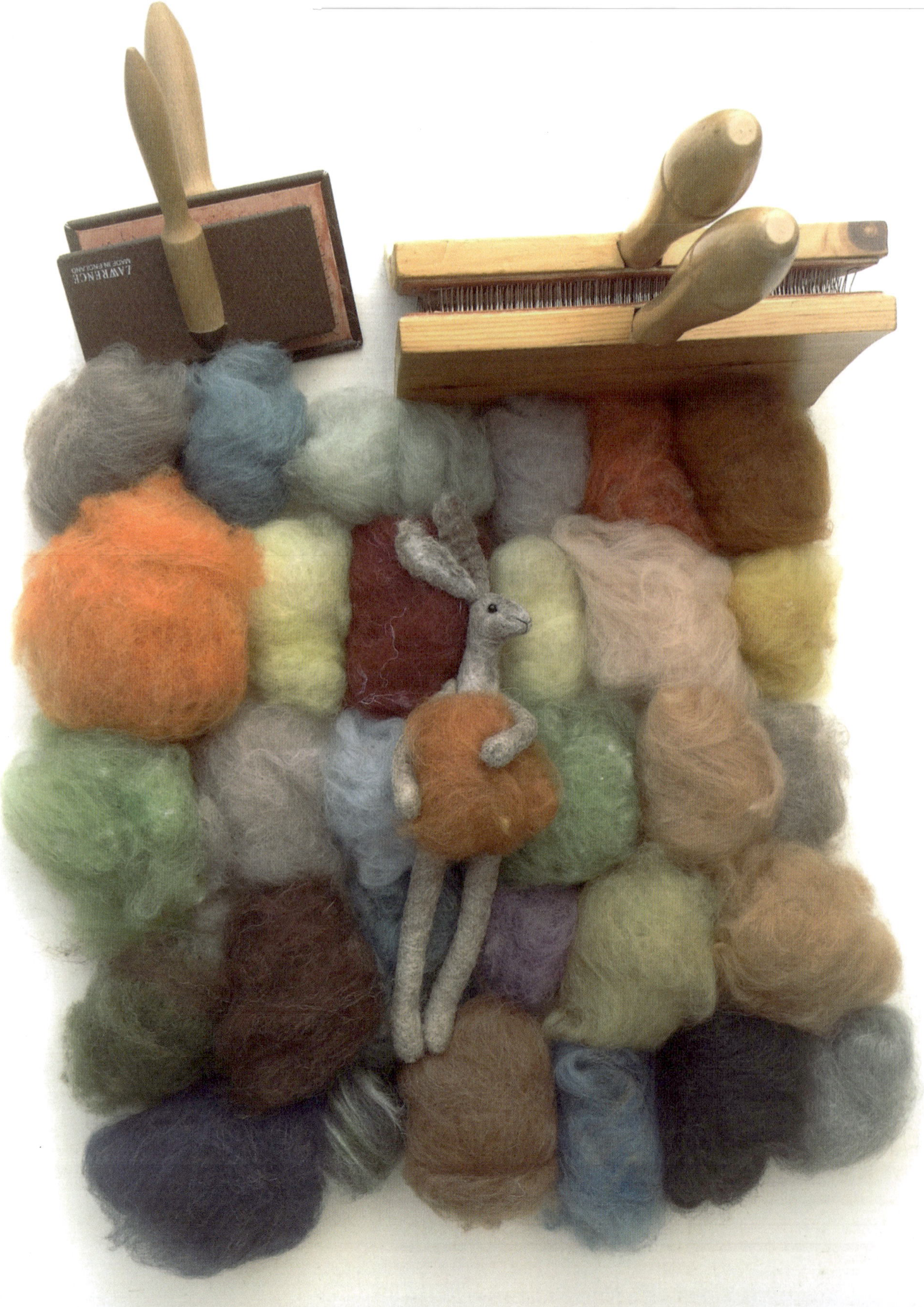
LAWRENCE
MADE IN ENGLAND

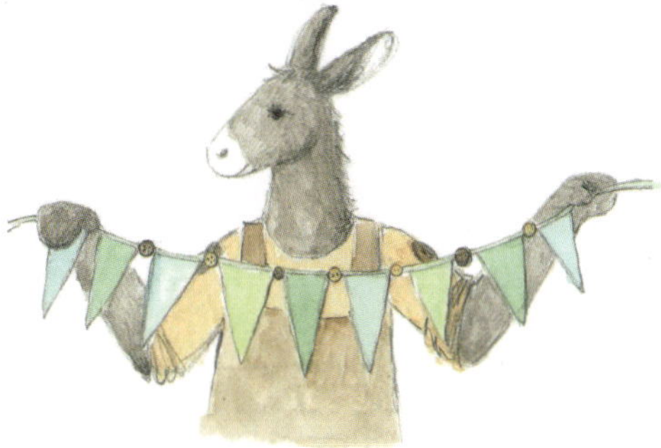

Introduction

Welcome to this book of workshops exploring the beauty and art of handmade felt.
You can create a range of charming items, using natural wool fibres and simple items from your home, some soap and water, and a gentle workout for your arms to turn the fibres into felt.
As wool felt tends to shrink a lot during its creation, some felt making techniques can take a lot of space and effort, and take ages to complete, so this collection is small in scale, and each item can be made in a limited space in one session of a few hours or you can enjoy the whole day making a group of several pieces all together.

The workshops can all be adapted, for example you can increase the scale and combine any of the techniques to dream up something new. You may like to include other materials in your felt, like beautiful fabrics, natural materials, threads, decorative elements, and keep your supply of beads, buttons and sequins handy for embellishing your artworks when felted.
All the workshops are suitable for any level of experience, but if you are a complete beginner, perhaps begin making some flat felt samples, decorative bunting, or simple flowers.

First you will find some explanations on how to achieve the different surface and structural effects like flat, decorative, textured felt, pockets, layers and three dimensional and solid forms.
You will become familiar with how your fibres and materials behave, and how much to felt the wool for a good quality result. Of course felt making isn't always exact, many factors will mean your results may vary. If things don't go to plan first time, don't be put off, just try again, make adjustments, find out what works best for you. You will be surprised when something turns out even more lovely than you planned.

The workshops are illustrated step by step with templates to use, and you can refer back to the techniques for extra tips, or why not adapt them and experiment with shapes and fibres as much as you like. There are no rules here, just exploration of what you can do.

Felt making is so satisfying, sensory and tactile, you can relax and take your time when setting out your designs. You'll need to roll your sleeves up for the felting part, enjoy watching the transformation in front of you from fluffy fibres into your own hand made felt.

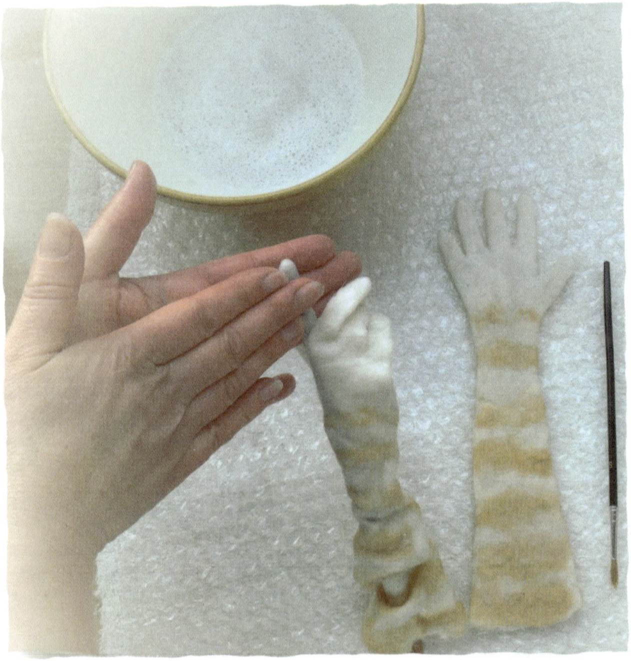

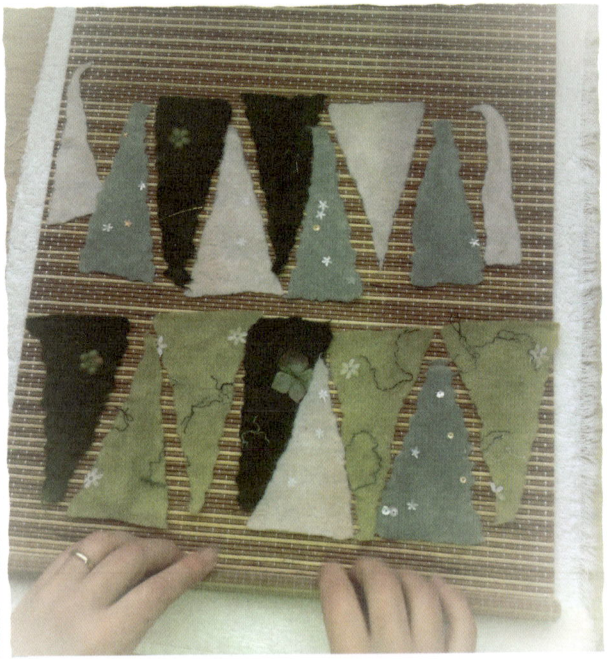

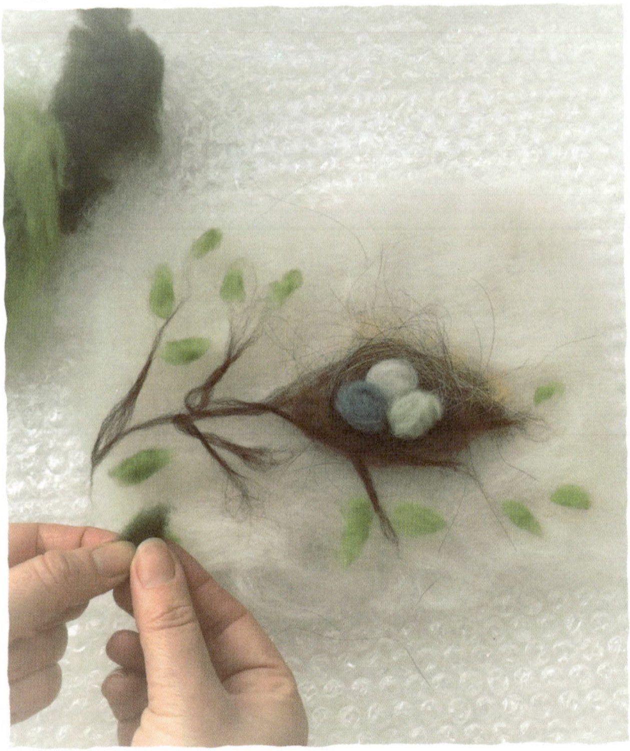

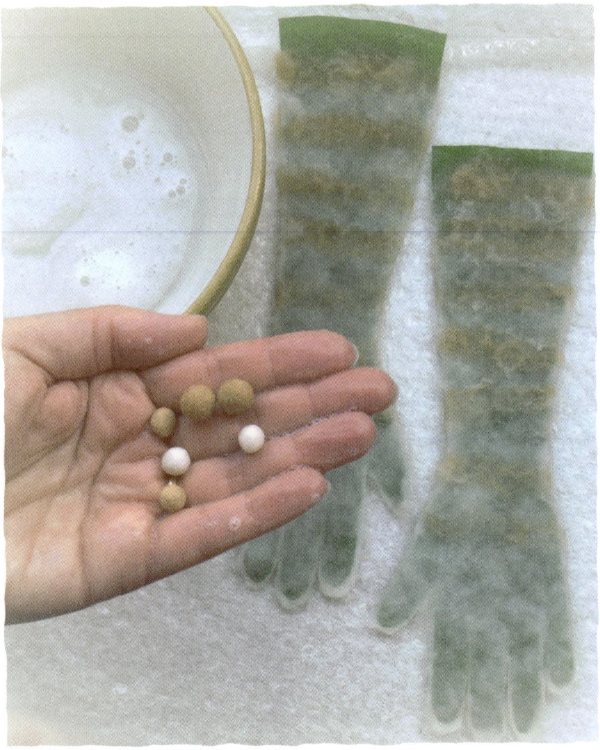

What is Wet Felting?

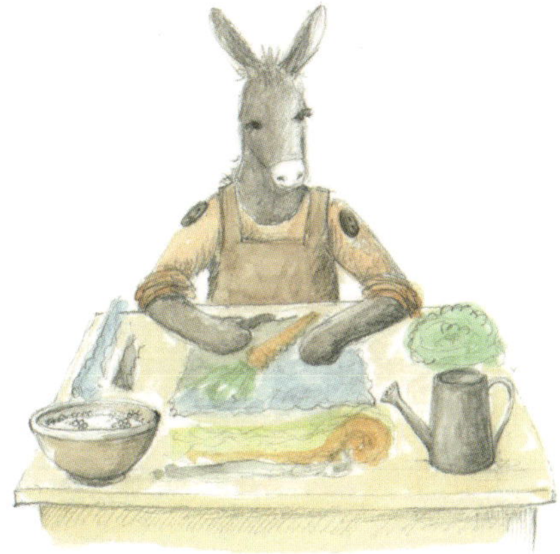

Wet felting is the combination of moisture and movement and also heat to turn natural fibres into a strong felted textile. Agitating or rubbing the wet fibres causes them to merge together and shrink into a matted material.
Wool felt is made with sheep fleece, but all sorts of other animal fibres can be used, or combined with the fleece to create a felt. Wool fibres have tiny scales on the surface, which open up in the warm soapy water, then close again after being moved around, rinsed and cooled, locking them together.

Felt is said to be the oldest non woven textile known, and has quite a history, being used in many ways for warmth and protection, decoration, clothing, cushioning, sound proofing, carpeting and even to build homes in the form of travelling tents. It's robust, can be water and chemical resistant, flame retardant, self extinguishing, will not unravel or fray, it's very 'green' too, being renewable, biodegradable, repairable and recyclable, what's not to like?

Dry fibres are layered together in random directions to the desired thickness for making a light and airy, cobweb~like felt or a thick, strong, durable felt. Any surface decoration, pattern or structure can be included, then the design is wetted through with warm, soapy solution.
The felting process can begin by gentle rubbing or hand rolling to cause the movement of fibres. Rolling in bubble wrap or bamboo mat causes more friction with the textured surface. The felt also shrinks in the direction it is rolled, so this needs to be varied for even shrinkage.
Felting can be paused to create a 'pre felt'. Partially felted pieces can be dried and later cut up and used to create intricate patterns to be applied to other pieces of felt.
Fulling, firming or milling is where you continue to shrink the wool into a good strong felt.
Different felting methods can be researched, experimented and invented, using various soaps, solutions and surfaces to agitate the wool, even a washing machine can be used to do the physical work for you.
Felting can be carried out on the worktop to make it flat, or your fibres can be placed over a template or a former like a bowl, hat block or even your own feet to create slippers and other three dimensional items. Lots of rubbing and massaging and adding very hot water will speed up the fulling, and also the wool can be thrown repeatedly onto the worktop, to further move the wool fibres and speed up the felting process.
When the wool has completely shrunk and you are happy with the degree of felting, the soap and water can be rinsed and squeezed out. It can be reformed, then steamed dry with an iron or left to dry naturally into your beautiful piece of felt work.

Fibres

Most wool fibres should turn into felt, but sheep fleece that has been carefully washed and prepared in natural shades or dyed, ready for spinning or felting is ideal, particularly the finer fibres like Merino, Gotland and Blue Faced Leicester. Other animal fibres like alpaca, llama, angora, and cashmere can also be used or combined with wool fleece to produce different qualities in your felt.

Some fibres will felt quickly, some will need more encouragement, and they will vary in shrinkage, anywhere between a quarter to half the size when felted.

Organic and synthetic fibres can also be trapped into the wool for surface decoration. As the wool fibres shrink, but the other fibres like silk do not, the result is a wavy, curly, marbling effect. This is most striking when the fibres are contrasting in colour or shade.

Fibres are available as tops or roving ~ long lengths of soft, clean wool, or as wool batts in a larger, random sheet form. Both are ready and easy to use, just gently tease out fine layers for building up your design.

If you have a supply of wool straight from the animal, the fleece will need to be cleaned and carded (combed through) ready for use. More information about these processes can be seen in tutorials online.

Amounts to use... Each workshop only requires a small amount of fibres, estimates are given ~ between 10 and 20 grammes should be plenty, to make them nice and delicate. Most fibres are sold by weight, so 100 grammes of each of a selection of colours will be plenty to choose from.

Hand carding and blending fibres.

Hand carders are large wooden~handled paddles covered in wire teeth, you can also card smaller amounts using two small, wire dog grooming brushes. Theses are great for mixing colours and shades and will make wool tops into a more random cluster of fibres, perfect for laying out your design.

Place some fibres to be carded onto one of the combs, then gently brush across them with the other comb on top.

Lift the fibres from one comb, and place them back onto the other and repeat, or reverse the combs, just continue to brush the fibres back and forth until they are nicely blended and fluffed up!

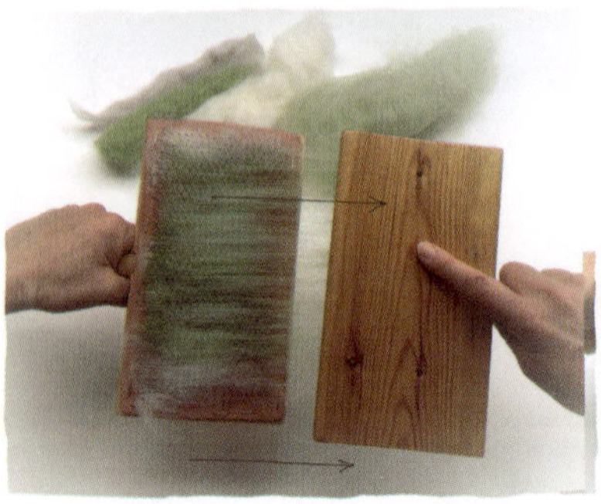

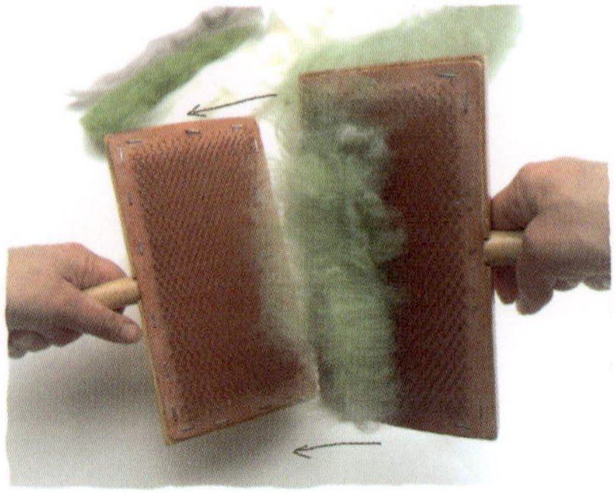

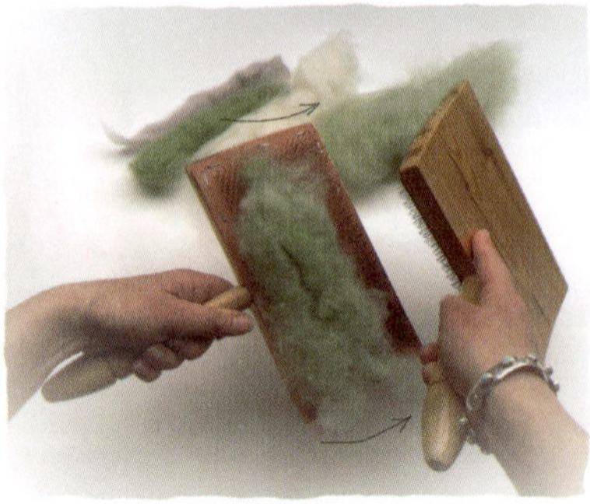

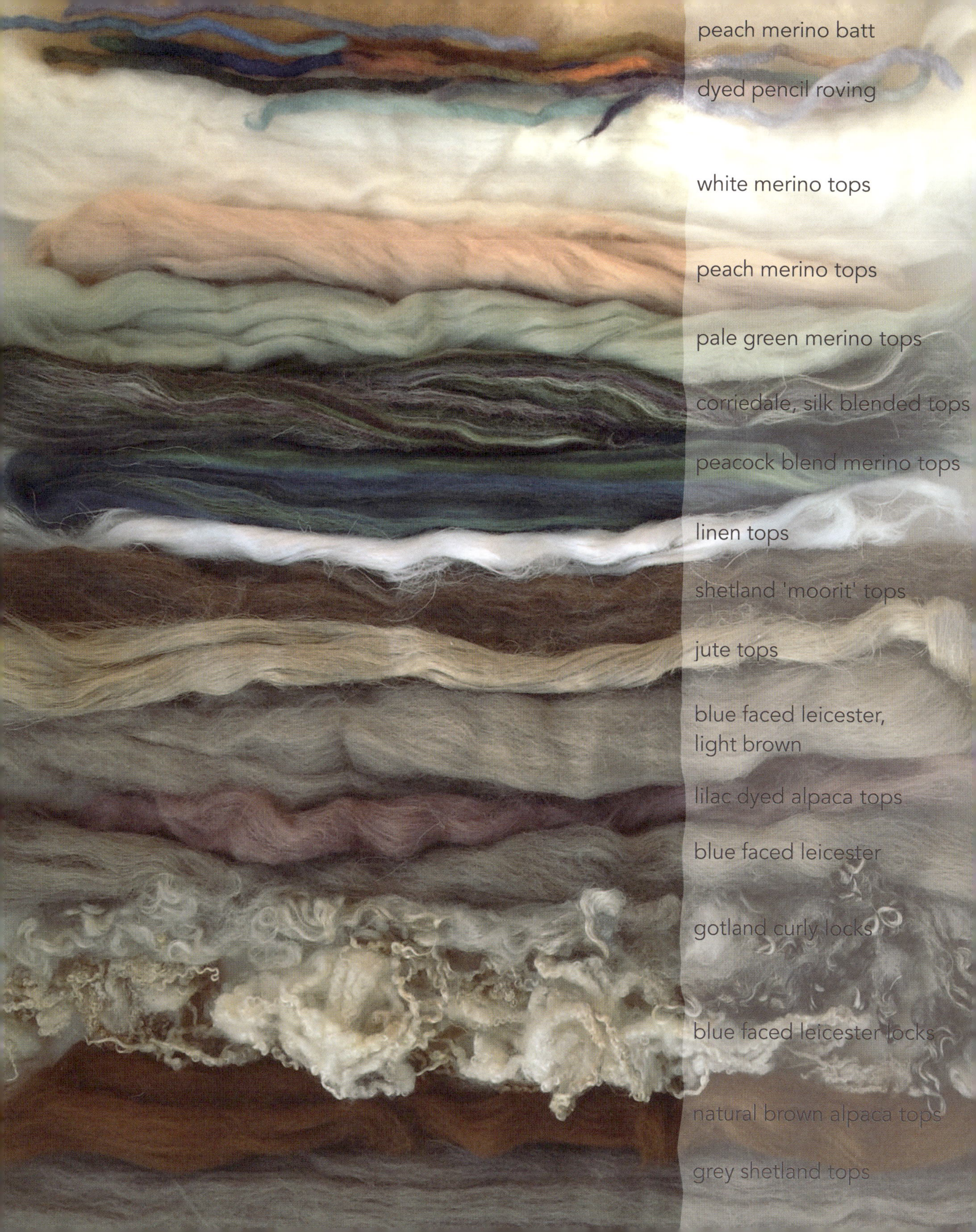
peach merino batt
dyed pencil roving
white merino tops
peach merino tops
pale green merino tops
corriedale, silk blended tops
peacock blend merino tops
linen tops
shetland 'moorit' tops
jute tops
blue faced leicester,
light brown
lilac dyed alpaca tops
blue faced leicester
gotland curly locks
blue faced leicester locks
natural brown alpaca tops
grey shetland tops

Tools and Equipment

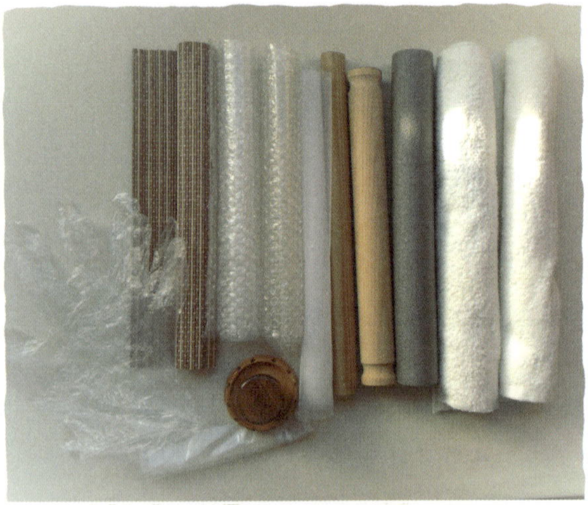

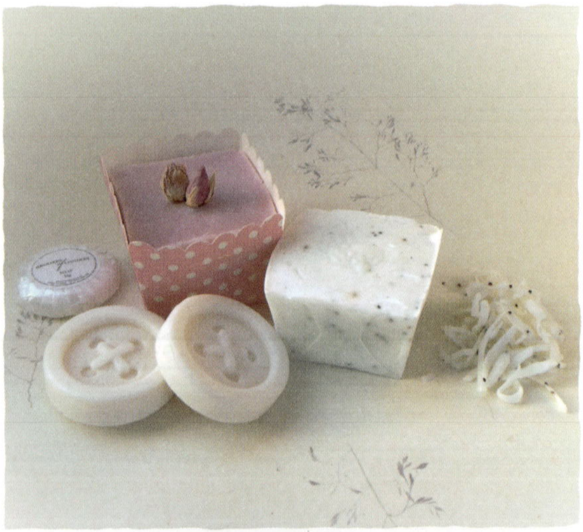

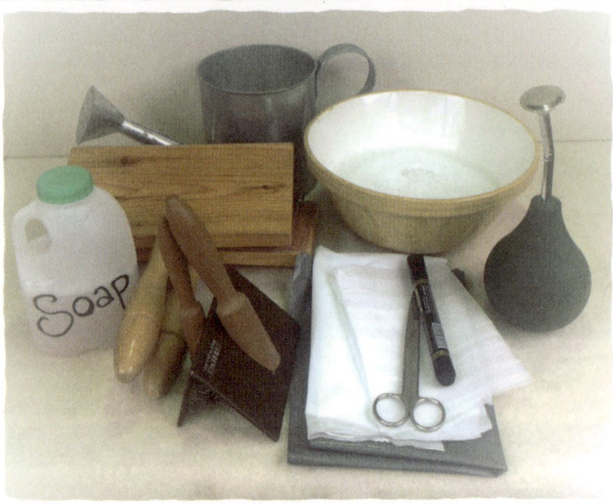

Choose from these for hand rolling.
Bamboo mat ~ place mat or small, cane roller-blind. (optional, but great for firming up the felt)
Bubble Wrap ~ use with the bubble texture facing your felt.
Netting ~ fine curtain netting to protect your design.
Wooden dowel for rolling inside the bubble wrap.
~or **Rolling pin**
~or **Foam roll** ~ pipe insulation tube
Towels ~ to roll around the bubble wrap, dry your hands and mop up spills.
Gloves ~ plastic or rubber gloves. (Optional)
Hand felting tool ~ optional, this can be used to rub/massage the fibres into felt.

Soap
Make a soapy solution by dissolving some soap in warm water.
Choose any soap that you like ~ handmade, liquid, use up leftover small pieces from the bathroom.
Some felt makers only use olive oil soap, others use dish soap.
Experiment with the dilution, it may be either too soapy, or not soapy enough. See how to fix this on page 110.
As a guide, try this mixture one teaspoon of grated soap dissolved in one pint of hot water.
Using warm solution aids the felting process, but it does still work if the solution has cooled.

Bowl ~ to hold soap solution.
Sprinkler ~ an empty plastic milk carton with small holes drilled in the cap, or a plant water sprinkler or small watering can.
Hand carders ~ or dog grooming combs for mixing colours and shades and carding wool.
Plastic resist ~ strong plastic carrier bag or mailing bag, or foam underlay sheet, or builders plastic.
Scissors
Marker pen

Things you will need

Materials you will need, and some other items you may find very useful.

Fabric and lace ~ any nice fabrics like old clothing, vintage lace, netting, remnants, doilies or hankies

Decoration ~ buttons, beads, mini pegs, and ribbons threads and yarn, sequins, fabric or dried flowers, skeleton leaves...anything can be used in the wool, as long as it can survive being wetted and rolled.

Sewing needle, pins, threads and scissors ~ various sizes

Wire and pliers ~ to make tiny clothes hangers. Try gardening/floristry/jewellery wire. Metal file (not pictured)

Small paint brush ~ for using to shape the fingers of felted gloves

Felting needles ~ barbed needles that tangle the fibres when repeatedly pushed into the felt. Great for repairs, details or embellishing the surface of your felt. Size '38 star' should be adequate.

Sketchbook and Pens ~ for keeping a record of your wonderful ideas and inspiration, and sketching templates.

Some other useful items, not pictured...

Tracing paper ~ to trace the templates from the book

Hot melt glue gun ~ lots of uses, like making wire coat hangers and flower stems. Pva glue for shoe boxes.

Spray starch ~ to stiffen fine felt if needed.

Apron, Iron, Kettle, Kitchen sink or bowls of water.

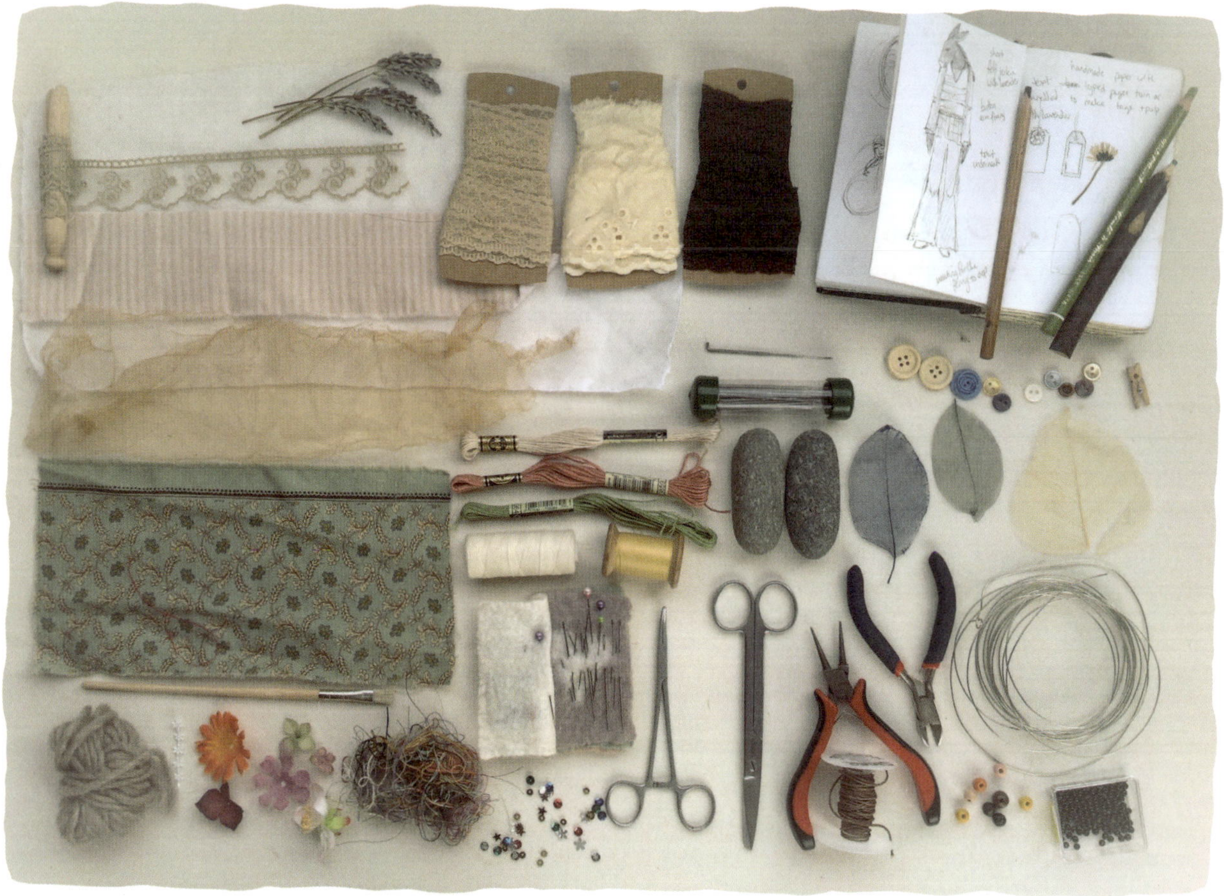

How to make Felt...

There are many varied methods of felting your wool, but remember the wool just requires moisture and movement, and some warmth to felt it. The following pages include some techniques to help when you choose a workshop from the book, so you can experiment with them, combine them or see what you prefer. Your chosen fibres may felt quicker or slower, and shrink anywhere between 25% to 50% but often about 40%, so you can adjust the amount of felting required, as long as you are happy with the results. To calculate the approximate shrinkage, see page 21 and how to increase template sizes on page 111.
Here are some hints and tips before you begin...

Prepare ~ Have everything laid out that you need for your project ~ towels, fibres, materials, soap solution, bubble wrap. Try to keep your hands and fibres dry whilst handling the wool, or it will stick to your fingers and become tangled.
Samples ~ Make lots of samples to try out your fibres and techniques. You can be creative with these, make them into bunting, bookmarks, coasters, mount them on cards, stitch together to make something new, book covers, needle cases...
Keep notes ~ Record how each fibre reacts to felting, including the time it takes, and the shrinkage, so you can scale up your templates to the desired size.

Things to try...
~ Vary the thickness, make samples using just one or two extremely fine layers, (cobweb felt) or thick, with two, three, four or more layers.
~ For flat felt shapes, try placing a paper template beneath the bubble wrap to guide you, or mark out a shape on the back of the bubble wrap in marker pen.
~ Remember that the felt shrinks in the direction of the fibres, and also the direction you roll/rub, so keep these random and varied, or try laying the fibres just in one direction to see what happens
~ To save time when making several items, place more than one together on one sheet of bubble wrap if they will fit. Or layer two sets of bubble wrap when rolling, you can roll more items at once this way.
~ Compare felting techniques, felt the wool with just the rolling method, or complete it with just massaging and rubbing the fibres.
~ Use a single colour or type of fibre to test and compare the amount of shrinkage.
~ Layer colours or blend them with hand carders for different shades/hues.
~ Use the fibres just like paint to make images, create patterns and shading.
~ Try different colours on the front and back, sometimes they will show through the layers.
~ Experiment with edges, leave them loose and natural, or fold the fibres over to create a straight edge. Try cutting the edges at different stages in the felting process, after wetting, half way through felting, and after felting.

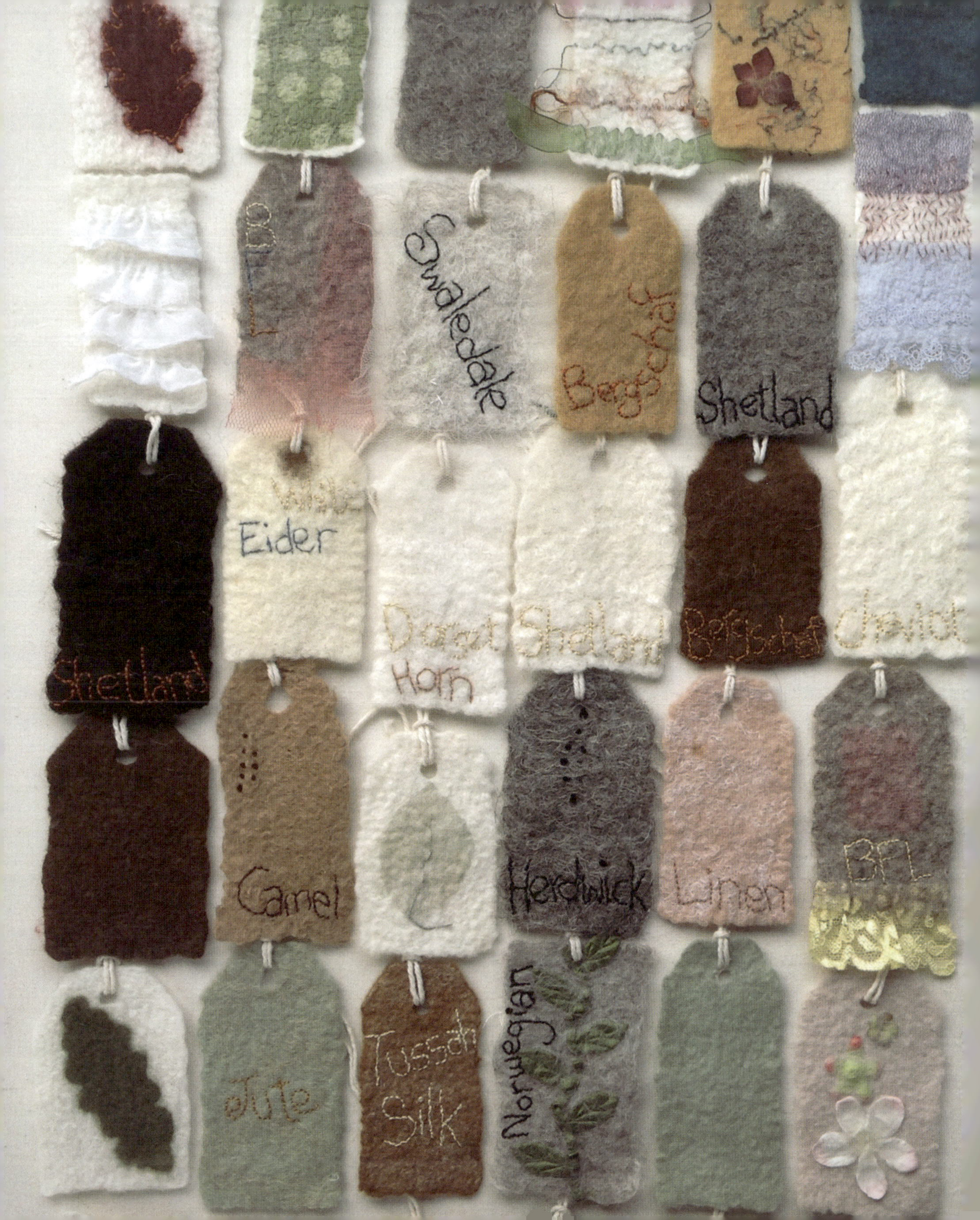
BFL
Swaledale
Bergschaf
Shetland
White
Eider
Shetland
Dorset
Horn
Shetland
Bergschaf
Cheviot
Camel
Herdwick
Linen
BFL
Jute
Tussah
Silk
Norwegian

Flat Felt

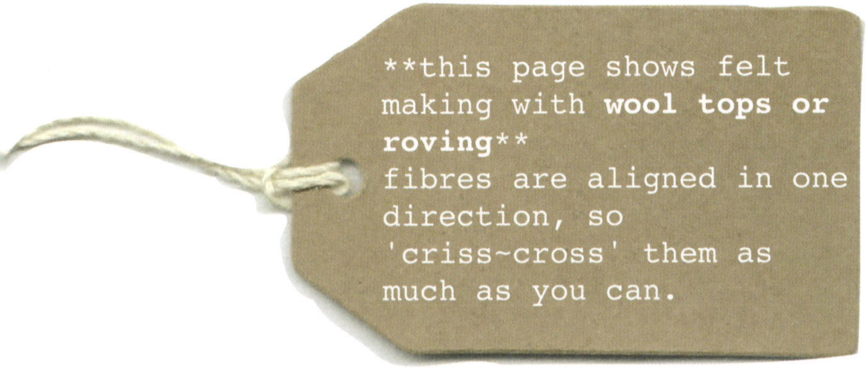

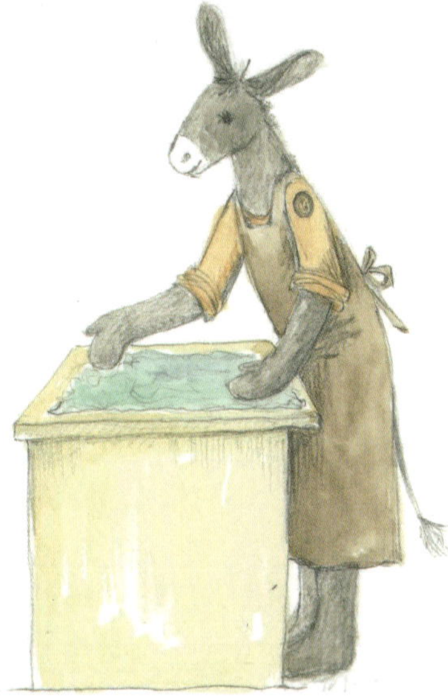

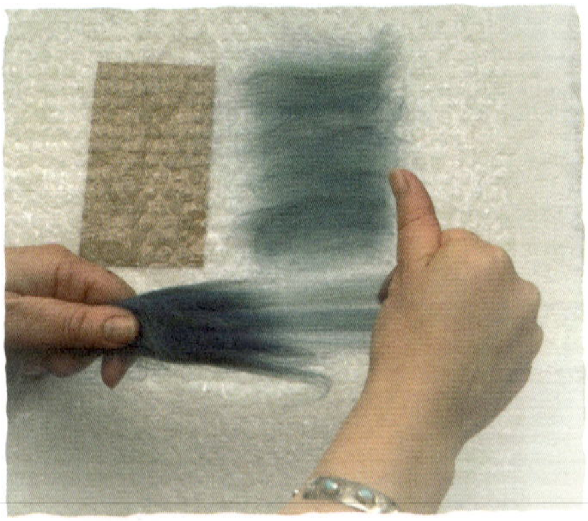

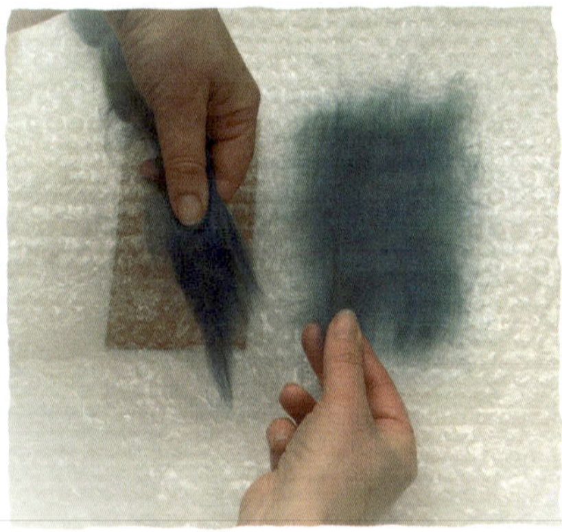

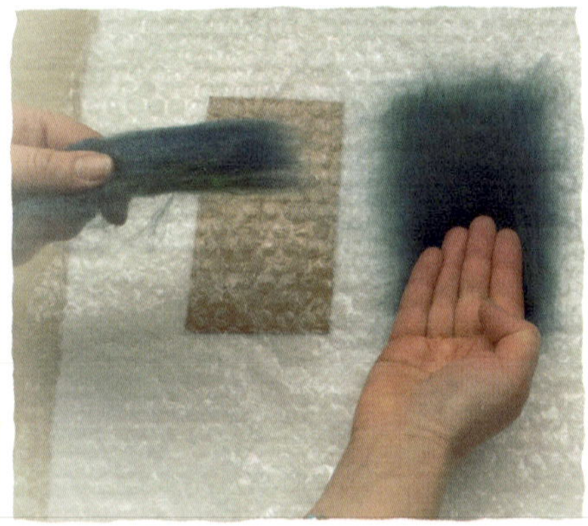

Lay out the fibres

Hold wool tops firmly in one hand, leaving between 10 to 15 cms overhanging and gently pull some fibres away with the other hand.
Lay them onto the bubble wrap with bubbles facing upwards. Repeat this, placing more fibres alongside each time, until you have filled the area you have planned.
Now in the same way, add another fine layer of fibres over the top of the first, in the opposite direction so that one layer is horizontal and one is vertical.
Gently pat down the wool with the back of your hand.
To make a fine felt, you can pause here, and begin the felting process.
To make a thicker felt, repeat above, building up three or four layers as desired.
Add any pattern or surface decoration, (see page 22) or leave plain and simple.
The fibres are now ready for felting, go to pages 18 and 19...

Tip~ *You can see the darker fibres better if you have a light towel beneath the bubble wrap.*

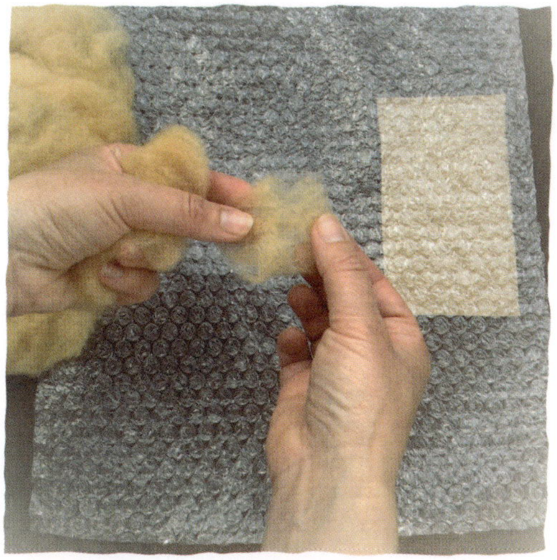

this page shows felt making with a **wool batt or carded wool

the fibres are more random, and tend to have a shorter length, so these are great for making tiny details like the fingers of the gloves on page 84.

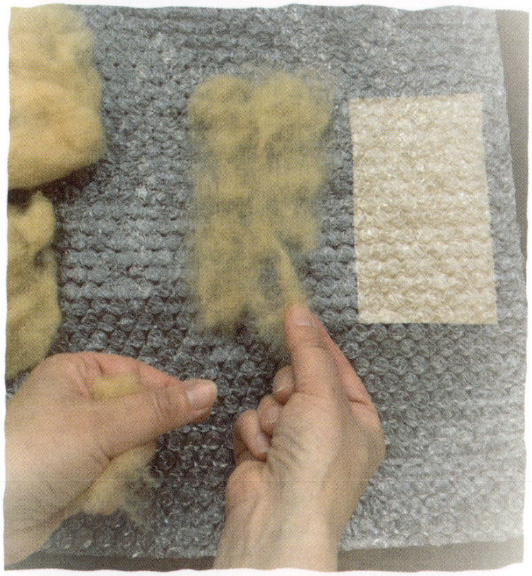

Take a pinch of wool from the batt, and tease it open as even as you can. Lay it onto the bubble wrap. Repeat this and lay more fibres next to each other until you have covered the area.
Sprinkle with soap solution, cover with bubble wrap, and press the solution through the fibres.
Peel back the bubble wrap, check it is wet through, and for any thin patches and add more fibres if needed. To make a fine felt, pause here and go to the felting stage. For a thicker felt, apply another layer of fibres over the first one.
Add any surface decoration, (see page 22) or leave plain and simple.
The wool is now ready for felting by rolling or rubbing, see following pages...

Tip~ *You can see lighter fibres well if you have a dark towel beneath the bubble wrap.*

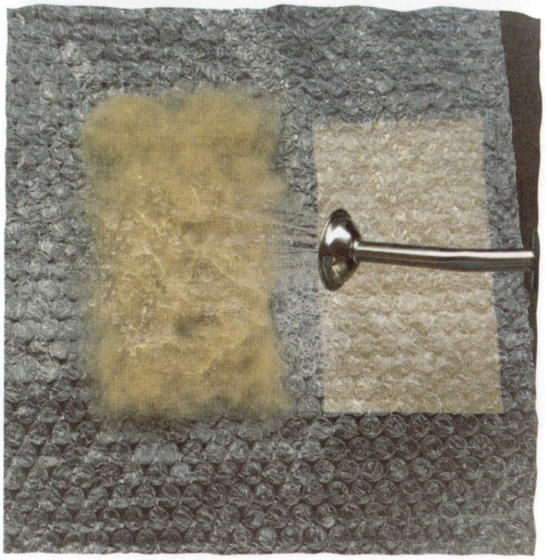

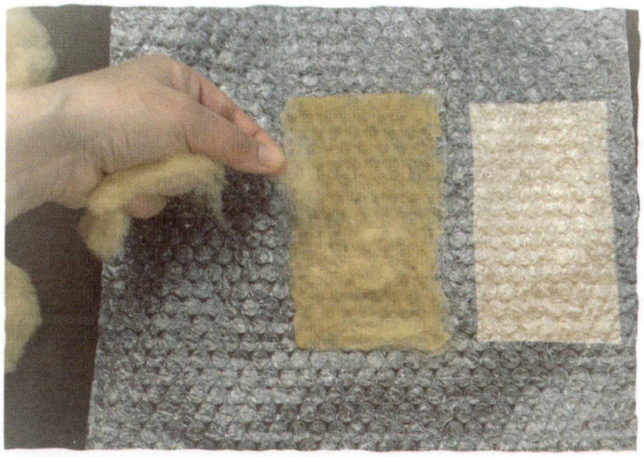

Hand rolling the Felt

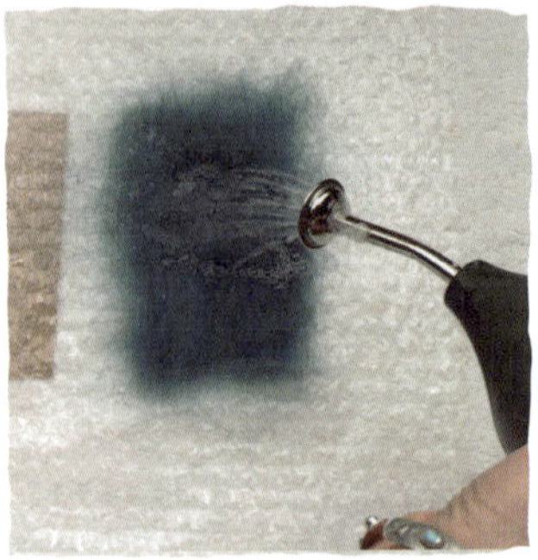

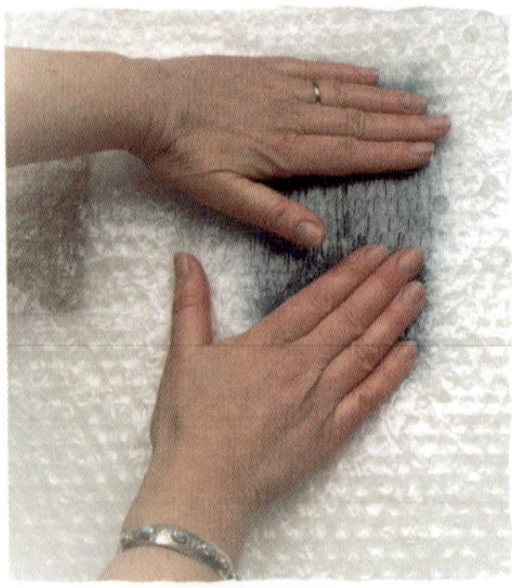

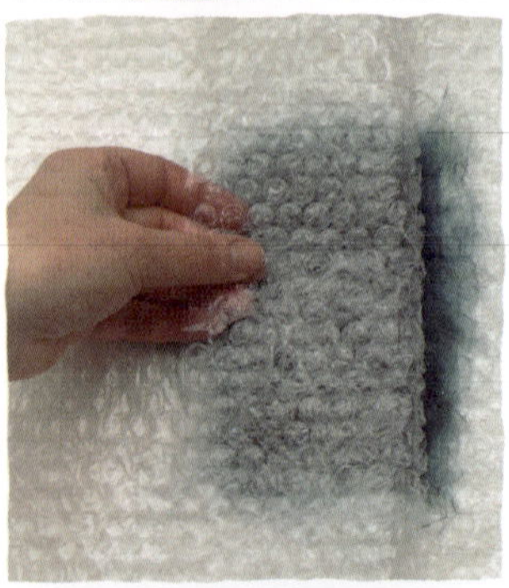

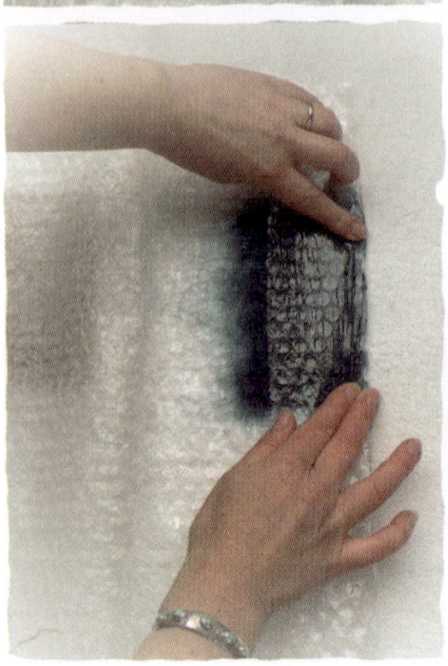

1. Gently sprinkle some soap solution onto the surface, enough to saturate the dry wool.

Tip~ if your design has a delicate surface design, you can place a piece of netting over the top to prevent anything moving out of place. Sprinkle the solution through the net, then gently press through and give the surface a gentle rub to set the design in place.

2. Lay the second piece of bubble wrap onto the first, bubbles facing down. Press the bubble wrap to push the water all through the fibres.

3. Peel back the bubble wrap taking care to unstick the fibres, and check the wool is fully wetted through. Sprinkle more solution if needed.

Check for any patches that look thin, and add a few more fibres. Cover and press through to wet.

4. For a straight edge, fold over the loose fibres inside the bubble wrap, and press them down. If you prefer, you can leave the edges loose and wispy and see what happens.

5. Roll the two layers of bubble wrap around the rolling pin. You can proceed to rolling, or ~

6. Roll up the bubble wrap and rolling pin inside the towel.

Ready to roll...

Begin gently rolling backwards and forwards, counting up to 50 rolls. Unroll the towel and bubble wrap.

Peel back the top layer of wrap, making sure the fibres stay on the bottom layer. Check for any folds, and push the wool flat.

Tip~ If your soap solution is a little thin, place a piece of netting over the wool fibres and rub a bar of soap onto the surface, to add more suds and start the felting action.

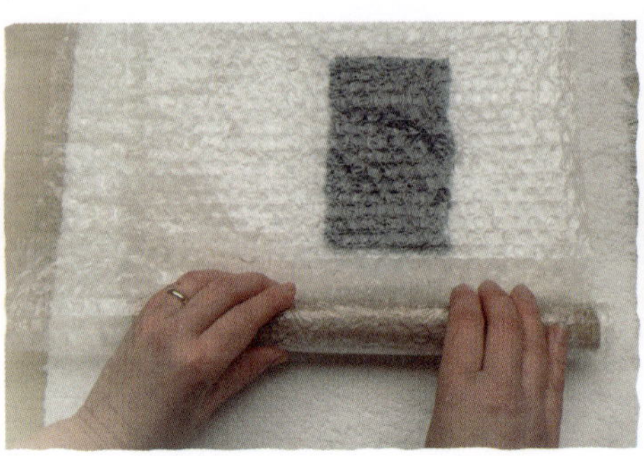

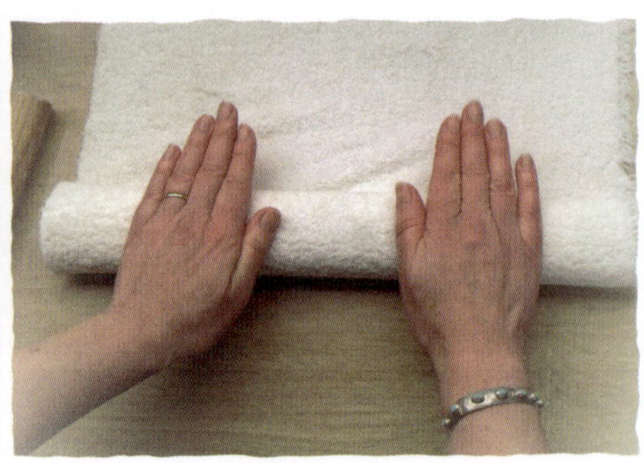

Keep rolling...
Turn the whole sandwich of bubble wrap 90 degrees clockwise, and repeat the rolling motion, counting to 50 again.
Check and turn 90 degrees again.
When you have rolled 50 times in each of the 4 directions, the wool fibres will be just starting to felt together. This is near the 'pre felt' stage, see page 25.
To continue with the felting process, you can now be more vigorous with your rolling, and turn the felt over (front to back) at intervals, so that you roll top and bottom sides.
Roll for another four turns, counting to 100 each turn.
You should now see the fleece is tightening, and turning into felt, but it will still shrink and felt more.
Repeat another 100 rolls in each direction, occasionally flipping the felt over.
You will now see a visible shrinking of the felt, but it can still be improved if you continue to the throwing or fulling stage, see page 20.

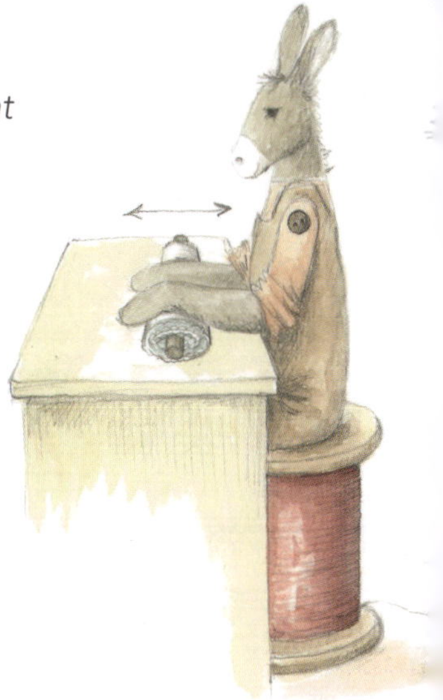

Massaging the Felt

The whole felting process can also be carried out by simply rubbing and massaging the wool fibres together, or with a combination of both rolling and rubbing techniques.

Cover the design with a piece of netting. (Occasionally lift the net, so the fibres don't attach themselves.)
You can use a massaging tool, or the flat lid of a jam jar, or some rolled up bubble wrap or simply with your hand in a plastic bag or glove.
Rub gently in a circular motion to create the movement of fibres for felting to take place.
Continue to rub, changing direction, and occasionally flip the work over, to work on both sides.
Keep going until the wool fibres merge together and everything shrinks into felt.

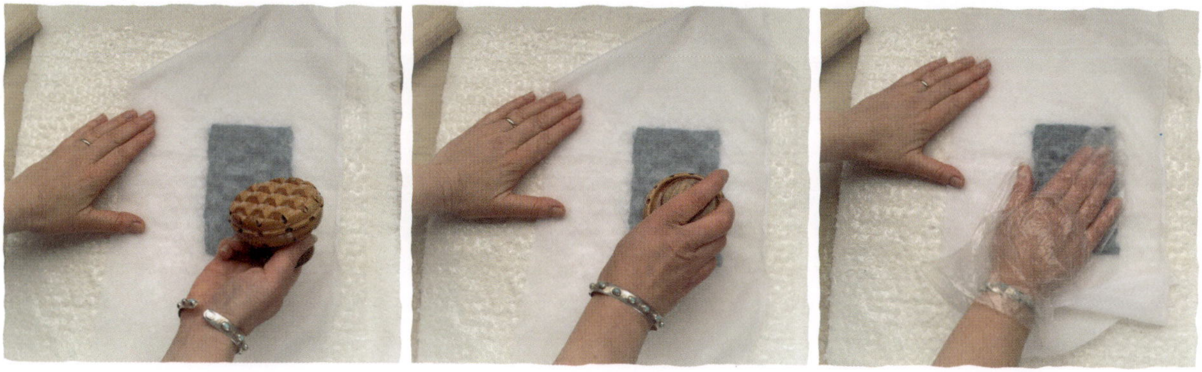

Fulling the Felt

To felt the wool as much as possible, and make it good quality and strong, it can be fulled, milled, or hardened with some or all of these techniques, and also heated then cooled. Your wool fibres may felt quicker or slower, so be prepared to adjust the amount of felting to suit the needs of your project or your preference.

*Try warming up your soap solution in the microwave, or carefully add very hot water from the kettle to the wool, rub a little more soap into the surface, and continue to roll.

Throwing the Felt

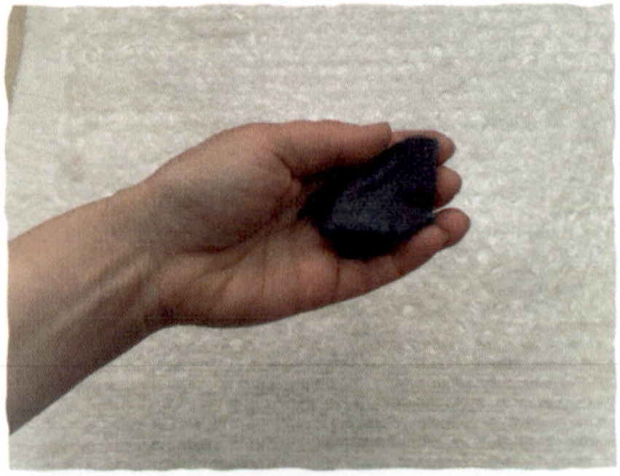

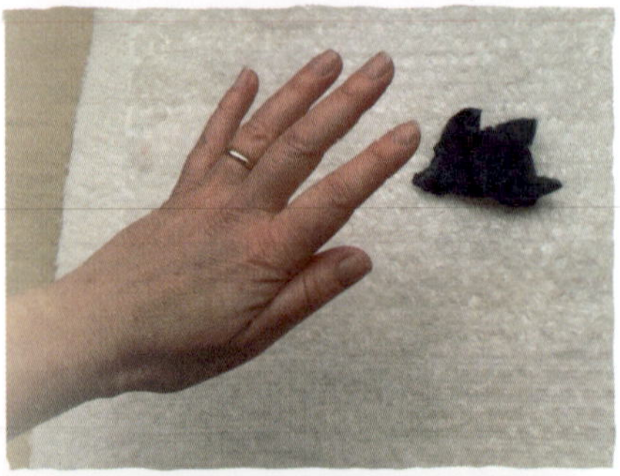

This really works!
Throwing the felt down with some force is not only fun, but creates more movement that will shock the fibres and cause them to lock together more, advancing the felting process.
If your design is very delicate, you may wish to avoid this stage, and just roll or rub the felt until you are happy with the result.
The throwing can be a bit splashy, so you may like to do it outside.
Remove the felt from the bubble wrap, but leave a sheet on the worktop or floor.
Throw the felt down onto the wrap. Pick up and repeat this several times. Continue for 25 to 50 times. You will see the felt visibly shrinking and puckering a little.

Fulling in the Bamboo mat

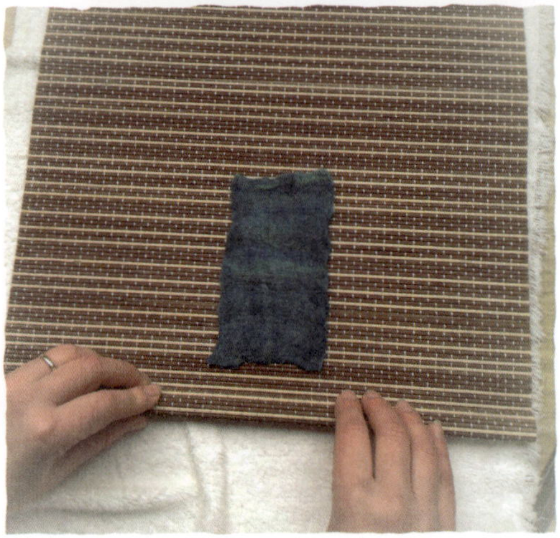

The felt can be reshaped, firmed and fulled with a little more rolling in the bamboo mat.
Place the felt onto the bamboo, and sprinkle with more hot soap solution if necessary.
Roll as before, counting from 25 to 50 rolls.
Repeat the rolling, turning 90 degrees and flipping over, until the desired shape and shrinkage is achieved.

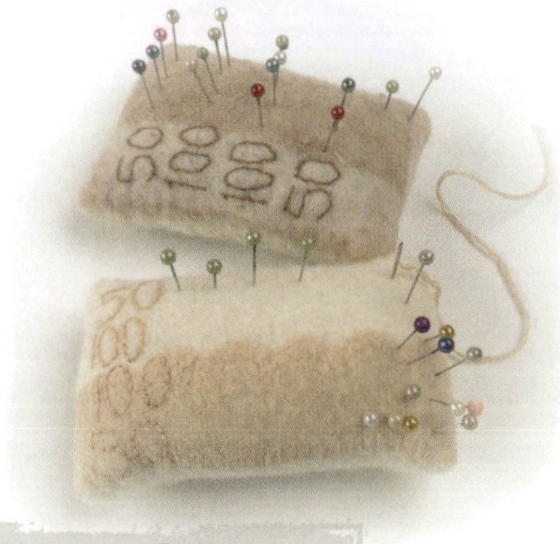

Tip~ It's easy to become distracted or interrupted when you are felting, so to help you keep track of where you are in the rolling process, you can make a simple pin cushion 'counter' to use with the felting workshops.
Mark out the different stages on the left, and place a pin in each section after each time you roll and turn the felt.
See how to make yours with the resist technique. on page 27.

Rinse and Dry

When you notice the wool has really shrunk and felted well, you can rinse out all of the soap in hot, then cold water. Some felt makers add a sprinkle of vinegar to neutralise the alkaline content of any soap residue.
Squeeze out as much water as you can in your hands. If the wool is still loose and fluffy, then it will perhaps need a little more fulling, so you can return it to the bubble wrap, and re~soap it and continue to roll.
If the wool looks tight, strong and well felted, you can reshape it and leave it to dry.
Your lovely felt can be blotted dry by wrapping inside a dry towel. Sit or stand on the towel for a few seconds to squeeze out as much water as possible.
Your felt can be placed somewhere warm to dry, or pressed dry with an iron, but avoid this if you have used sequins, as they can melt!

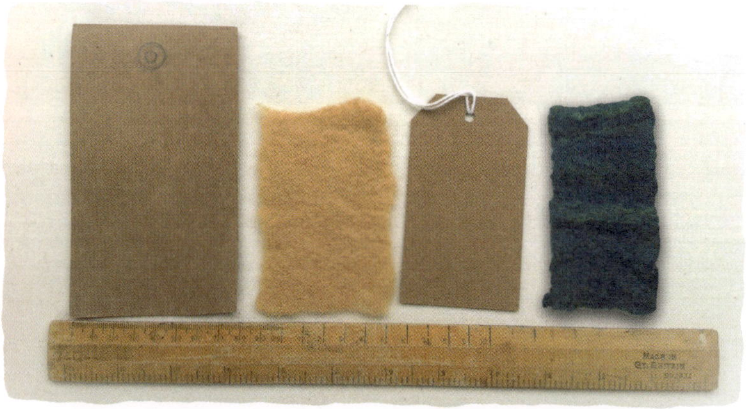

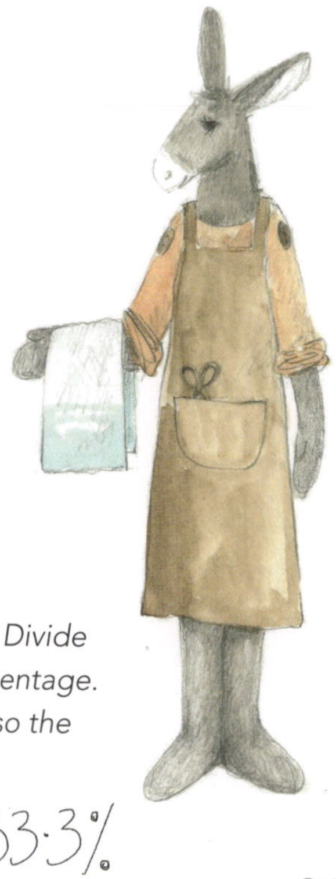

To estimate the shrinkage of your felt, you need your 'before' and 'after' measurements.
Subtract the finished size from the original size, which gives you the difference. Divide this number by the finished size, then times the result by 100 to give you a percentage.
E.g. the width of the template above was 8cm and the finished width was 6cm so the difference was 2cm. The calculation gives a shrinkage of 33.3%

$2 \div 6 = 3.33 \times 100 = 33.3\%$

Surface Design

There are many decorative effects and textures you can use to make your felt beautiful. You can 'paint' with the wool as you lay out your coloured fibres, make pre felt (partially felted wool) to cut up pieces to create layers or patterns of design, or add other materials like threads and fabric. You can also embellish the finished felt with stitching, needle felting, beads, buttons and anything else you can think of.

Things to try

~ Paint with the wool. Lay out different areas, or pinches of wool to create an image or pattern.

~ Place other materials like thread, fabrics, sequins, leafs onto your design. Add a very fine layer of fibres over them to trap them into the surface.

~ Add organic or synthetic fibres and materials for effect, blend them with your wool using hand carders, or place them directly onto the surface of your design, add fine wisps of wool fibres to trap them.

~ Create a textured surface adding extra pieces of felt, strings, balls etc, or embedding other objects like mirrors, pebbles or gemstones into the wool, with layers of felt over the top. Cut through the finished felt to reveal layers of colour, objects or cavities.

~ Embellish the finished felt with buttons, beads, hand stitched embroidery, sewing machine stitching, or needle felt onto the surface.

~ add structure using the resist technique on page 27, try layers, pockets, folds, pleating, constructing into other items....the possibilities are endless.

Surface design sample...

This felt picture has been made on a background of white merino, wetted through and the edges folded over in the bubble wrap. You can see the different textures added before felting below, then with finishing touches (opposite) with freehand machine stitching, needle felting, and hand embroidery stitches. 1~Viscose nepps on prefelt, some lace is later added to the cuff opposite. 2~wool fibres pinched round into a circle, applied to prefelt. 3~Angelina fibres carded with pink merino, applied to the background, and threads onto prefelt, trapped with some extra fibres on top. 4~sequins onto prefelt, covered with fine fibres. 5~sequins onto loose wool, covered in a few fibres to trap them. 6~net curtain nuno felted onto background. 7~fabric flower and wool locks with fine fibres on top. 8~skeleton leaf on loose fibres. 9~netting and lace nuno felted onto background. 10~resist pocket and white linen fibres carded with green merino.

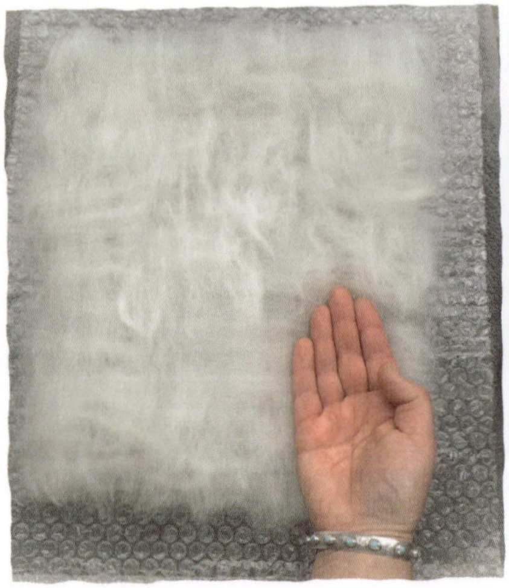

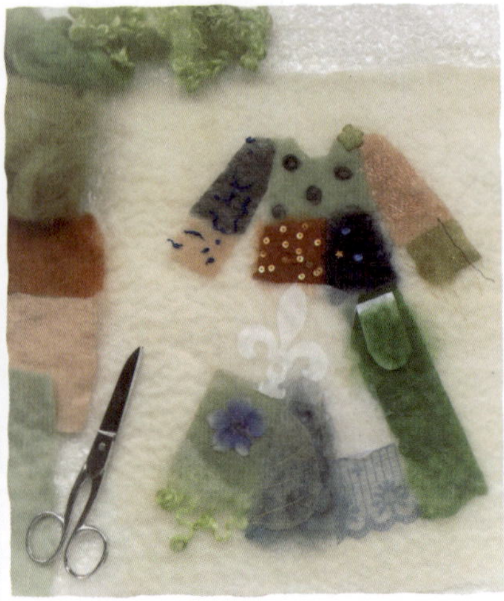

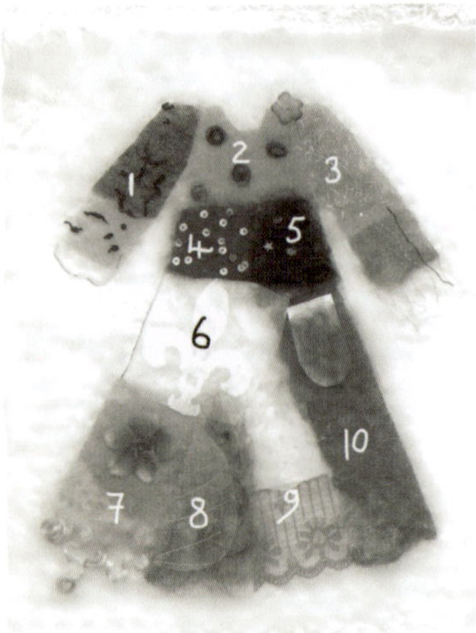

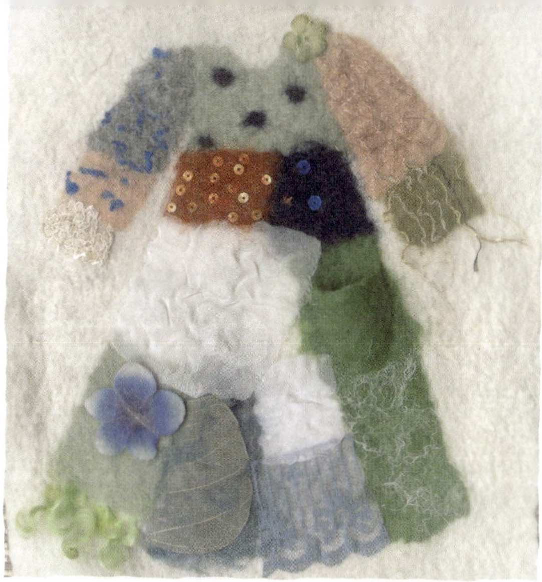
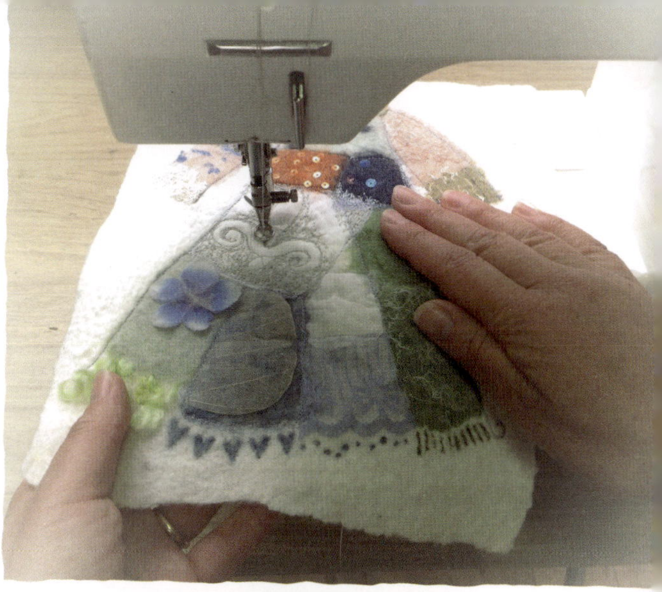
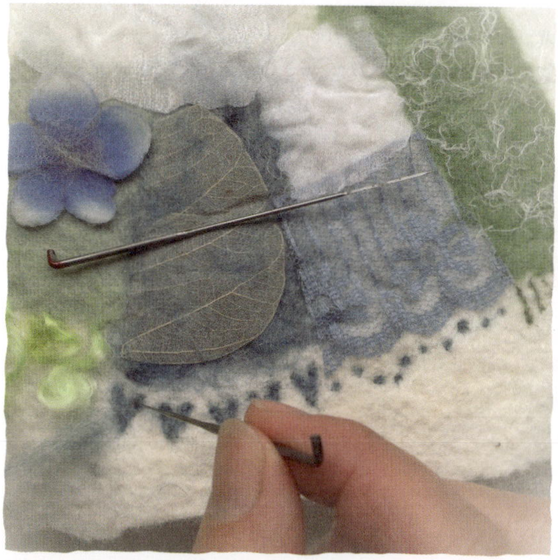
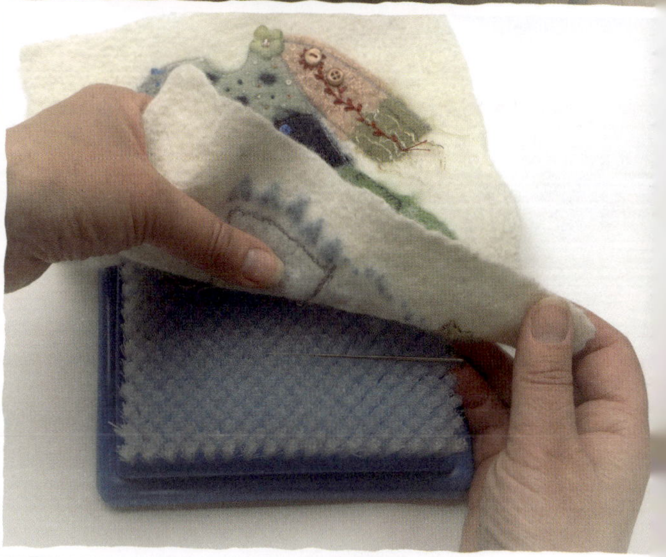
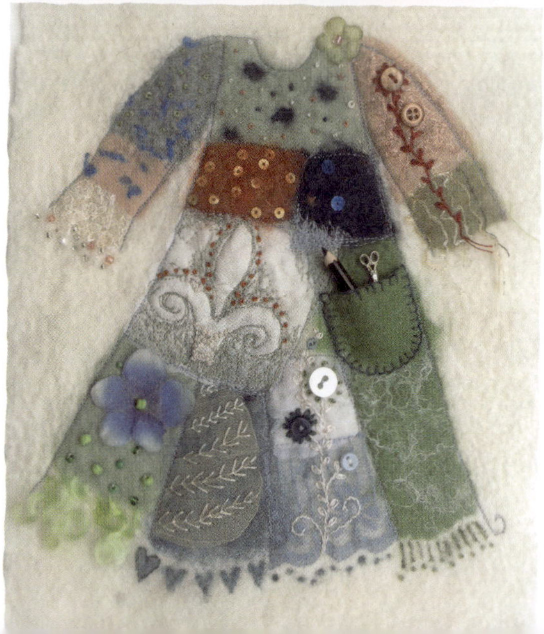
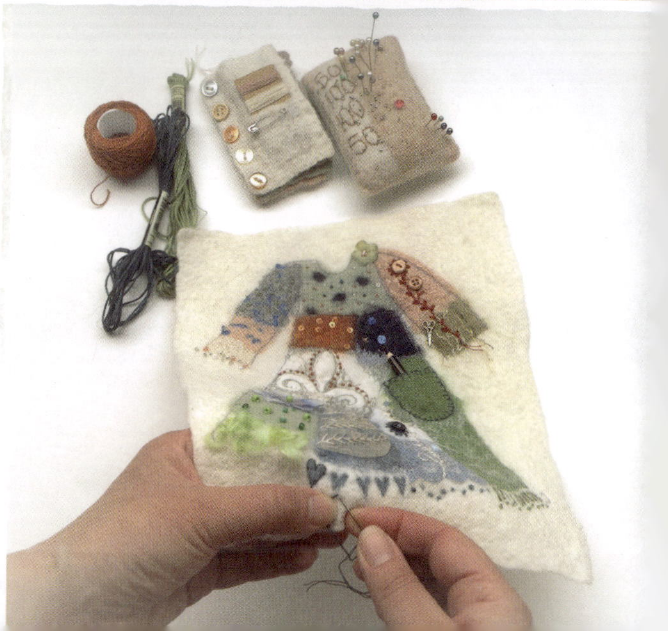

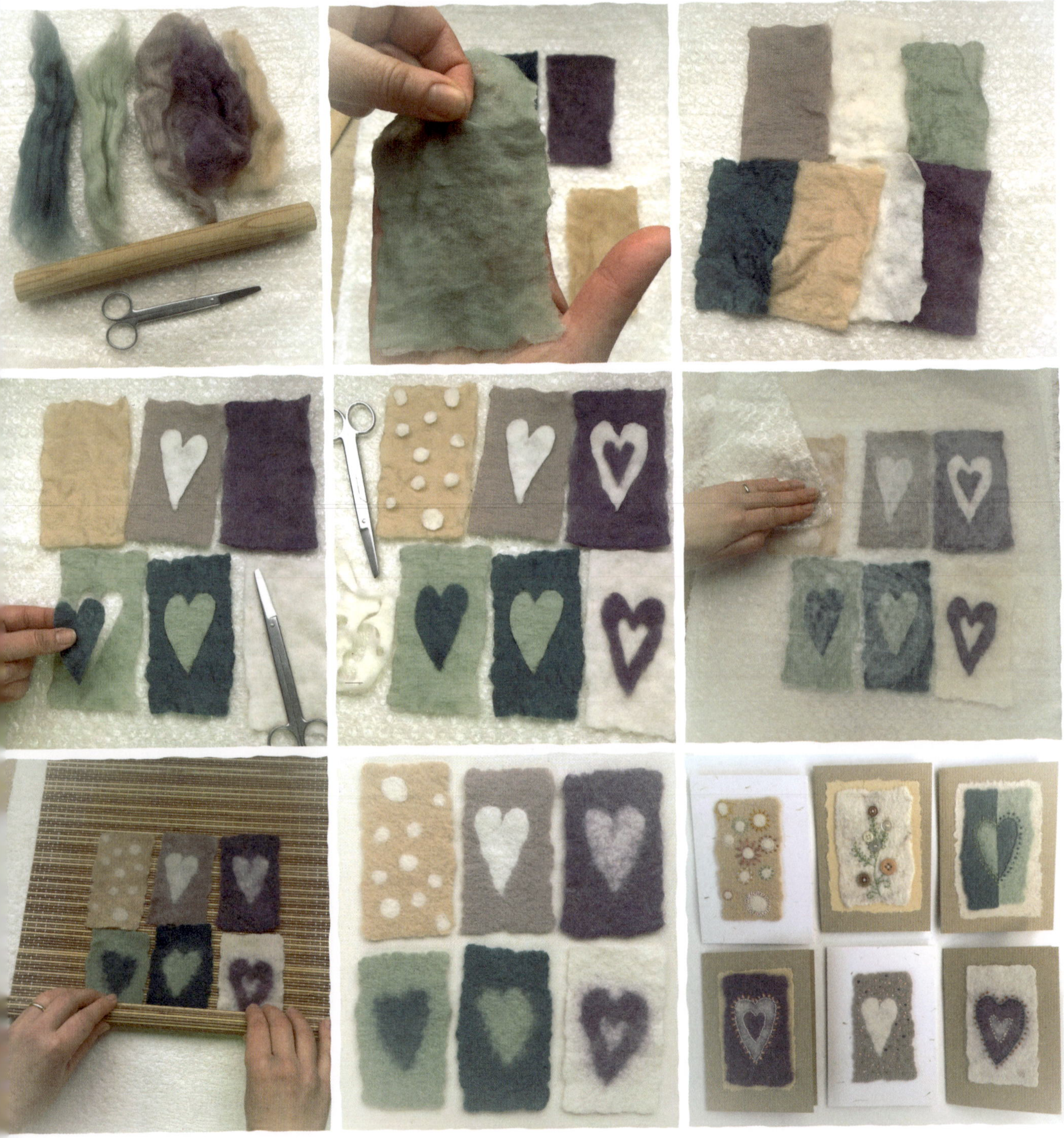

Making Pre~felts

Pre felts are pieces of partially felted wool that can be used in your design, creating definite shapes with clear edges. The wool is felted only to the point before it shrinks, but it can be handled and cut, and it will still merge with other fibres. If the wool is felted too far, is it difficult for the layers to bond. Try making a range of pre felts, rinse and dry and store for future projects. Pre felts can be cut up to use on the surface or as inlay, layered together, even cut into strips and woven to form a lattice or chequer board effect and other patterns.

Pre felt samples...

Lay out your fibres.

You can make several pre felts together of various colours and thickness.

Make them as large or small as you wish, edges can be left wispy, or straight and any shape you like.

Wet the fibres through as before, and begin the felting process, either rubbing or rolling.

Roll for 50 times in each of the four directions, or rub with a felting tool or bubble wrap until the fibres begin to bond together.

Pinch test.

A good way to test if the fibres are beginning to merge is to gently grab some fibres with your finger and thumb, and if individual fibres come away, keep rubbing or rolling. When you can pinch the surface and the fibres are connected, the felt will lift, and felting has begun. (See top row)

Pause the felting and gently rinse the pre felt, squeeze dry and blot with a towel.

Store extra pre felts until you need them.

You can can add your pre felt onto a fresh layer of fibres or mix them together. (See middle row)

Cut out shapes and switch them, or place them together. Fresh wool fibres and other decorative details can also be added to the surface.

When you are ready to felt the wool, wet through with soap solution.

To help the layers bond together, cover with netting and give the whole surface a gentle rub with a plastic bag, bubble wrap, or a felting tool. Keep rubbing until the design stays in place.

Felt the wool.

Continue to rub the wool more vigorously, or go to the next sated in the rolling process, see guide below. (You've already done the first 50 rolls each of 4x turns)

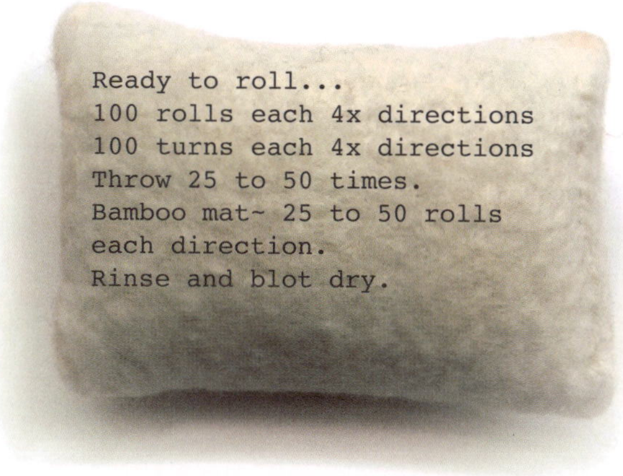

When you are happy with the amount of felting, rinse and dry your pre felt samples. You can decorate them and use to make pictures or handmade cards. (See bottom row)

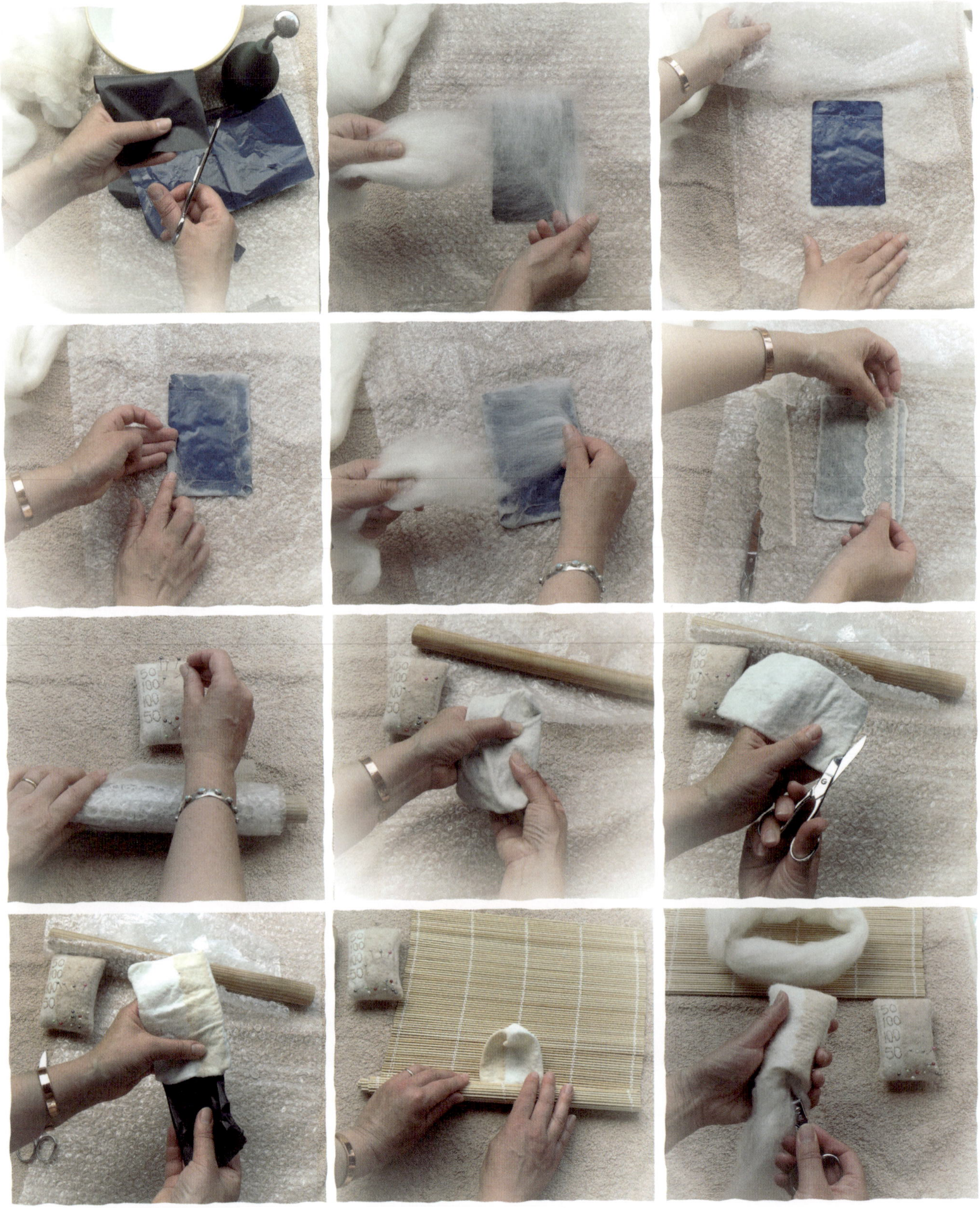

Resist Technique

The resist technique is where plastic bag or any similar material is used prevent two layers of fibres from felting together, which means you can make pockets, bags, layers, and three dimensional hollow forms.

~Dark coloured plastic is useful when covering with light coloured fleece, as you can see any thin patches.
~White opaque plastic is good if you are using dark fibres, so you can see the layers.
~When you make more complicated shapes, it helps to cover the template in sections, not all at once, this will help when folding fibres around tight corners, and help stop different sections from joining together, like the fingers of gloves.
~Remember the wool shrinks, so measure perhaps a third or 33% larger for your project.

Pin cushion/counter

1. Cut a simple pillow shape from your chosen resist material. This one is 15cm x 10cms
2. Place your resist shape on the bubble wrap. Lay out your fibres as on pages 16 and 17. Be sure to overlap the edge of the resist shape with some fibres as shown.
3. Sprinkle with soap solution, cover with bubble wrap, and press to wet through.
Turn both layers of bubble wrap over, peel back the top layer to reveal the back of the template.
4. Starting form one side, lift some of the wet fibres that are showing form under the resist, and fold them over onto the top of the template.
5. With dry hands, place some fibres over the exposed resist, filling in the gap. Then add another layer of fibres over the whole surface, overlapping the edge as in step 2.
Sprinkle this with more soap solution, cover with bubble wrap, and press through.
Turn the whole sandwich back over, peel back the bubble wrap and again fold over the outside fibres onto the surface.
Add one more layer of fibres to the centre of the resist, where it may be thin.
6. Add any design to the surface of the felt, don't forget to turn over and fold any more overlapping fibres over the edges
7. Roll up the felt inside the bubble wrap and roll 4 x 50 rolls in each direction as on page 18.
8. In between the next 4 x 100 rolls, move the template inside the felt to avoid thick seams. This is done by pinching the wool between fingers and thumb, and pushing the felt to the left or right, so it turns around the outside of the template as shown. Repeat the next 4 x 100 rolls.
9. Cut an opening in the felt, along the edge is good as this can be stitched back up after stuffing the cushion.
10. Remove the plastic resist.
11. Firm up the felt by rolling inside the bamboo mat for up to 50 rolls each direction.
12. When the felt is rinsed and dried, you can fill with wool fibres and stitch the pin cushion closed.
To help with counting your rolls when felting, just sew the numbers on with a simple back stitch.

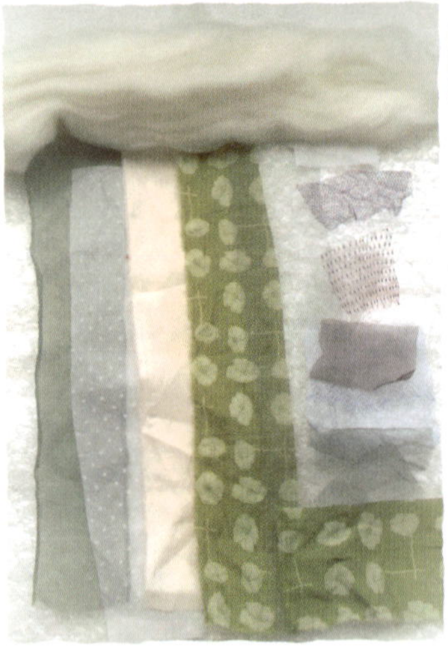

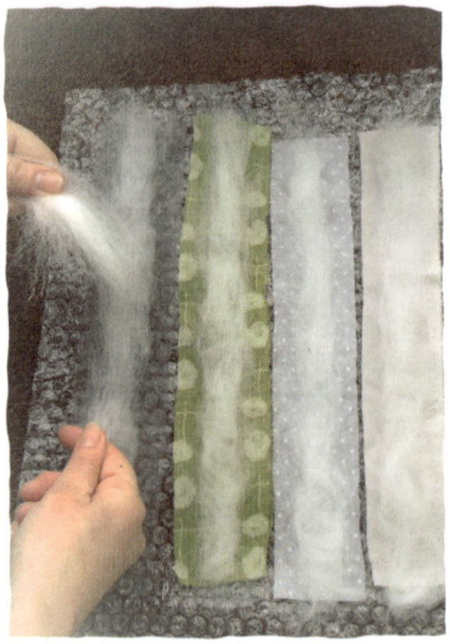

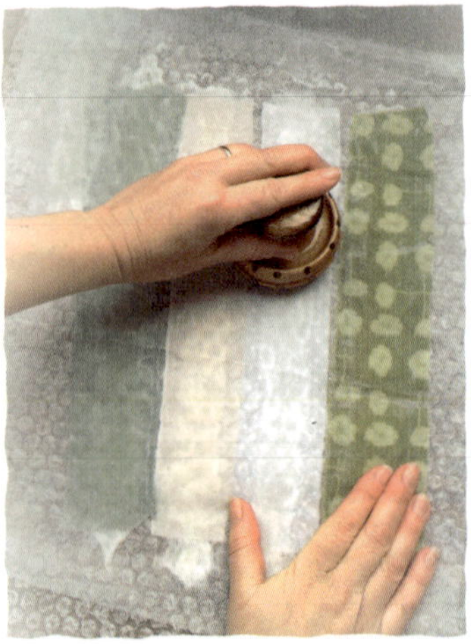

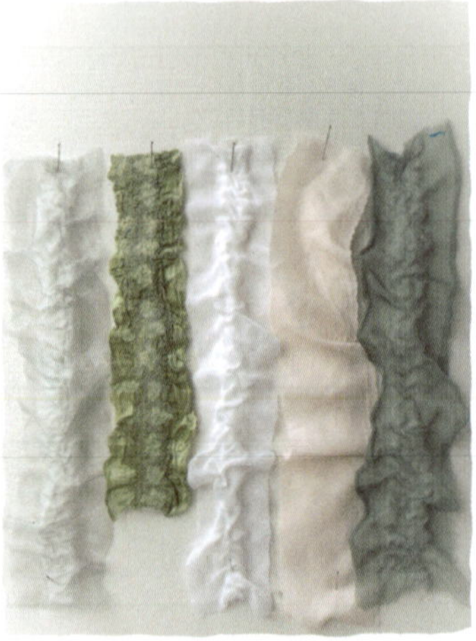

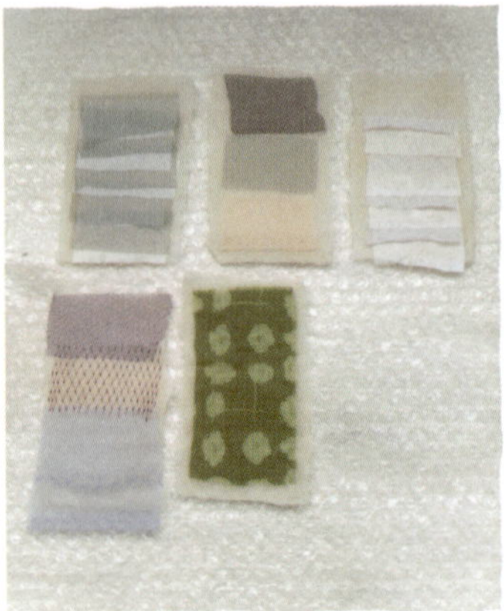

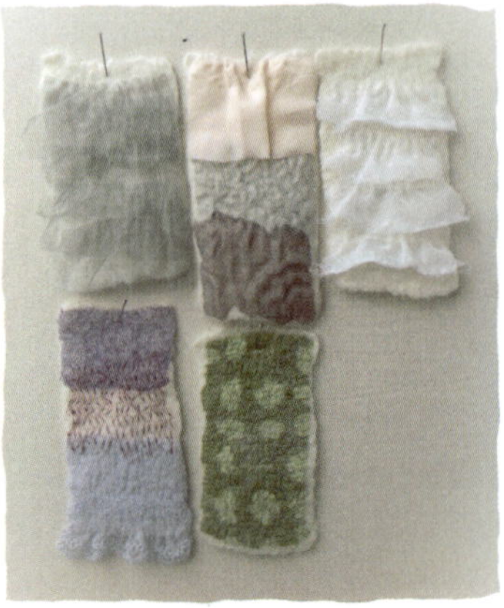

Nuno felting

Nuno is the name given to felt when it is made with the addition of woven fabric or netting, or other textiles that are trapped into the fibres, either with a layer of wool above or below, or totally embedded between layers. This creates a felt that drapes well, so nuno felting is often combined with silk and gauze to make scarves and other wearable items.
As the wool shrinks, and the fabrics do not, some interesting textures and patterns can appear, like puckering and gathering of the material as shown in these samples and the dresses opposite.
Nuno works well with loose~weave, and natural textiles like muslin, tule and really fine textiles like silk, and organza but it can be surprising how the wool fibres will find their way through the weave of some thicker textiles like tweed, and cotton.

Nuno felt samples

You may like to check that your chosen fabrics will be compatible with your fibres. Try different thicknesses, and different positioning and direction of fibres for varied shrinkage.

Lay out your fabric and fibres, and wet through with soap solution.
Cover the layers with a sheet of netting, and give everything a gentle rub to encourage the fibres through the fabric.
Felt the wool as you wish from the directions on pages 18 and 19, but additional rubbing will enhance this technique.

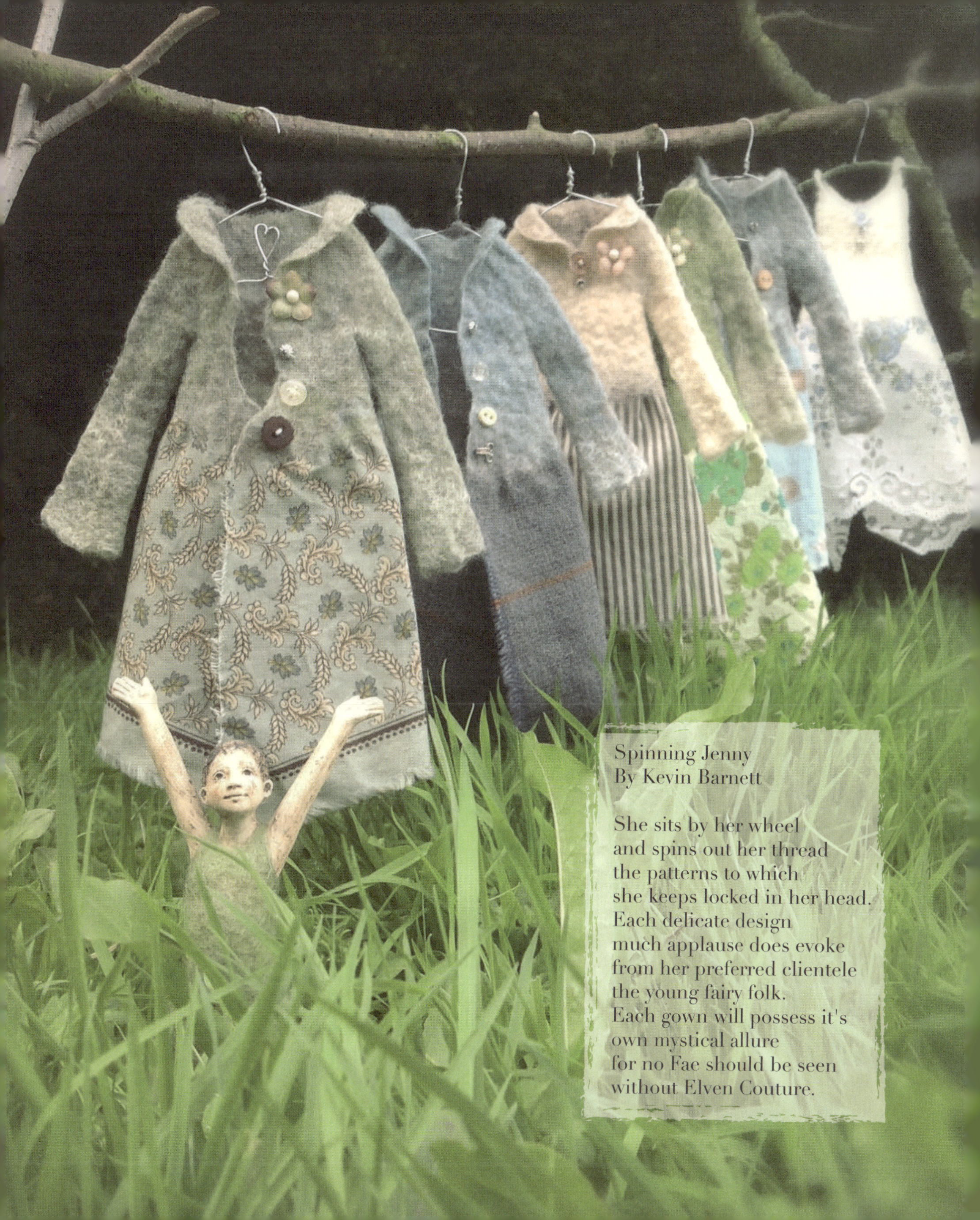

Spinning Jenny
By Kevin Barnett

She sits by her wheel
and spins out her thread
the patterns to which
she keeps locked in her head.
Each delicate design
much applause does evoke
from her preferred clientele
the young fairy folk.
Each gown will possess it's
own mystical allure
for no Fae should be seen
without Elven Couture.

Making solid shapes

Wool fibres can be formed into solid, three dimensional forms, with the same combination of warmth, moisture, rolling and massage. You can form beautifully round beads for jewellery, cords, ropes, belts, laces and long shapes for flower stems, handles or tails, arms and legs for figures. Make small patches of felt to cover anything you like, a vase, soaps, pebbles for paperweights. Flat felt that has been made to measure with a resist template can be moulded into shape by transferring onto a hat block or shoe last.

Round beads *(top row)*

Separate some fleece into roughly equal amounts and put to one side. Try different sizes with more or less fibres.
Have a towel handy, and put some warm soap solution into a bowl. Beads take just a few minutes to make.
Take one amount of fleece and pinch it over into a tight little ball, then dip it into the soap solution.
Place between your finger, with your hands flat and start to roll the wet fleece around very gently, with not too much pressure as it can split the bead. Continue rolling, dipping into the solution to keep the fibres wetted. Then add more pressure and roll in your palms, or onto some bubble wrap until the ball firms up. When you are satisfied with the size and firmness, you can rinse out the soap, squeeze water out in a towel, reshape and leave to dry.
Thread beads onto a cord using a large sharp needle to make an unusual necklace like the one on page 34.
Try mixing colours, or adding other fibres like sparkly or silk.
Start with one colour, add a contrasting colour and repeat, building up layers of colours like a geode.
This can be cut through to show the pattern of colours inside.

Things to watch out for...
If the bead splits, you can always take some more fibre, wrap this around covering the whole split bead, and continue to roll, and felt.
If you would like all your beads equal size, start with the same amounts of wool. If one seems smaller, add another layer, if one is bigger, try rolling some more to shrink.

Shaped beads *(middle row)*

Try squashing the ball flat, rubbing the bead in your palms or on bubble wrap before it is too firm, to flatten into a disc shape.
Rub your hands backwards and forwards, like you are warming your hands, to create a long, pointed bead.
Rub one end onto the bubble wrap to round off for an egg/acorn shape.
Experiment with different ways of rolling and rubbing on the bubble wrap to alter the shape.

Ropes/cords/tails/sausage shapes *(bottom row)*

Here are several ways to make them...
With bamboo mat ~Lay your fibres out to the chosen length and thickness onto the bamboo mat. Wet the fibres through and fold the mat over onto the top, gently draw the top layer across the bottom layer towards you, repeat this and check the fibres are gathering into a sausage shape. Then be more vigorous rubbing the mat forwards and backward to roll the sausage thinner.
With bubble wrap ~Place your fibres onto the bubble wrap, wet through and roll up inside the wrap, rolling to form a sausage.

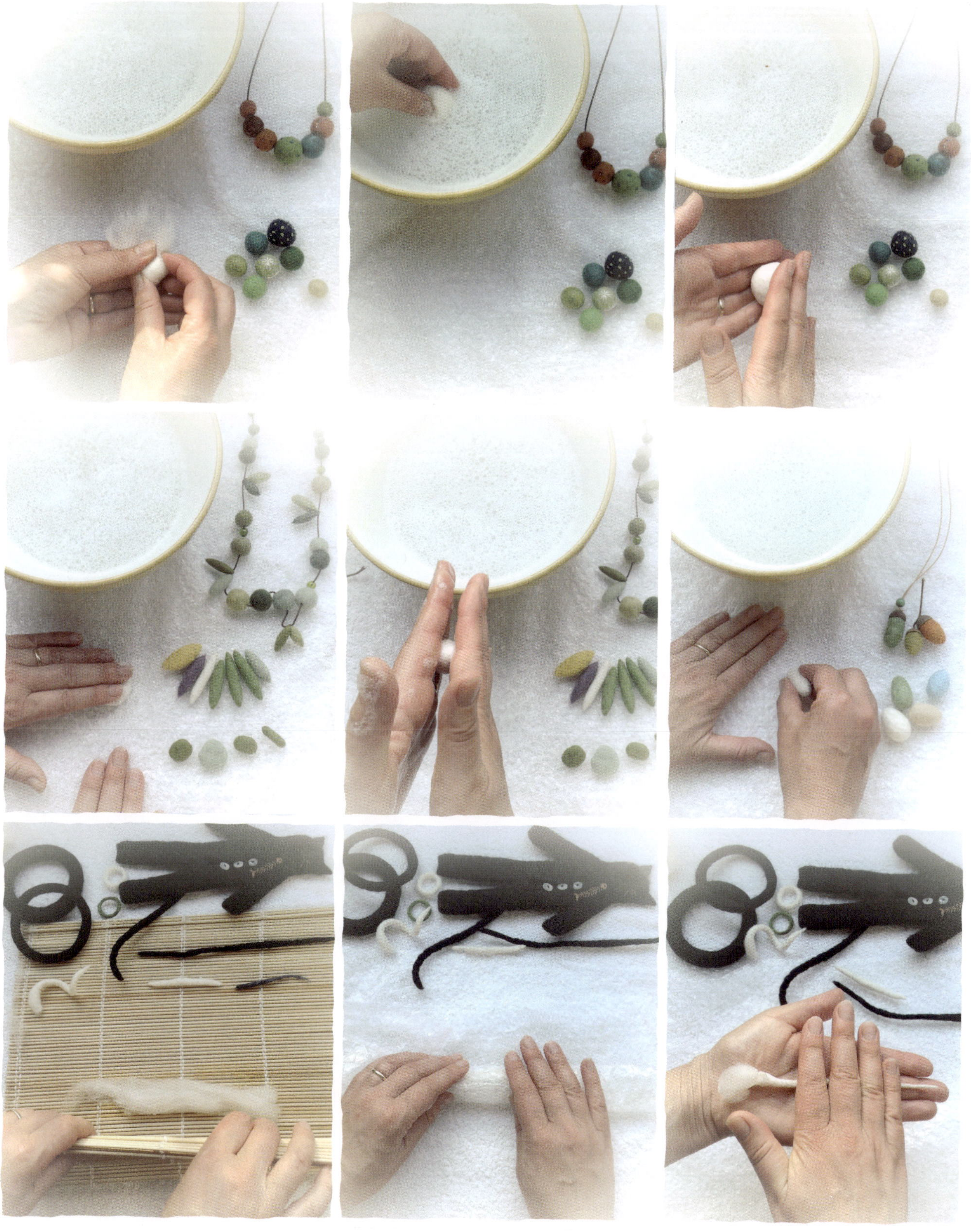

With hands ~Dampen your hands with soap solution and begin to rub the fibres between your palms, backwards and forwards, like rolling a clay sausage.
Dip into the soap solution and continue to roll to firm up the rope.
For longer lengths, just leave the end fibres loose, and connect more fibres so they merge together during felting.

Things to try...
Vary the thinness/thickness by adjusting the amount of wool, or add more wool to thicken.
Make a loop, chain or bangle , by rolling the middle of the length first, leaving the ends dry. Form into a loop, and join the dry ends together so they overlap. Wet hands and roll this section to join, then dip in the soap solution and continue to roll the whole loop all around to firm up.
Try joining the felt rope or handle or tail to the other felt as it is being made, so leave the ends dry, place them onto the main piece and felt together by rubbing.

Wrapping 3D shapes

A curious idea is to encase items in your handmade felt. You can also choose to remove them after felting to create hollow forms, like a pod, a bowl or a vessel, its also a way to make larger items like hats and slippers to wear too.
Cover pebbles to make a paper weight, cover three golf balls to practice juggling, make a cat toy with jingle bells inside.
Make plenty of patches of fibres, enough to cover and overlap all sides of your chosen object.
Choose your item and follow the directions below to cover it with felt. Felting takes about ten minutes, but carry on longer if you think it's necessary.

Sea shell rattle (opposite)

Find two limpet shells about the same size.
Place some small pebbles into one shell, place the other on top and bind the two together with yarn. Wrap as much as you like, to make a nice shape, and prevent them separating. (Top row)

To cover your object
Lay out several patches of fibres to cover the object. These can be roughly round shaped
Lay one or two more patches to include your chosen pattern/colour for the outside surface.
Wet, cover, and press through the fibres.
Lift one of the patches of wool and drape it over the shape. Turn over and add the second patch of wool. Keep turning the form over and overlapping the remaining patches of fibres, so the whole bundle is covered all around. Add your surface decoration last, covering the outside of the form.
All surfaces should now be covered and overlap. (Middle row)

Felt the wool. *(Bottom row)*
Gently wrap the form inside some bubble wrap, and move it around in your hands. Rub and massage the surface to felt the wool onto the object. Rub slowly to begin with, unwrap to check progress, then you can be more vigorous, rolling and rubbing until the wool is well felted and shrunk. Felting should take bout ten minutes.
Rinse and squeeze all the soap out and blot with a dry towel.
When fully dry maybe add more decoration with stitches or beads.

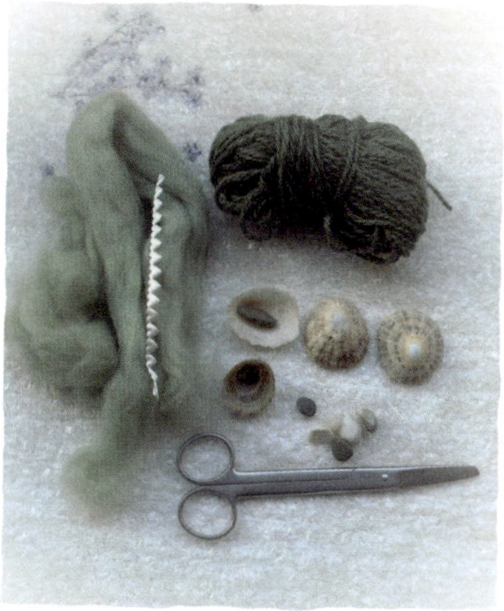
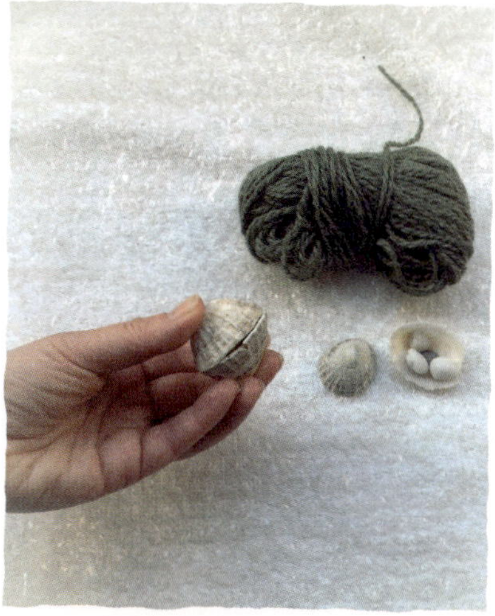
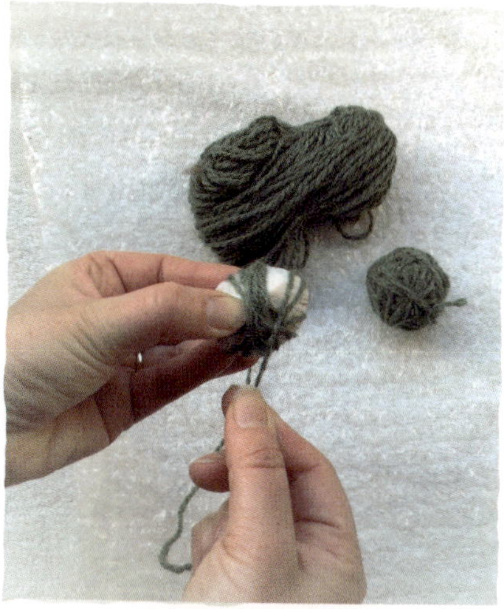
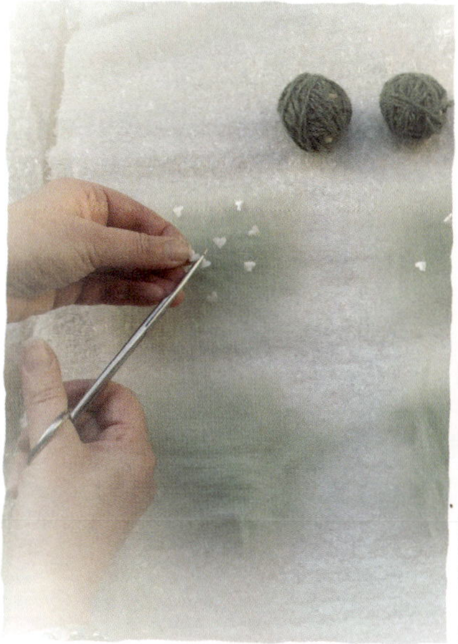
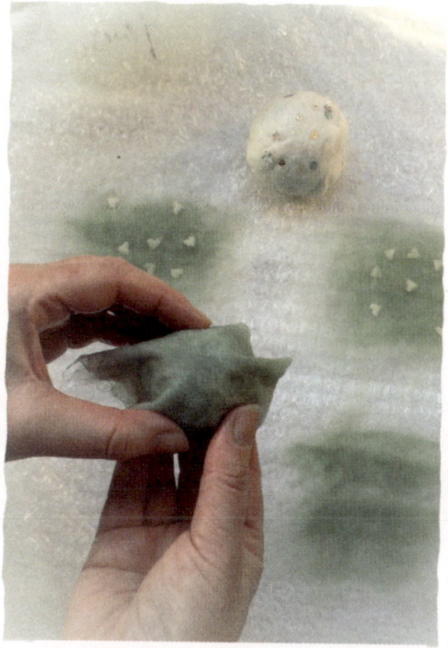
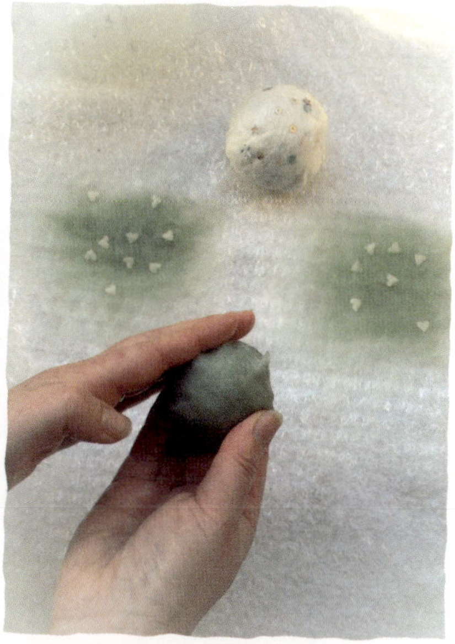
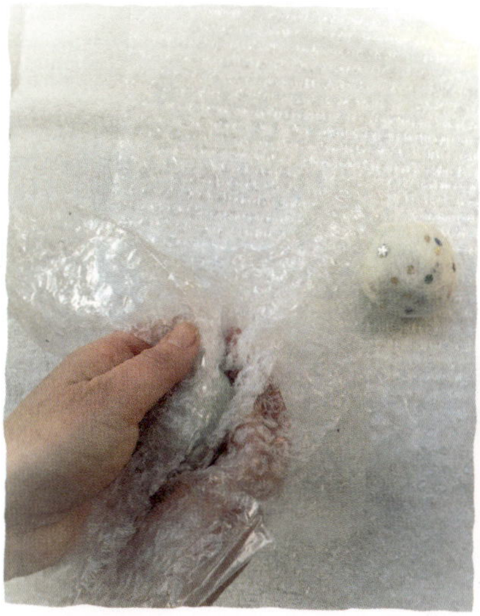
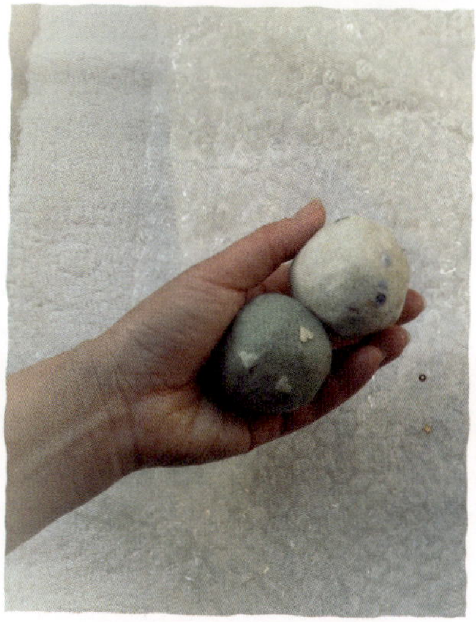
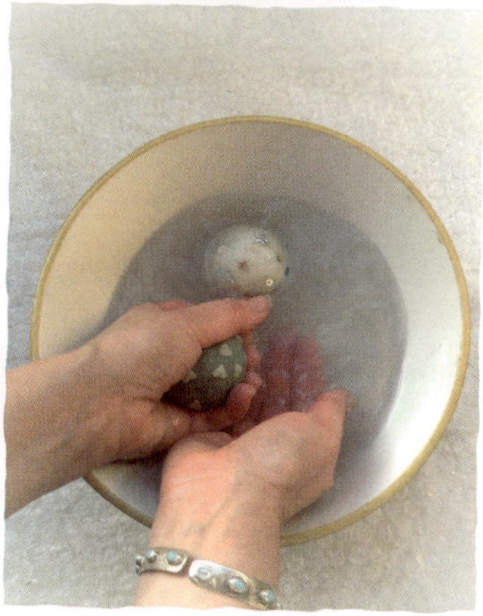

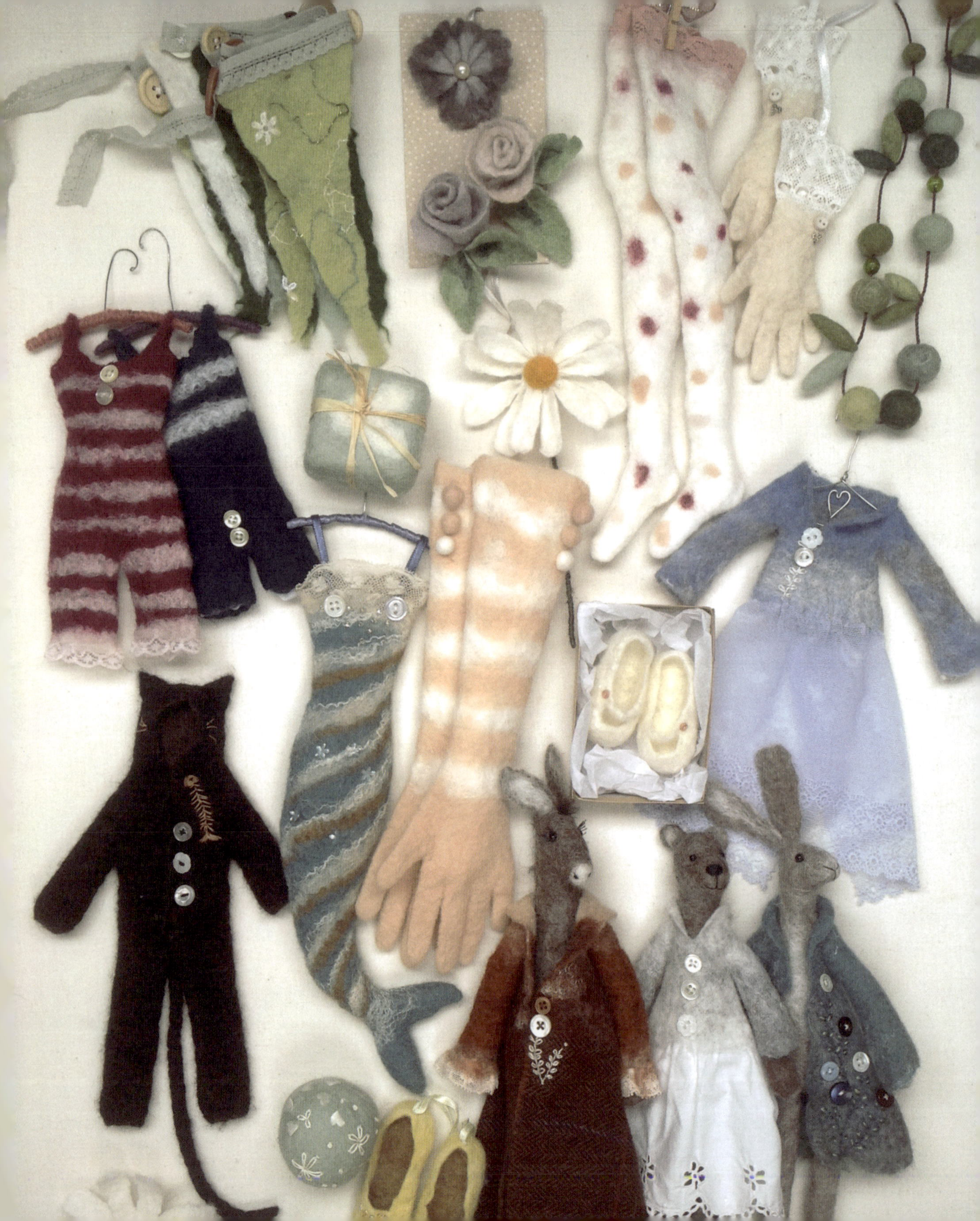

The Workshops

Here is the collection of lovey items for you to make. With each workshop there are photographs of an example, to see how it may look during creation, and illustrated steps for you to follow some of the more complicated designs. Each can be adapted to your choice of colours and materials. Enjoy choosing them and take time laying out the fine layers of fibres.

As suggested, most workshops only require about 10 to 20 grammes of wool. The amount of rolling is a guide and can be adjusted if your fibres felt quicker or slower.

If you get stuck, don't panic just refer to the techniques at the beginning of the book, or problem solving on page 110. Good luck!

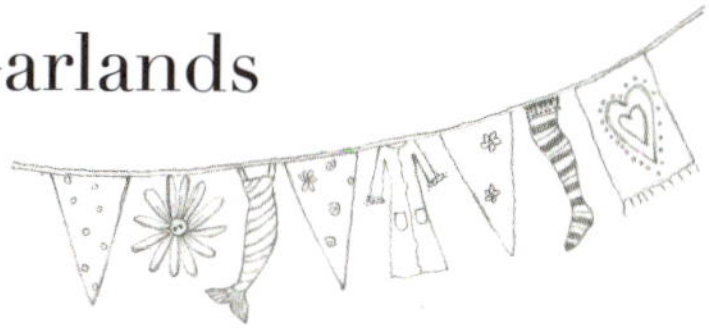

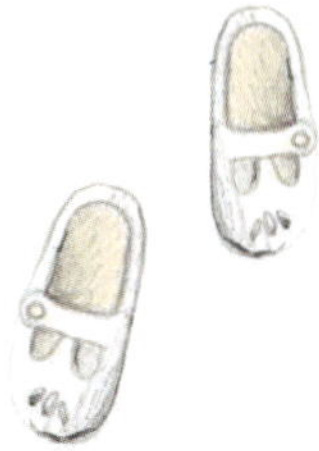

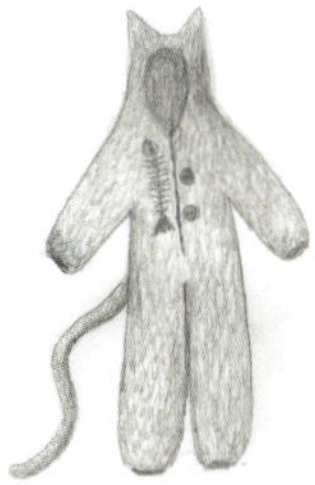

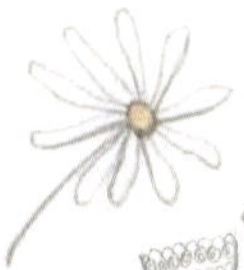

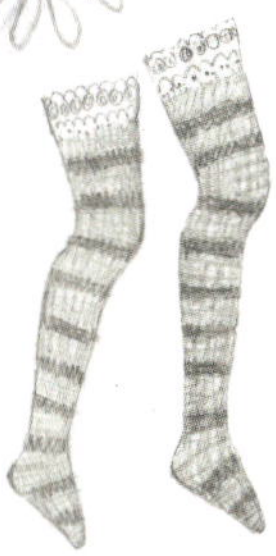

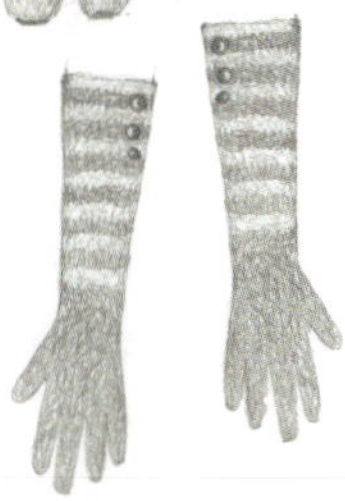

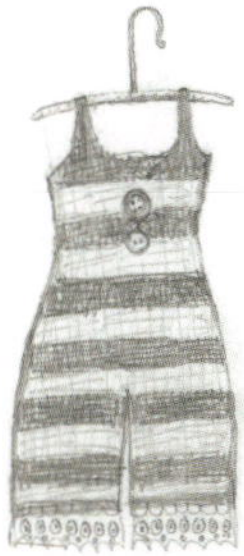

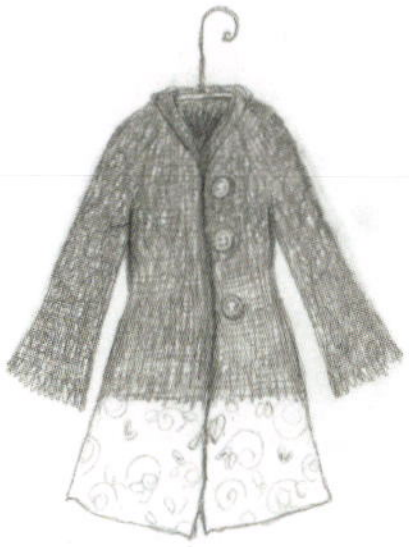

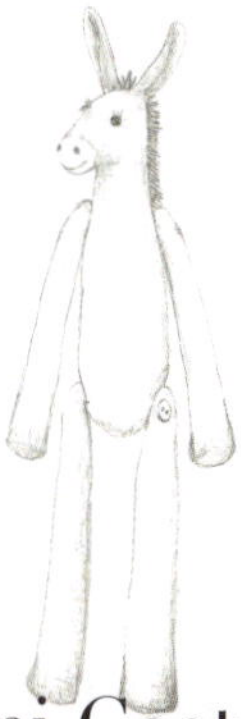

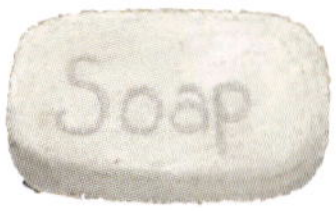

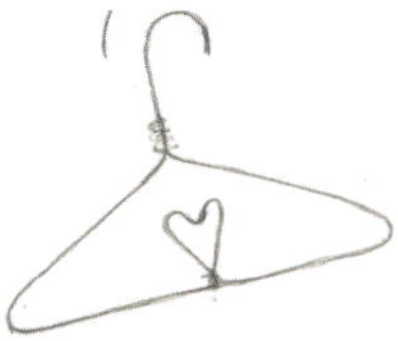

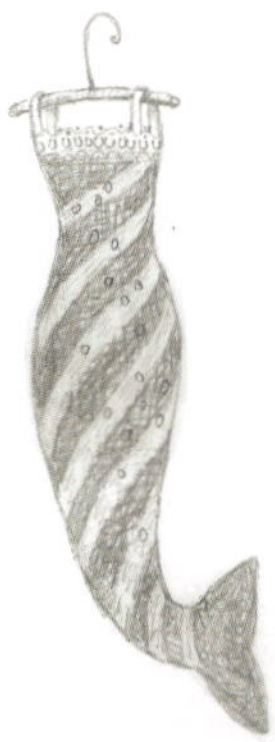

Bunting and garlands

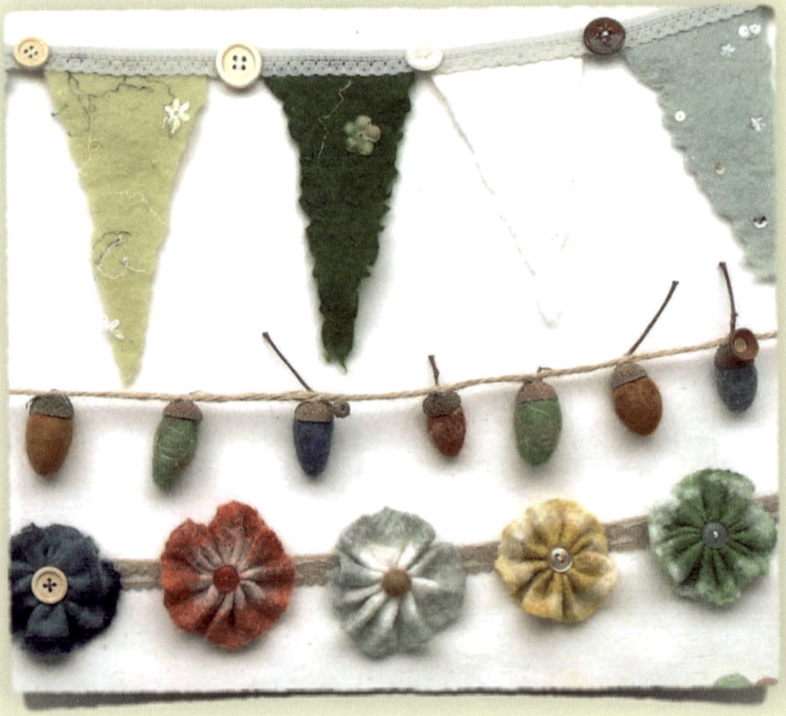

Celebrate with traditional triangle shaped flags, or make different shapes and sizes ~ tiny bunting, square prayer flags, leaf shapes, scallop shells, hearts, paper chains...
Add your own patterns, designs, or cut pre~felt lettering to spell a message ~ welcome, happy birthday, new baby's name...
Make garlands using some of the other items in the book.

Materials and tools

Wool fleece, about 20 grammes for 12 flags.
Colours of your choice.
2 pieces of bubble wrap per template
Soap solution, sprinkler.
Rolling pin, Bamboo mat, Towels
Scissors
About 1m or more of lace, ribbon or tape.
Buttons or beads

Notes on technique...

Experiment with edges, try cutting the flags at different stages of felting for different effects.
Decorate the flags when finished using buttons/beads/embroidery.
Stitch or glue onto tape/ribbon or lace trim. Space as wide as you like, add beads buttons in between.
Design your own shapes.

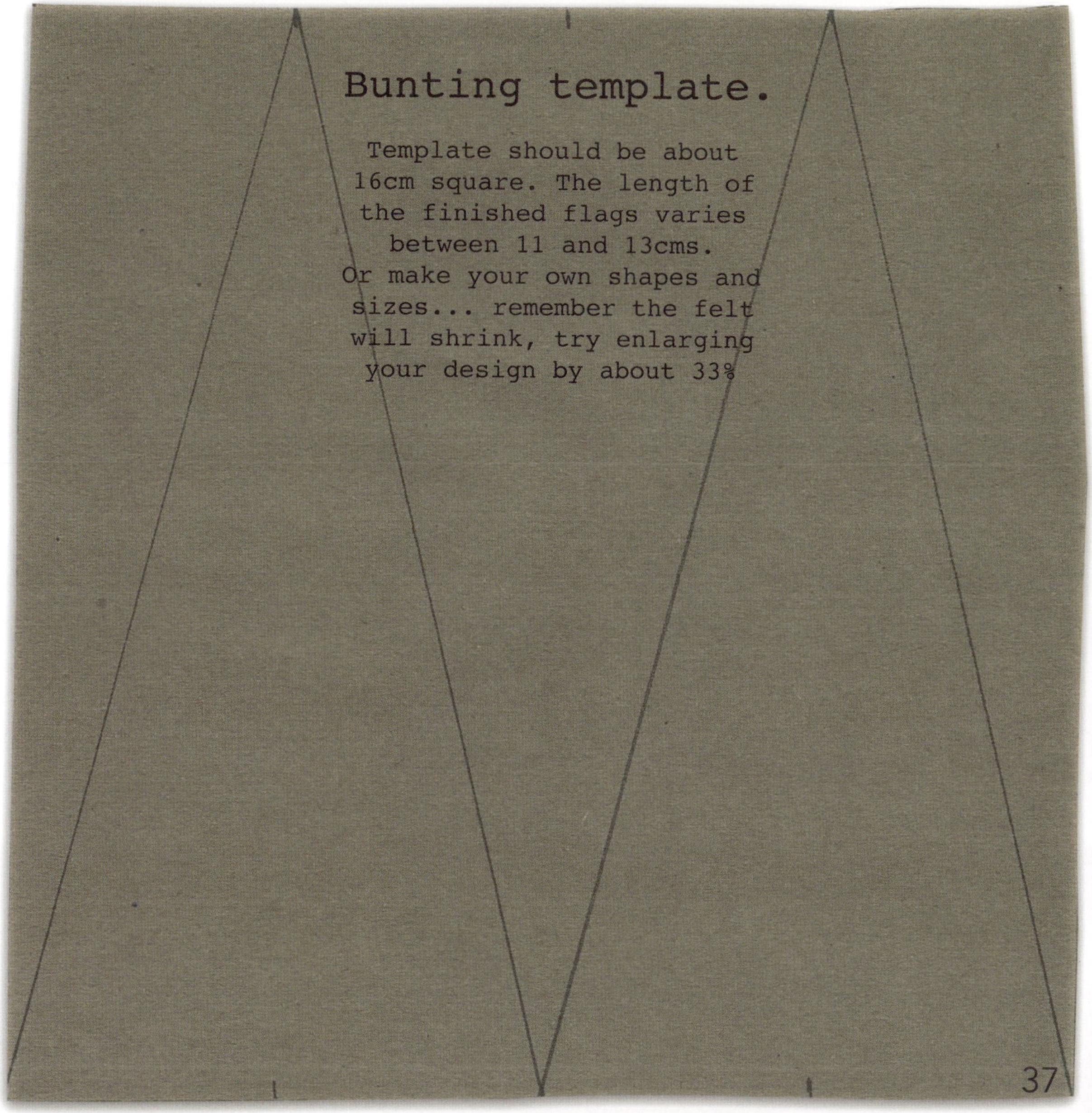

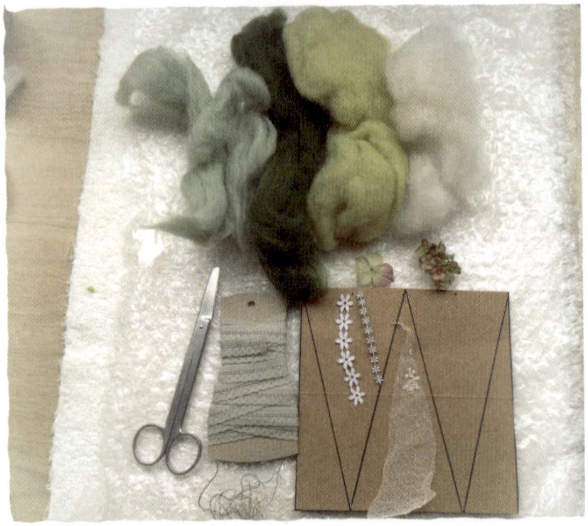

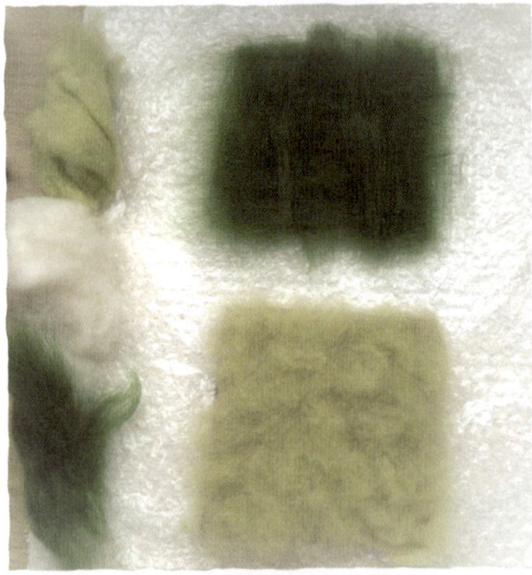

1

This bunting is made with four sets of different colours/design, to make 12 flags.
You can try cutting the flags at different stages in the felting for different edges, or even cut them after the felting is done.

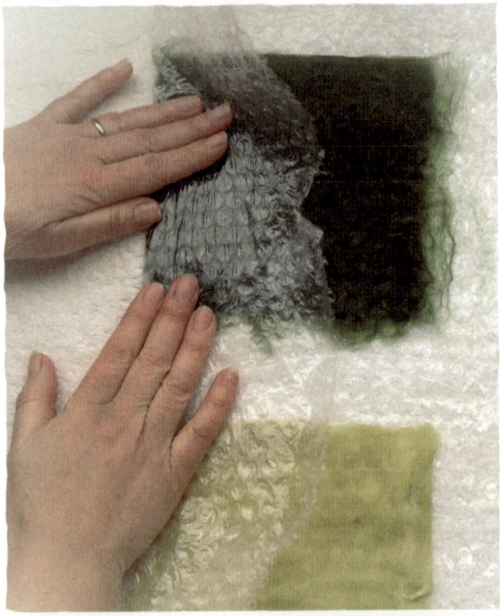

2

Lay out your design.

1. Place your template beneath the bubble wrap so you can see the shape and size to follow. Or you could draw the shape directly onto the back of your bubble wrap with marker pen.
Place a fine layer of fibres over the area to be covered.
You can slightly overlap at the edge. Add another fine layer in the opposite direction.
Wet the fibres, cover with bubble wrap and press through.

2. Peel back the top layer of bubble wrap.
Use the lower sheet of bubble wrap to fold over the edge of the fibres and create a straight edge. Repeat this for all of the edges.

3. Check for any thin areas and fill them in.
You can add any surface decoration at this stage, or add some pre felted designs like lettering. Refer to the tips for making pre felts on page 25.

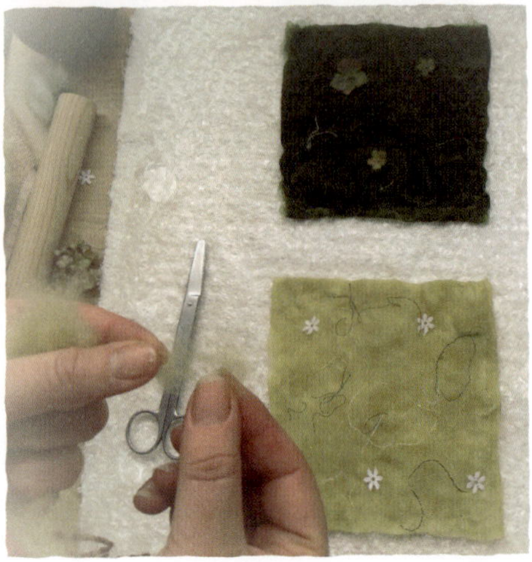

3

Felt the wool. *(refer to the felting guide below)*
Fix any surface decoration in place and begin the felting process by covering with netting and rubbing gently.
Roll up the bubble wrap for the first 50 x rolls in each direction. The felt will now be at the pre felt stage, ready for cutting. This will create a soft, slightly wavy edge.

Cut the flags.
4. Remove the top layer of bubble wrap.
The felt should still be about the size of the template.
Place the template on the top and mark the point of each triangle with a snip of the scissors.

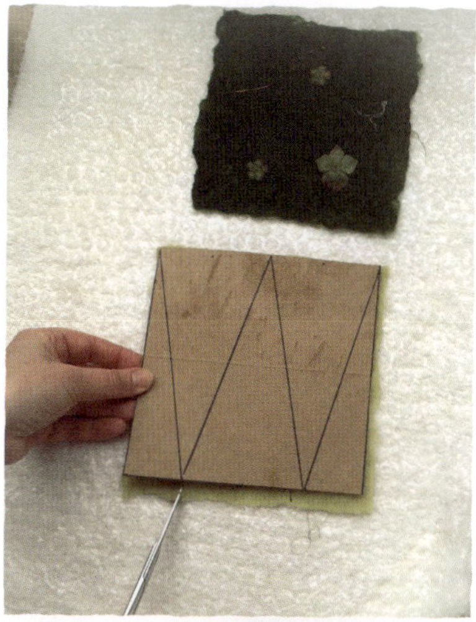

4

5. Remove the template and cut a straight line from each point to create three whole triangles. Use a ruler if needed. There should be two halves of triangle at each end.
Space the triangles apart a little.

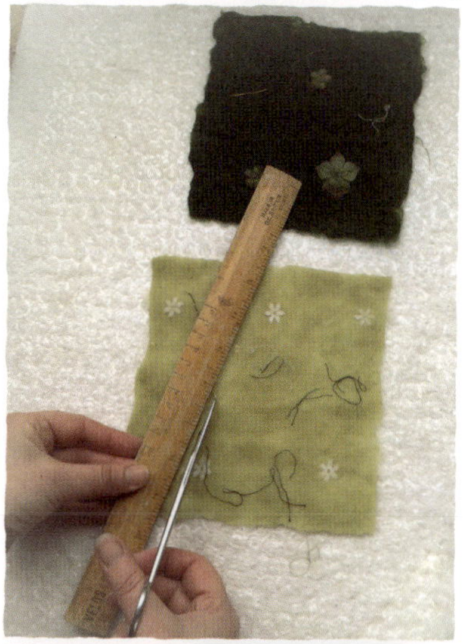

5

6. You can make an extra triangle with the two spare halves by overlapping them slightly. Cover this one with net and rub with bubble wrap to help the two halves merge together.
You can still add some details like patterns or lettering with fresh wool fibres or pre felt at this stage.
To make sure they adhere, cover with net and rub a little more.

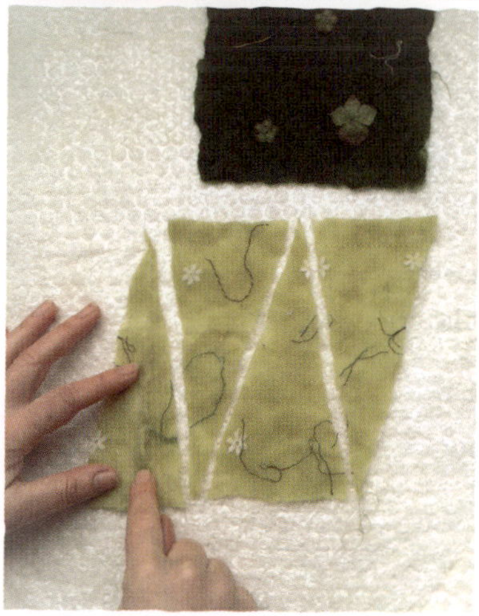

6

Repeat the cutting for all three sections of felt, or you can leave some for cutting at later stages in the felting to create sharper edges.
Complete the felting of the flags as below.

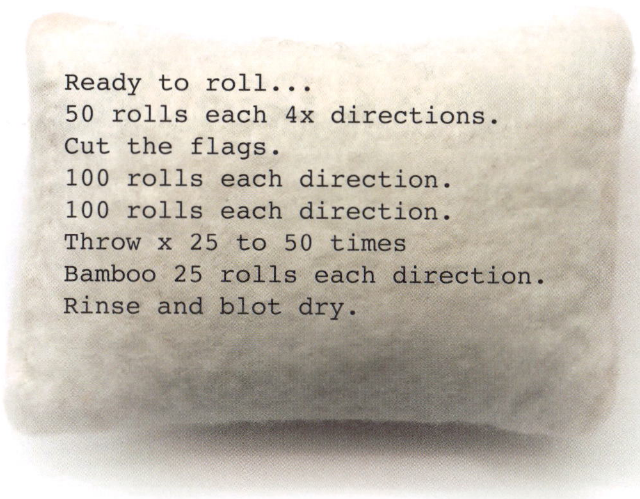

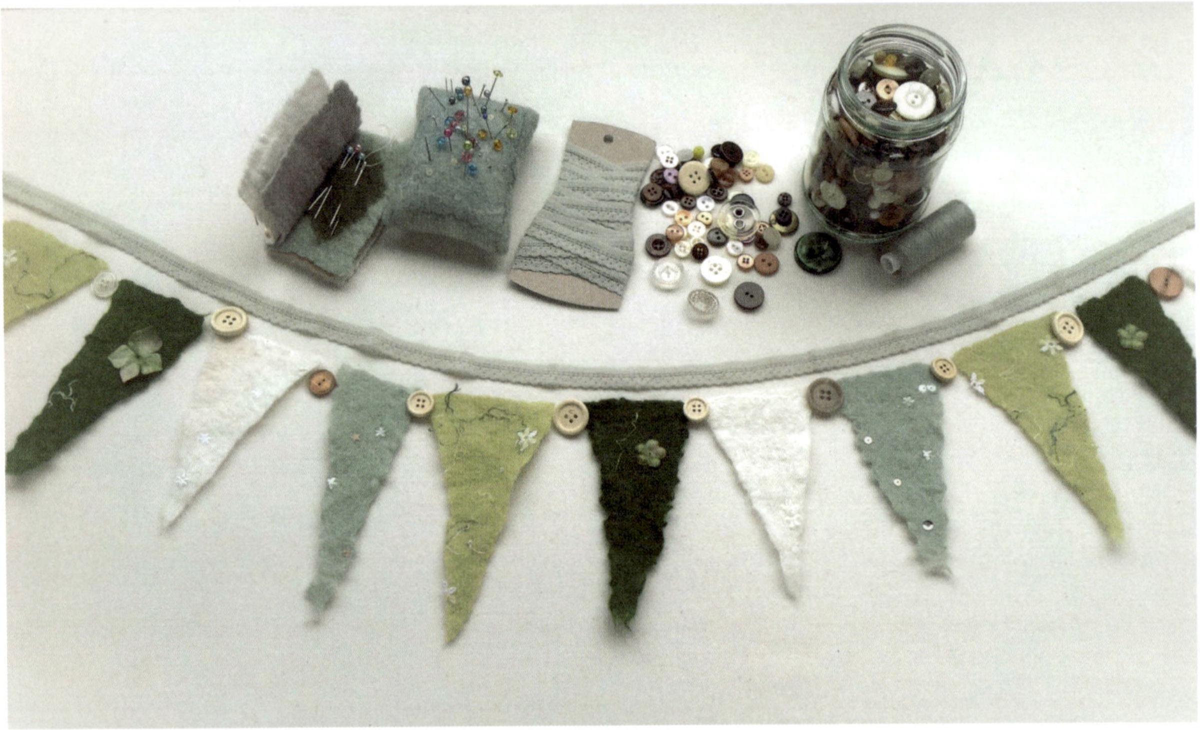

Press your flags flat with an iron. (Avoid this if there are sequins involved as they can could melt, not pretty! Or place a piece of tissue paper on top first)
Space the flags along your worktop and rearrange the combinations of colours as you like. Try different spacing, adding decorative elements to the gaps, like buttons or beads.
Measure enough tape or ribbon to include a loop at both ends for hanging, or joining to other lengths of bunting. Sew the flags in place or cheat with glue if you prefer.

Garlands

To make garlands with any of the other designs in the book, have fun choosing colours and layout.
The paper chain style garland is made with simple strips of felt, stitched or glued into links with a glue gun.
For the acorn garlands, make various size and colour acorns using the techniques on page 30.
Match them up with real acorn cups to fit and glue them in place. A hot melt glue gun works well for this, and you can carefully glue the cups to a length of rustic twine.
Flower garlands can be stitched or glued onto a length of ribbon or lace.
Beads can be threaded with a large sharp needle onto nylon thread or fishing line.
Mix and match to your heart's content.

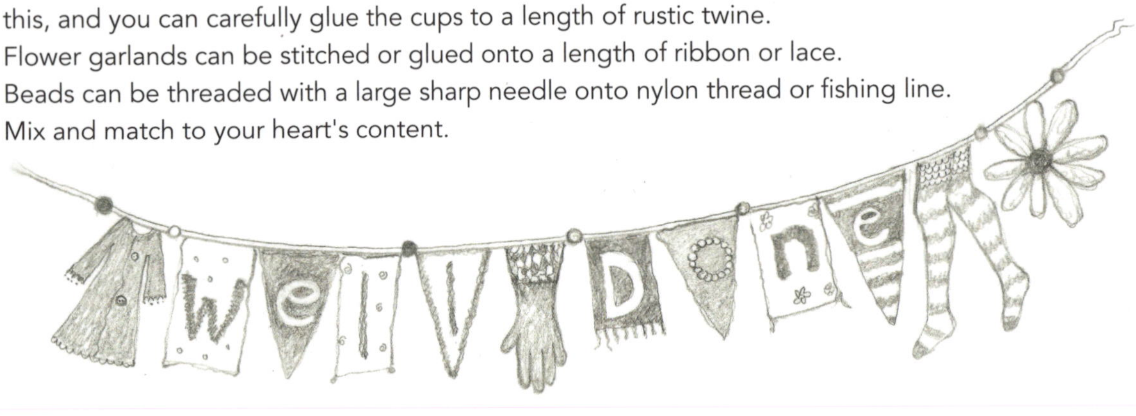

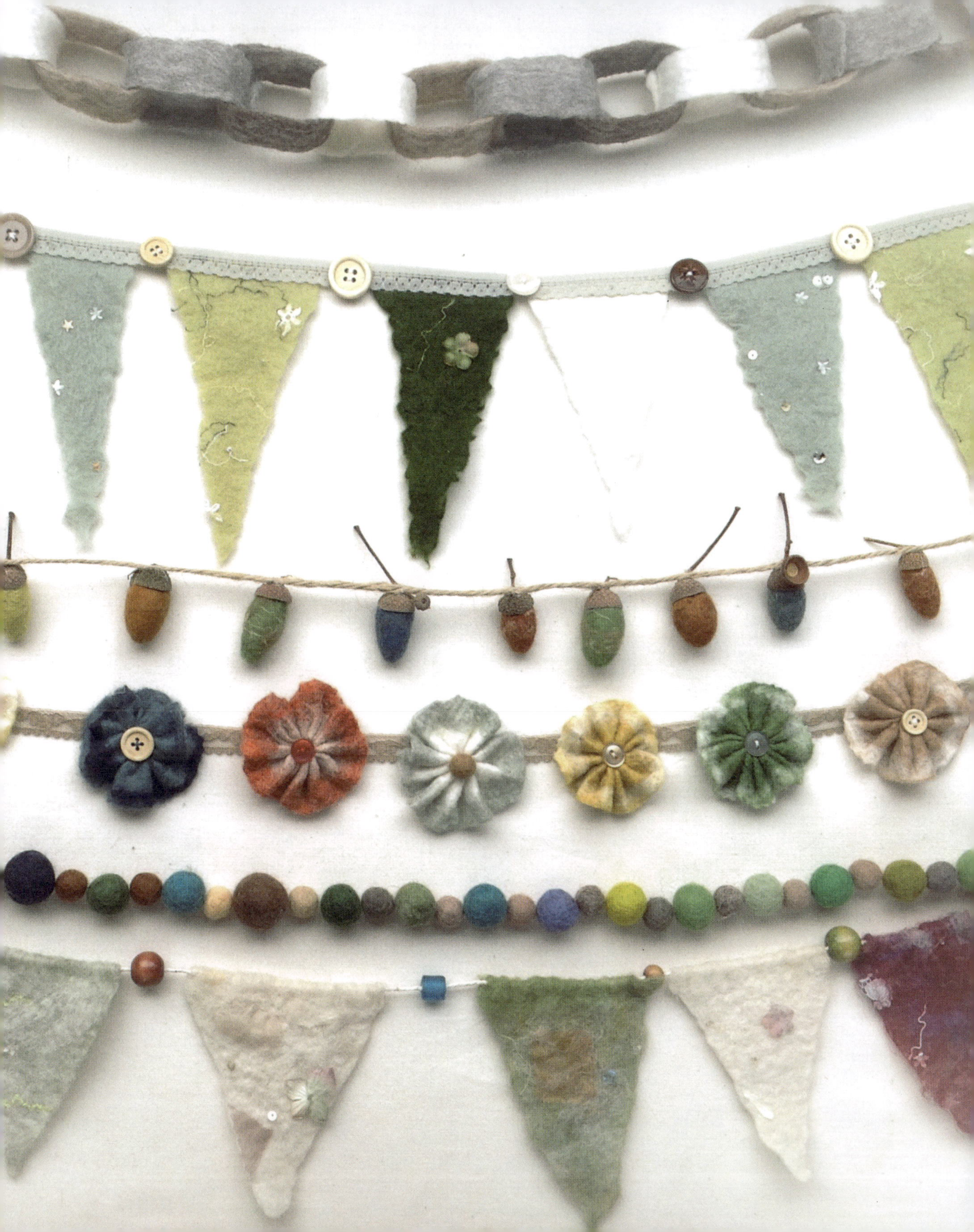

Flowers

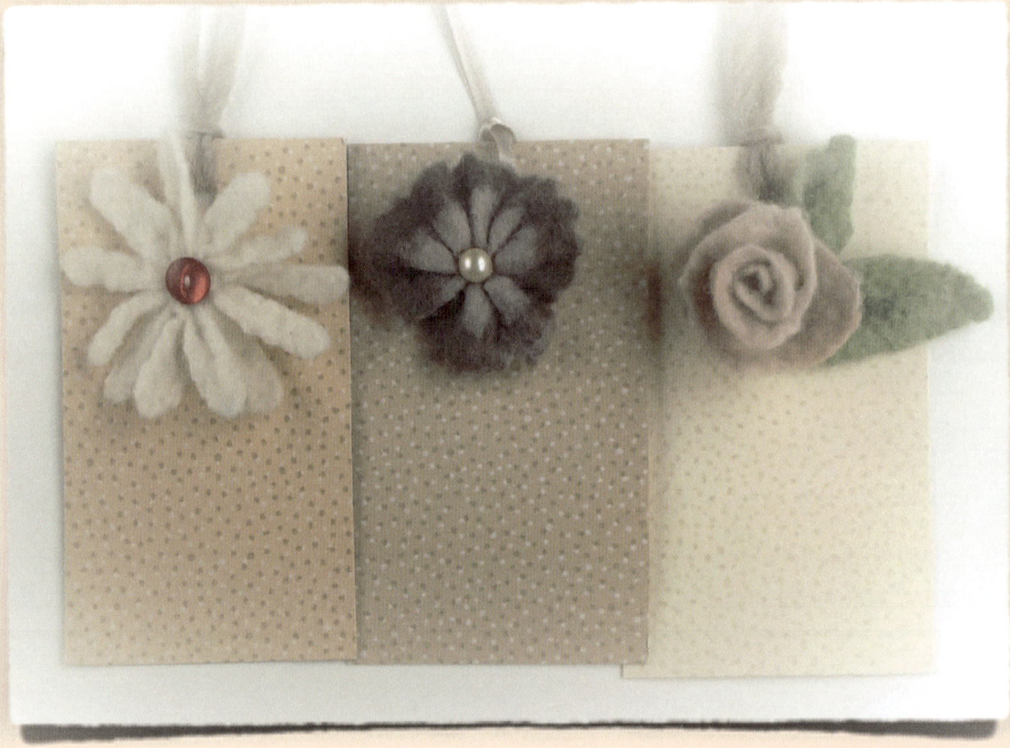

Create a bouquet to last. Invent your own species, lay out random amounts of fibres for different size, shape, length petals. The flowers can be made into a pretty garland. Make them into beautiful brooches or hair accessories, or pin onto your favourite hat.

Materials and tools

Wool fleece, a few gms per flower ~several different colours
Several pieces of bubble wrap
Soap solution, sprinkler, bowl
Rolling pin
Bamboo mat
Towels
Card to make templates (optional)
Buttons or beads
Wire, cutters, pliers
Ribbon, string or yarn
Scissors
Glue gun
Sewing needle and threads
Brooch pins, hair clips etc. optional

Notes on technique..

Try a different scale, like larger petals for big moon daisies.
Try combining flat felt and 3D shapes to make different styles ~ trumpets, leafs, stamens and stems. Try layering petals.
Have a look at different flower structure.
Try different colour fibres top and bottom, to create different shades at the edges of petals and leaves.
Add a wire, bound with thread for a stem.
Fold daisy petals at the base and secure with a stitch.
Use small amounts of wool to make the felt quite thin and delicate.

Choose your own size for petals, with or without a template. Examples here are about 5 to 6 cm long.

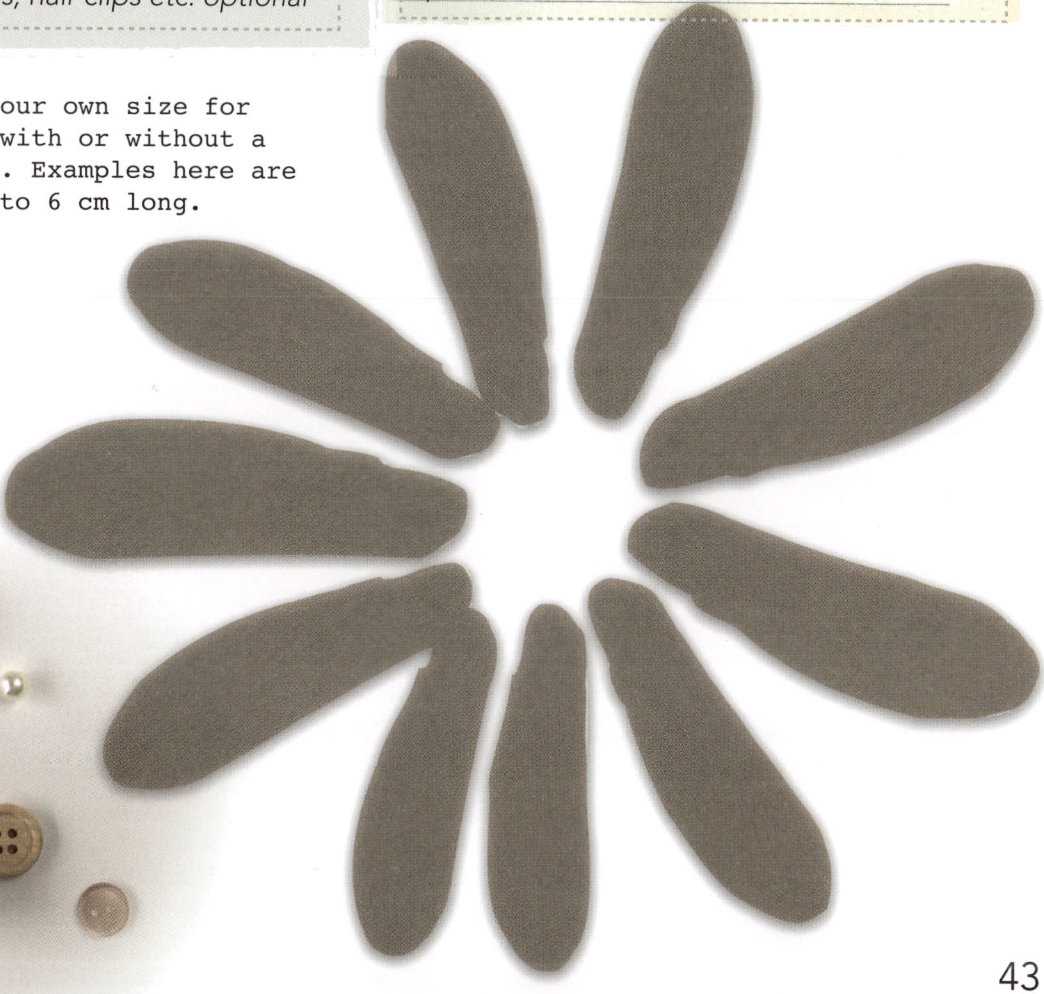

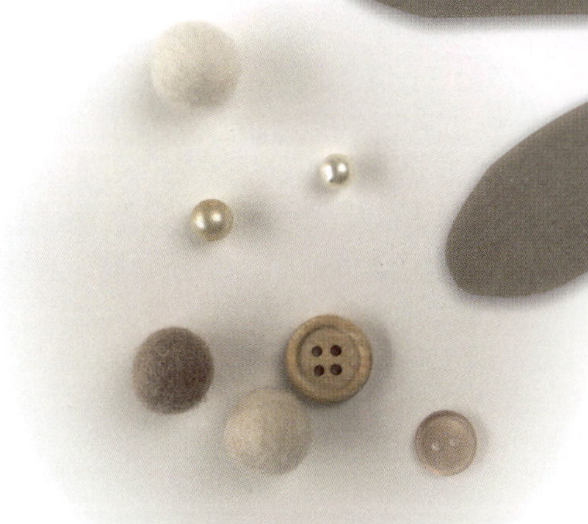

Making Daisies

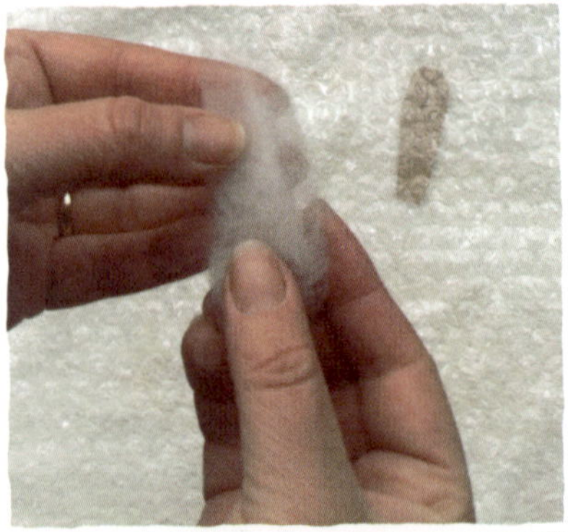

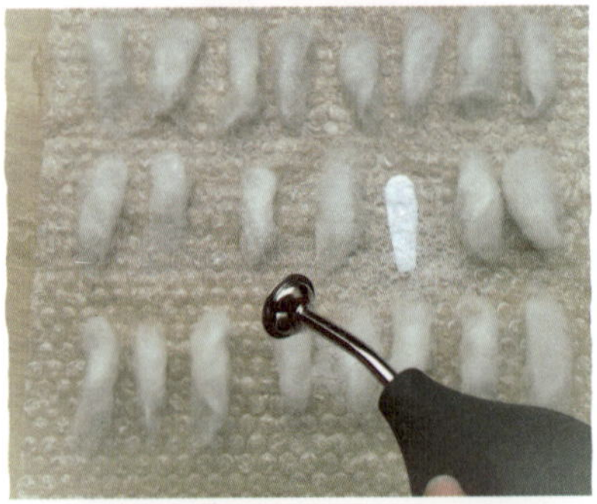

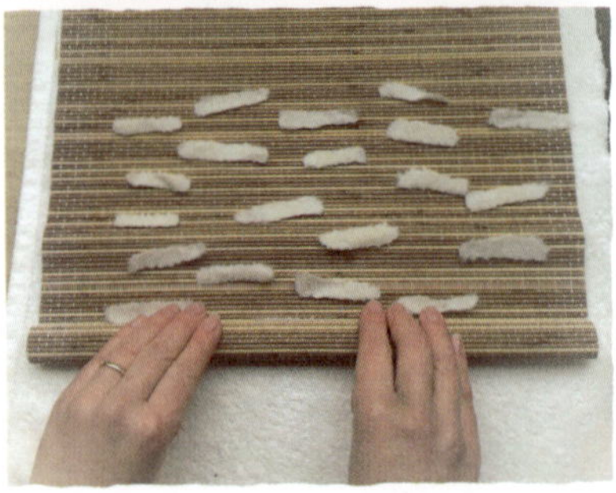

Make plenty of individual petals to be joined together.
The examples are made with about 12 petals.
Add a brooch pin or hair clip, or make a wire stem.

Lay out your fibres.
You can place some card templates beneath the bubble wrap, or just try different amounts of fleece for various sizes.
Lay fibres onto the bubble wrap, try rolling them over to shape them a little. Space them out so they don't join together during felting.
Wet with soap solution, cover with bubble wrap and press through.
Unpeel the bubble wrap to look at the shapes.
You can try leaving a natural wispy edge, or fold the outside edges inwards to create a more definite shape.
Felt the wool. *(refer to the guide below)*

Press petals dry with an iron.
Sew a thread through the base of each petal, adding a fold if you can (see below) and stitch together in sequence, or try a glue gun if you prefer. Add a contrasting felt bead or a button for the centre.

To make a stem, bind along the length of some wire with cotton or wool thread and glue the ends. Bend one end into a circle and glue to the underside to your daisy with a hot glue gun.
Try other petal shapes and combinations for variety.

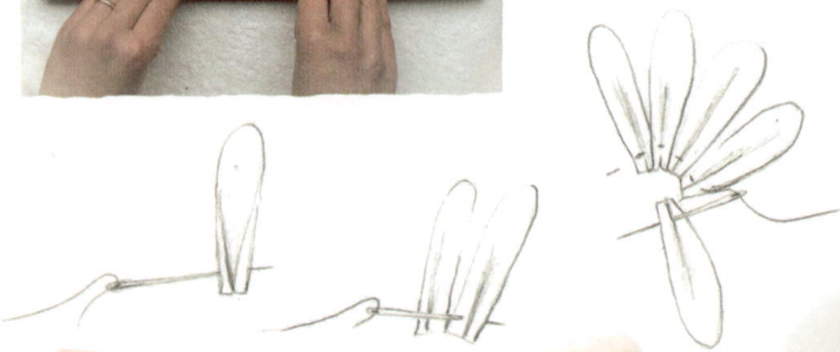

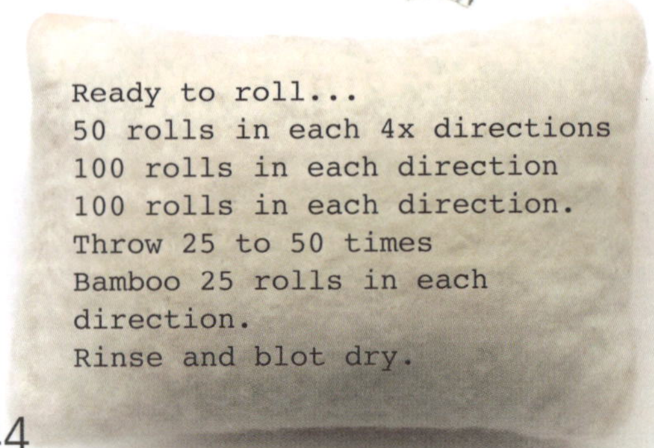

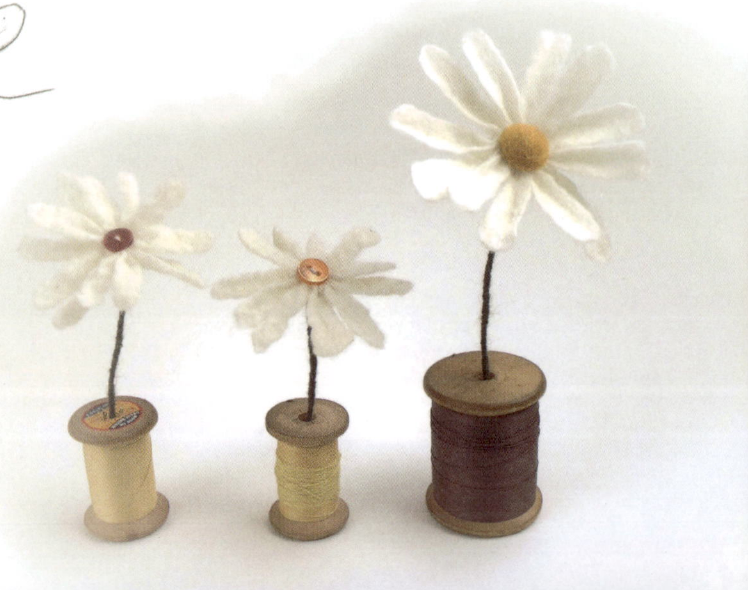

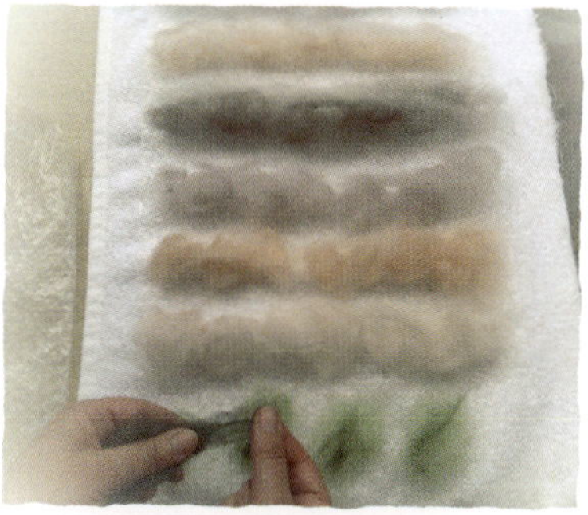

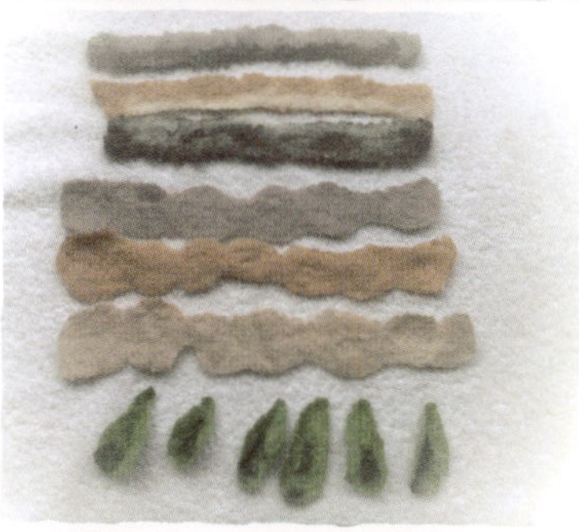

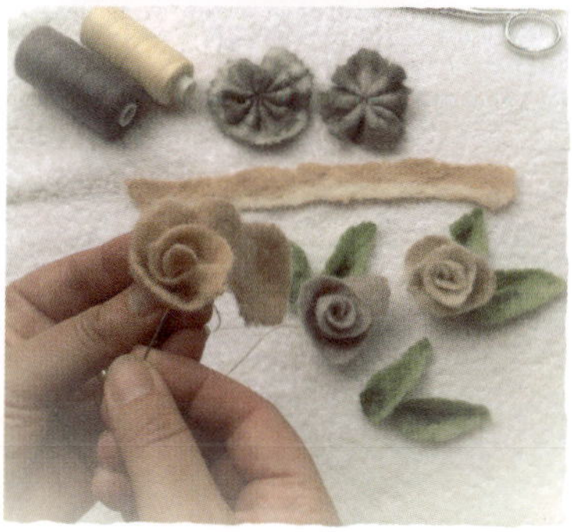

Making gathered and coiled flowers.

Gathered or coiled flowers can be simply made from strips of felted wool. Experiment with different lengths and depth, add shading and two~tone colours for variegated blooms.

Lay out your fibres.

Place a layer of fibres onto the bubble wrap in a long length, with or without a template to guide you. The examples began about 26 to 28 cm x 3cm.

Wet with soap solution, cover and press through.

Peel back the bubble wrap to look at the edges.

You can leave a natural wispy edge, or fold the outside edges inwards, or move the fibres around to create a more wavy shape for the rose.

Try a thin layer of fibres for a delicate flower, or thick felt for something more rigid.

Lay out 2, 3 or more strips on each sheet of bubble wrap to make several flowers.

Felt the wool. *(refer to the guide on opposite page)*

Press the felt strips dry with an iron.

For the gathered flower, knot a strong thread, then simply sew a running stitch along one edge and pull, gathering the wool together. Stitch the ends together to hold in place. For the centre, use buttons, beads or make a felt bead, cut in half and glue in place.

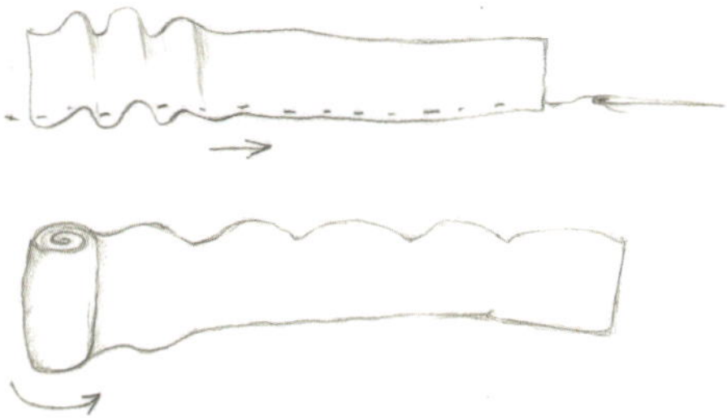

For the rose flower, start at one end and roll the felt up.

Pin to hold and sew through the bottom edges of the felt to secure in place. Pull the tips of the felt outwards to open up the rosebud.

Make some felt leaf shapes to add, using green fibres.

Make stems for individual flowers by binding some wire with thread, or arrange in different formations and quantities, to create an accessory or garland.

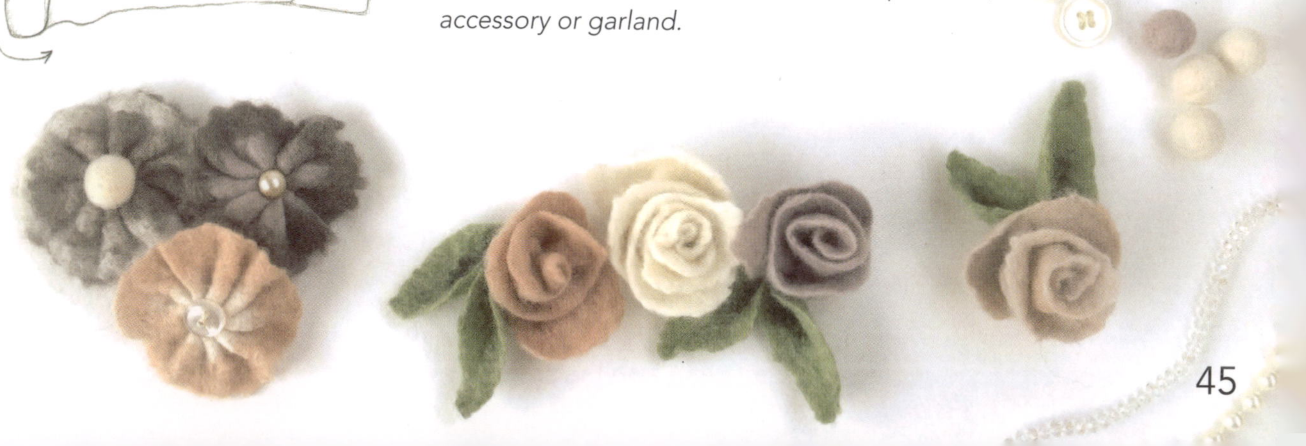

Stockings

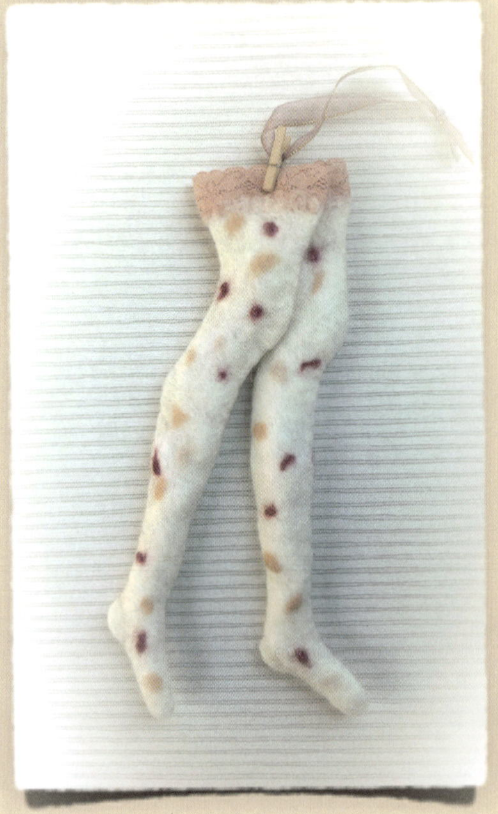

Delicate lace~topped felt stockings, patterned with stripes or spots or sequins.
Use some white vintage lace for a bridal gift.
Fill them with fragrant lavender or other dried flowers.
Make in festive colours to hang on a Christmas tree.

Materials and tools

Wool fleece in your chosen colours, about 10 gms per pair
2 pieces of bubble wrap per pair
Soap solution, sprinkler
Rolling pin, Bamboo mat, Towels
Plastic resist
Length of lace, ribbon or tape.
Scissors
Long paintbrush

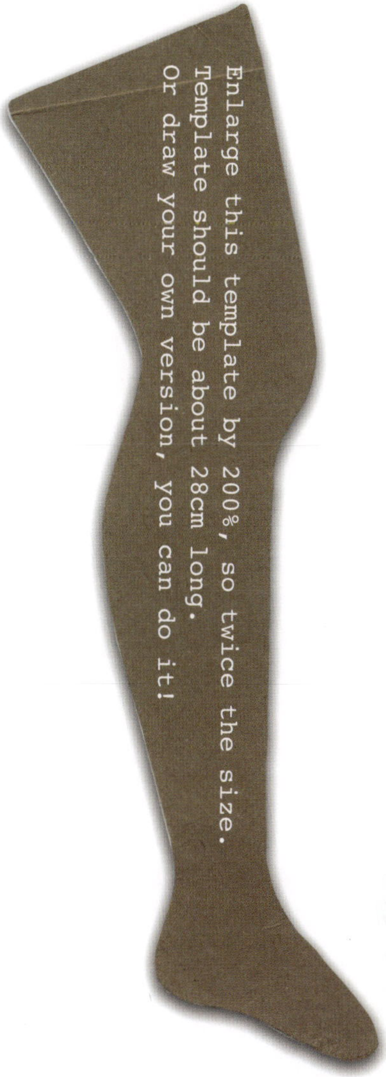

Notes on technique...

Cut two resists from the template to make the pair.
Measure and cut your lace so that it wraps around the top of the stocking template.
This design includes the nuno felting technique on page 28.
Take inspiration for your colour and pattern from your chosen lace for the top of the stockings.
Make sure your fibres are random, not just across the width, or they will shrink unevenly and may distort.
If you are adding horizontal stripes, be sure to make the base layer with more vertical fibres, for even shrinkage.
Join together with a mini peg, and attach a ribbon for hanging.

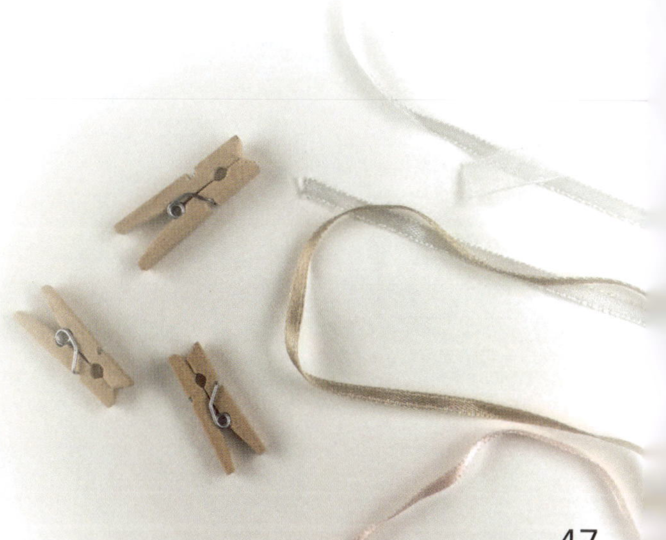

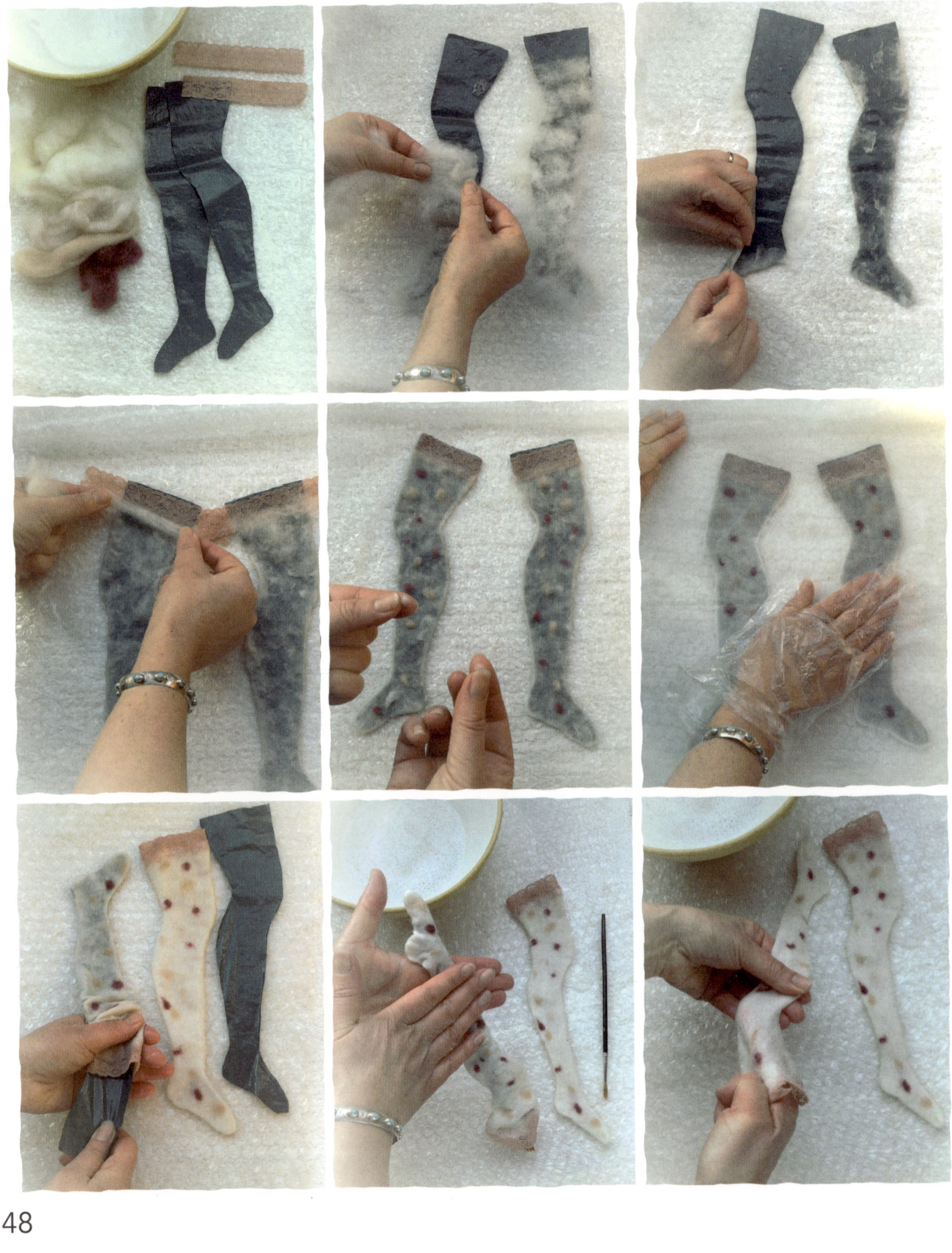

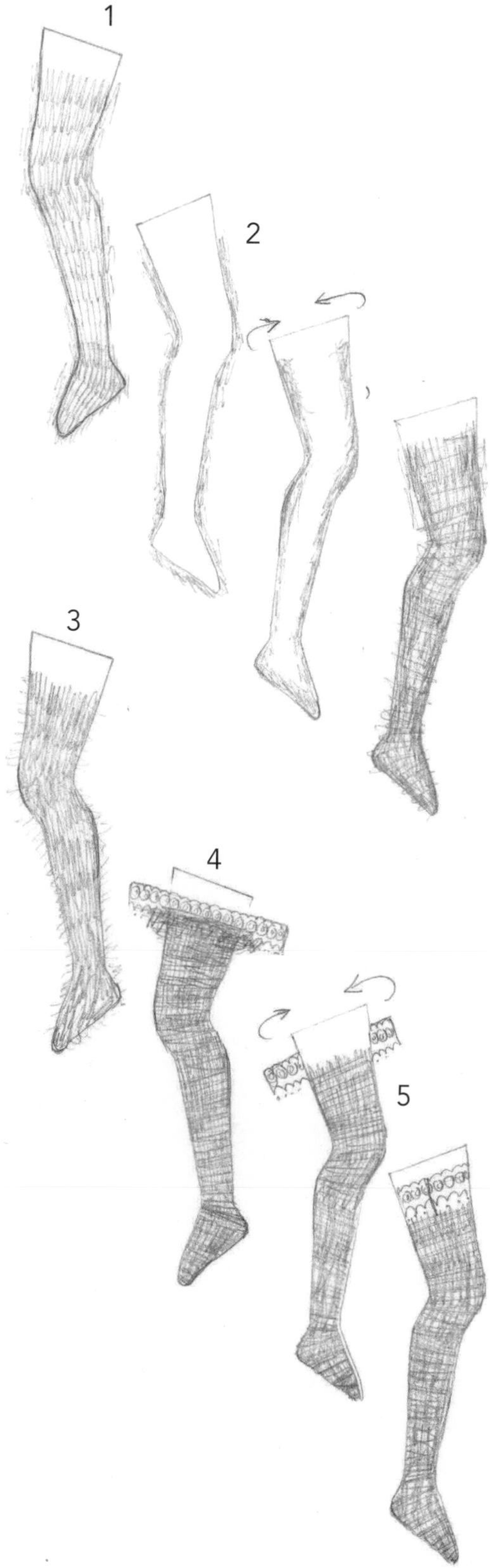

Lay out your design

1.Front

Place your templates on the bubble wrap, you can work on both stockings together.
Start at the toes, place a fine layer of fibres over the surface of the template, overlapping the edge slightly.
Stop about 2cm from the top
Wet the fibres, cover with bubble wrap, and press through.
Turn the whole piece over to the other side.

2. Back

Peel off the top layer of bubble wrap. Starting at the toe, Fold the outside fibres onto the surface of the resist. Fill in the gap with a fine layer of fibres. Add another fine layer over the first, overlapping the edge slightly.
Wet the fibres, cover with bubble wrap and press through.

3. Front

Peel off the top layer of bubble wrap. Starting at the toe, Fold the outside fibres onto the surface of the first layer of fibres. Add one more fine layer over middle of the first. This should be enough, but check for any thin areas and fill them in.

4. Lace trim

Place the strip of lace over the top edge of the fibres. Place a thin wisp of fibres over the top of the edge of lace.
Cover with bubble wrap and press through. Turn the whole piece over.

5. Back

Peel off the top layer of bubble wrap. Fold the outside lace and fibres over onto the back. Add one more fine layer over middle of the lace .
Cover with bubble wrap and press through. Turn the whole piece over.

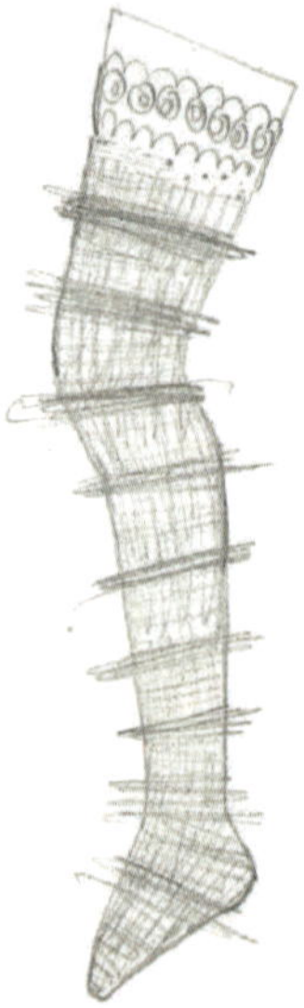

6. Front
Peel back the bubble wrap.
Fold any remaining outside fibres over onto the front of the covered template.

Now add any pattern or surface detail like stripes, spots, sequins etc. To set them in place, cover with fine netting and give this a gentle rub, to encourage the surface fibres to merge.

Nb, if you add horizontal stripes, they can shrink the width, so make sure you first layer has plenty of vertically placed fibres.

Felt he wool. *Refer to the guide below.*
After about the first 400 rolls, the wool will begin to felt, and shrink around the template. Hold the wool with fingers and thumb and twist the felt, so it slides around the resist a little to avoid lumpy thickness at the seams. *(see page 26, 27)*

After another 400 rolls, you can remove the resist template. Place the rounded end of a paint brush into the stocking and roll between your palms to firm up the felt. Reshape the stockings after rinsing by pushing the knee out with your finger.

When dry, peg together with a miniature clothes peg and some matching ribbon to hang. Fill with fragrant dried flowers like lavender or rose petals, or stuff with a little tissue paper.

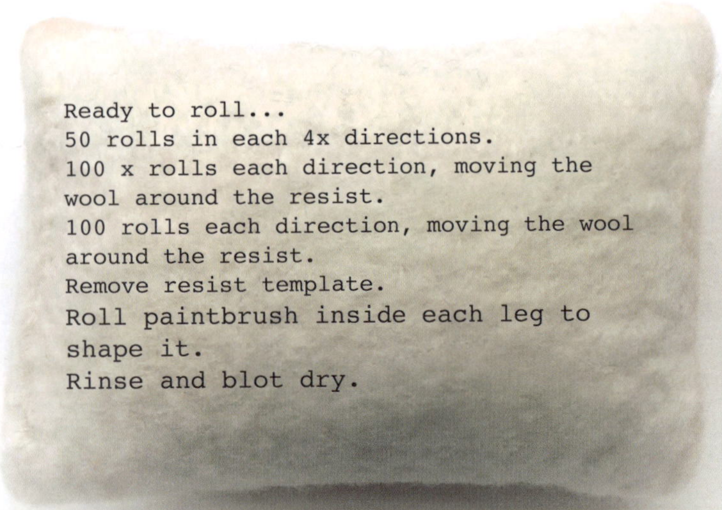

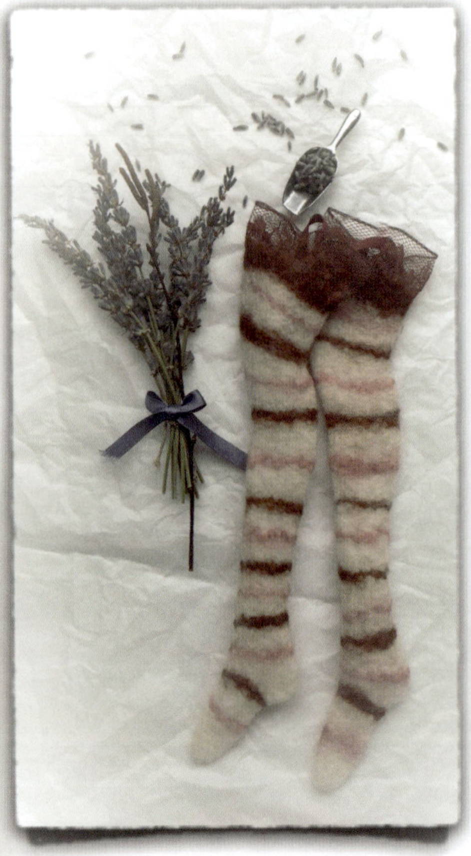

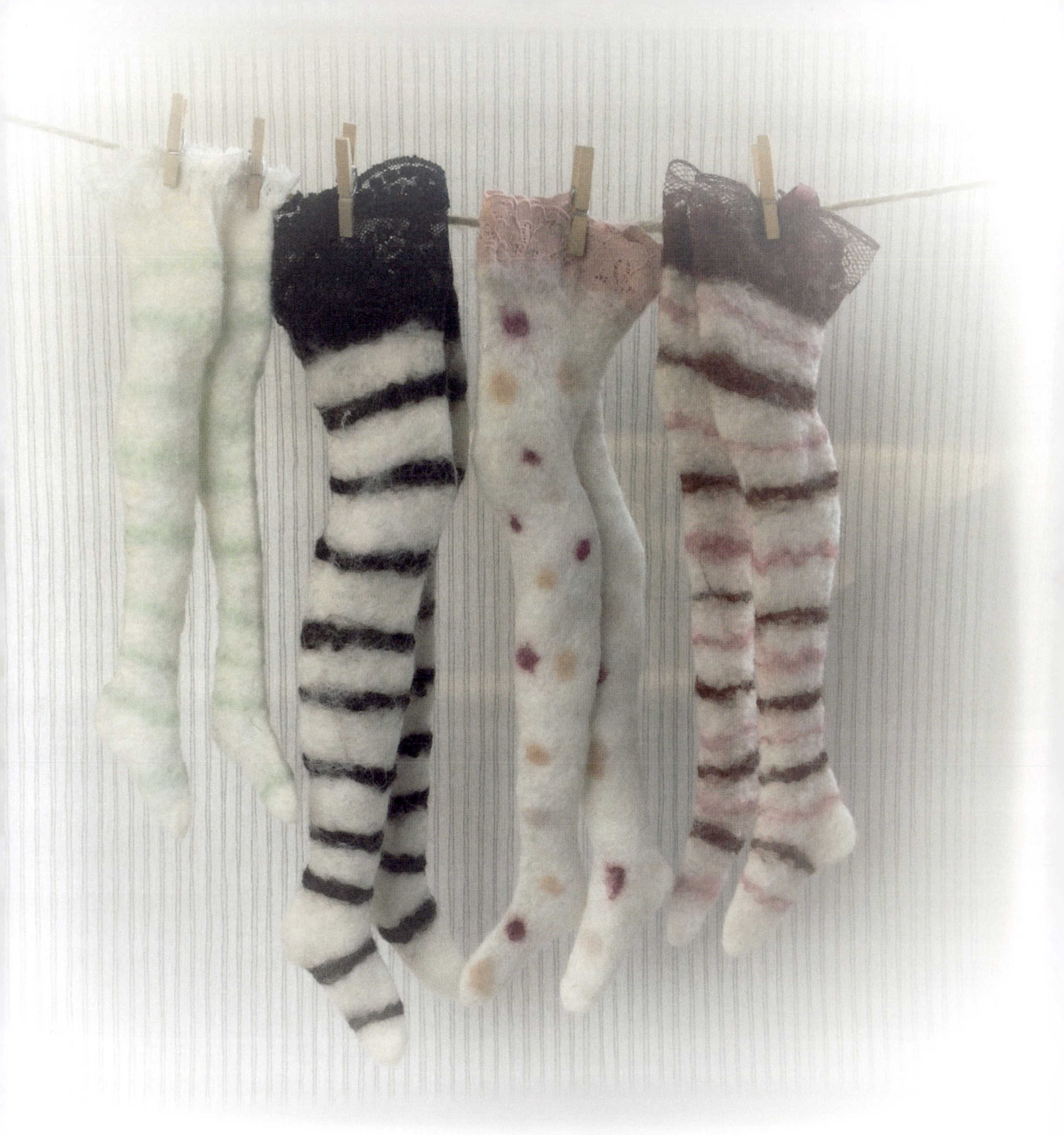

Swimsuits

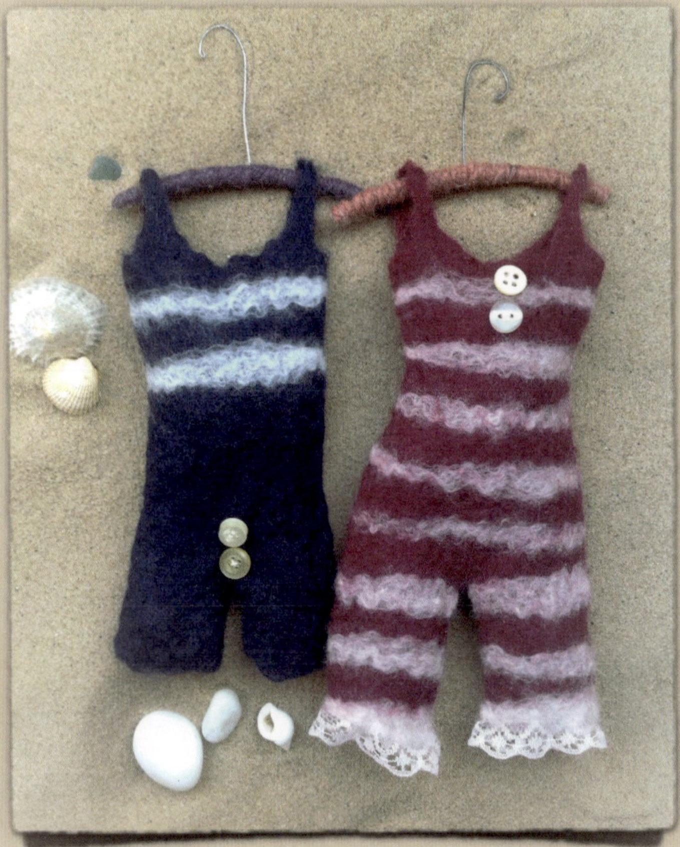

His and Her's old fashioned swimming wear and costumes
inspired by the Victorian and Edwardian era.
Choose your own colours to create a complimentary pair.
Try vintage buttons and lace to decorate.
Finish with tiny wire hangers.

HER swimsuit.

HIS swimsuit

Materials and tools

Wool fleece in chosen colours
10 gms per swimsuit
2 pieces of bubble wrap
Soap solution, sprinkler
Rolling pin, Bamboo mat
Towels
Plastic resist
Length of lace
Scissors
Buttons or beads

Notes on technique..

When adding horizontal stripes, be sure some of the base layer of fibres are vertical, so the wool shrinks evenly.
Choose colour combinations to complement each other.
For 'her' lace trim, measure the width of each leg, and double for the length of lace required... about 10cm each leg.

Actual size.
'His' template should be about 19.5cm long.
'Her' template should be about 21cms long.
Or draw your own version, you can do it!

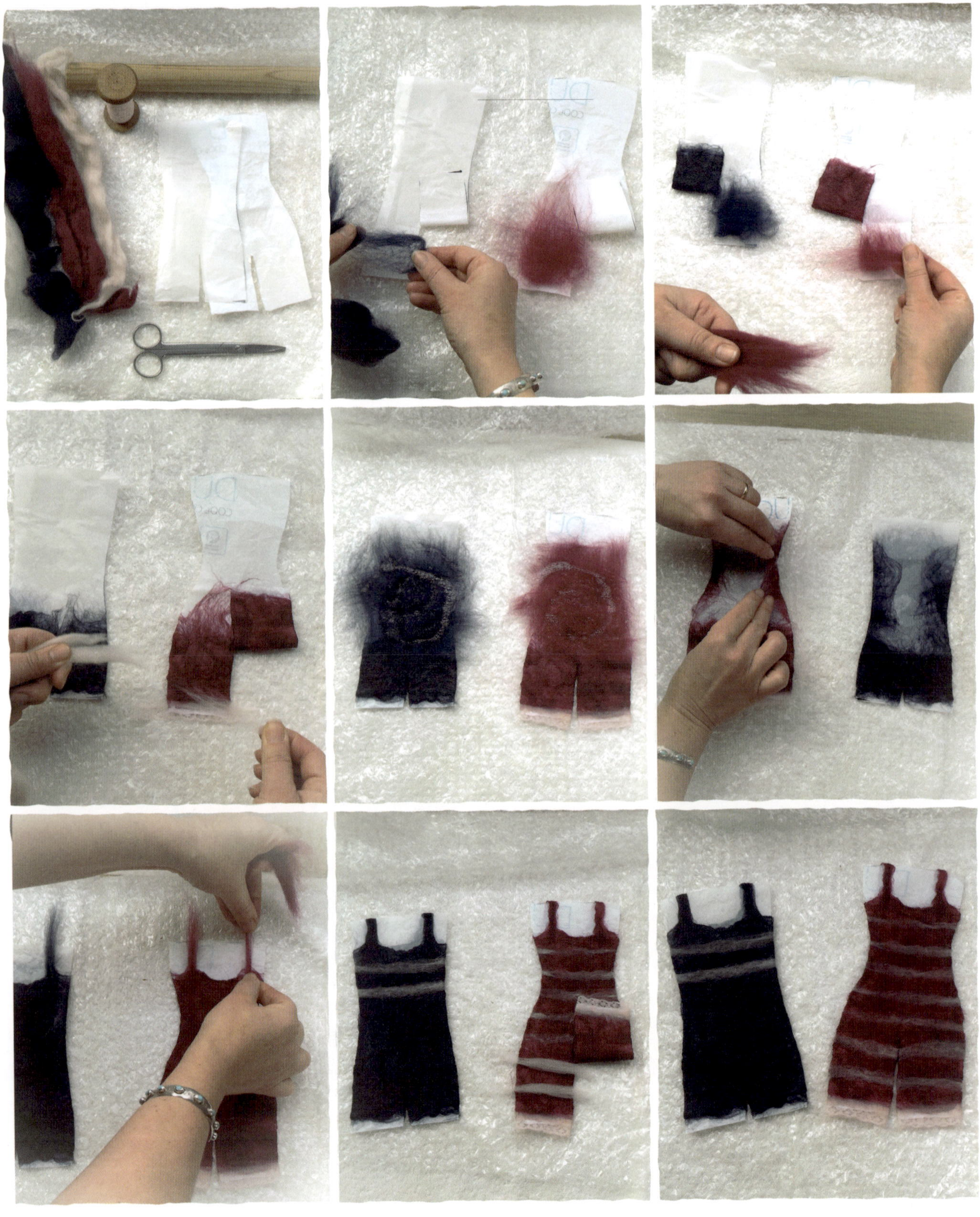

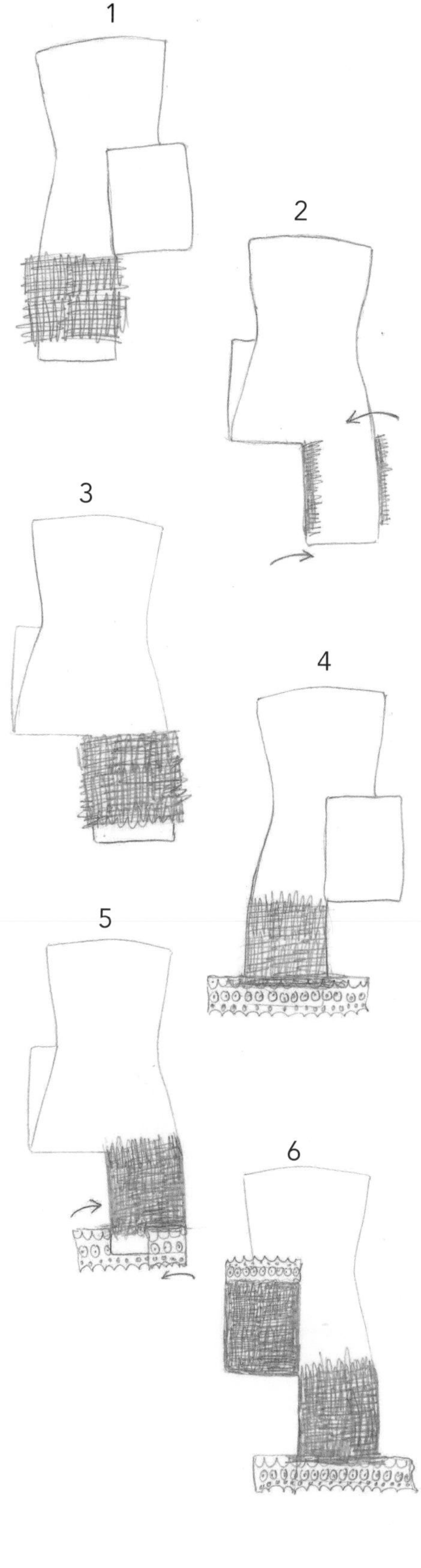

Lay out your design

1. Place your template on the bubble wrap and fold the right leg of the template upwards so it's out of the way. Place a fine layer of fibres over the bottom of the template, covering the left leg and overlapping the edge slightly.
Wet the fibres, cover with bubble wrap, and press through.
Turn the whole piece over to the back.

2. Peel off the top layer of bubble wrap. Fold the outside fibres onto the surface of the resist.

3. Fill in the gap with a fine layer of fibres. Add another fine layer over the first, overlapping the edge slightly.
Wet the fibres, cover with bubble wrap and press through.
Turn the whole piece over to the front
Peel off the top layer of bubble wrap. Fold the outside fibres onto the surface of the first layer of fibres. Add one more fine layer over middle of the first. This should be enough, but check for any thin areas and fill those in.

4. Lace trim (optional)
Place the strip of lace over the bottom edge of the fibres. Place a thin wisp of fibres over the top of the edge of lace, so it's sandwiched between fibres.
Cover with bubble wrap and press through. Turn the whole piece over.

5. Peel back the bubble wrap.
Fold the lace and fibres over onto the edge of the back fibres. Add a small wisp of fibre to cover the edge of the lace where it meets the wool and press through.
Turn the whole piece over.

6. Fold the right leg down, and fold the covered left leg up and out of the way.
Repeat steps 1 to 5 so that both legs are covered and the lace is in place.

7. Fold the covered leg down flat.

7

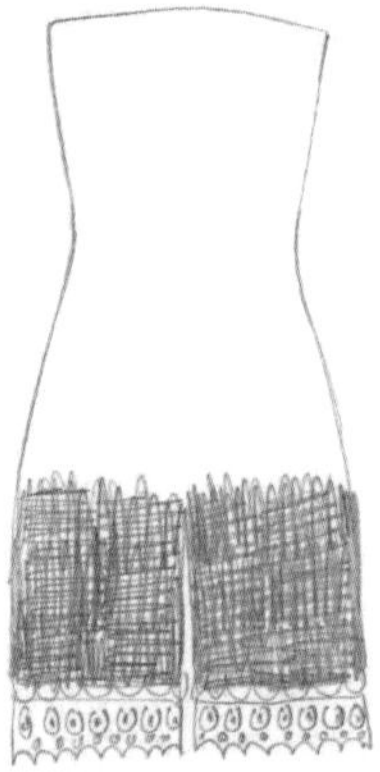

8. Starting from the top of the legs, continue to add a fine layer of wool over the body of the swimsuit. Allow the fibres to overlap the edge slightly. Stop about 2 cm from the top to leave space for the straps.
Wet, cover and press through.

8

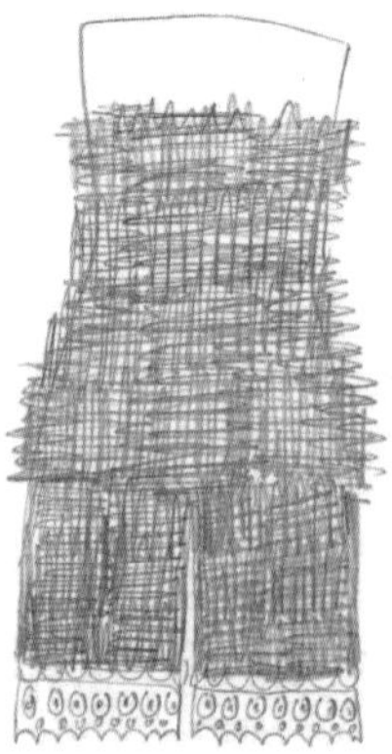

9. Peel back the bubble wrap and add a thin length of fibres to the top of the shape to form straps. Allow these to overlap the top, they will be folded over to join the back.
You can add small amounts of fibre to the strap where it joins the neckline, to create a curved edge.
Cover again and press through.
Flip the whole piece over.

9

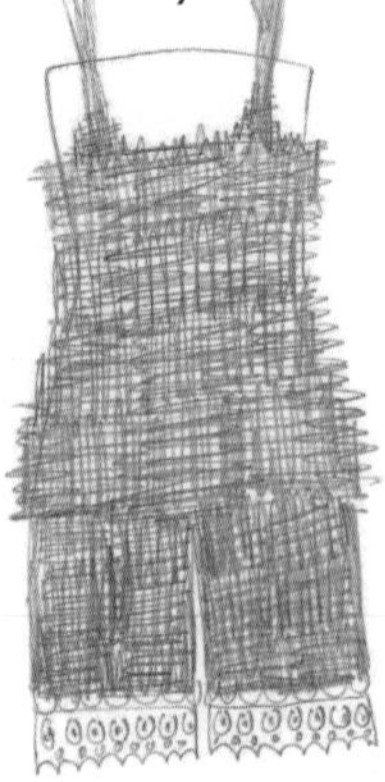

10. Peel off the bubble wrap. Fold over the outside edges of fibres onto the resist, including the ends of the straps.

10

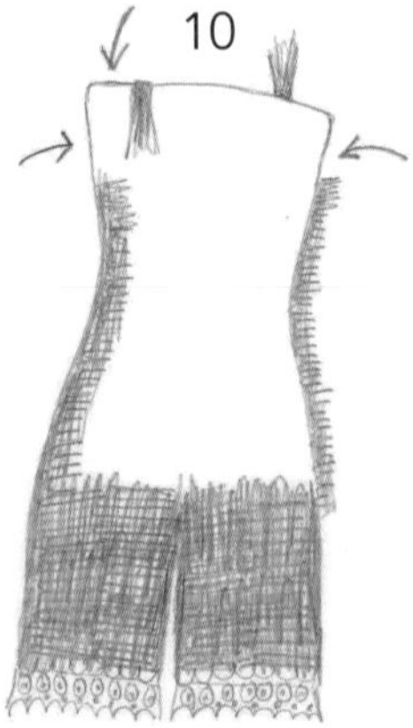

11. As before, fill in the space with wool. Add another fine layer of fibres, allowing them to overlap the edge of the template.
Add some more thin lengths of fibre to fill in the back of the straps and overlap at the top.
Wet, cover, press through.
Turn whole piece back over to the front.

11

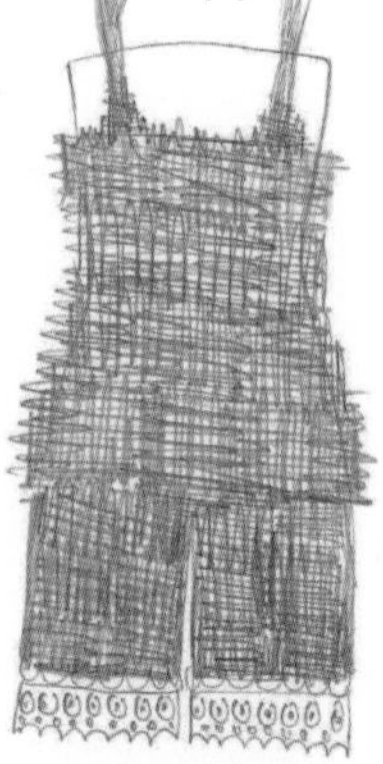

12. Peel back the bubble wrap.
Fold over the outside fibres onto the surface of the front. Place one more fine layer over the middle of the shape, check for any thin areas, and fill them in.

12

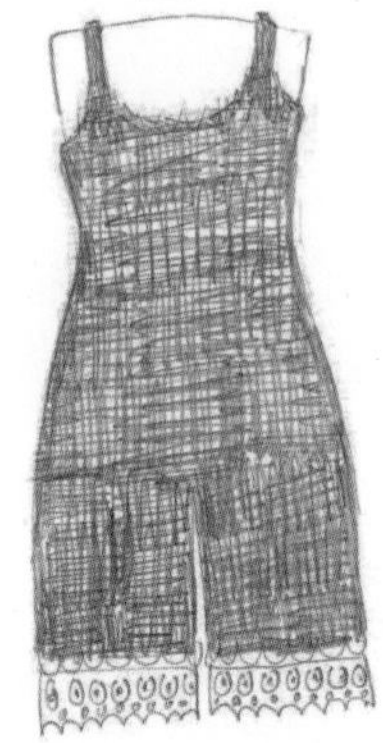

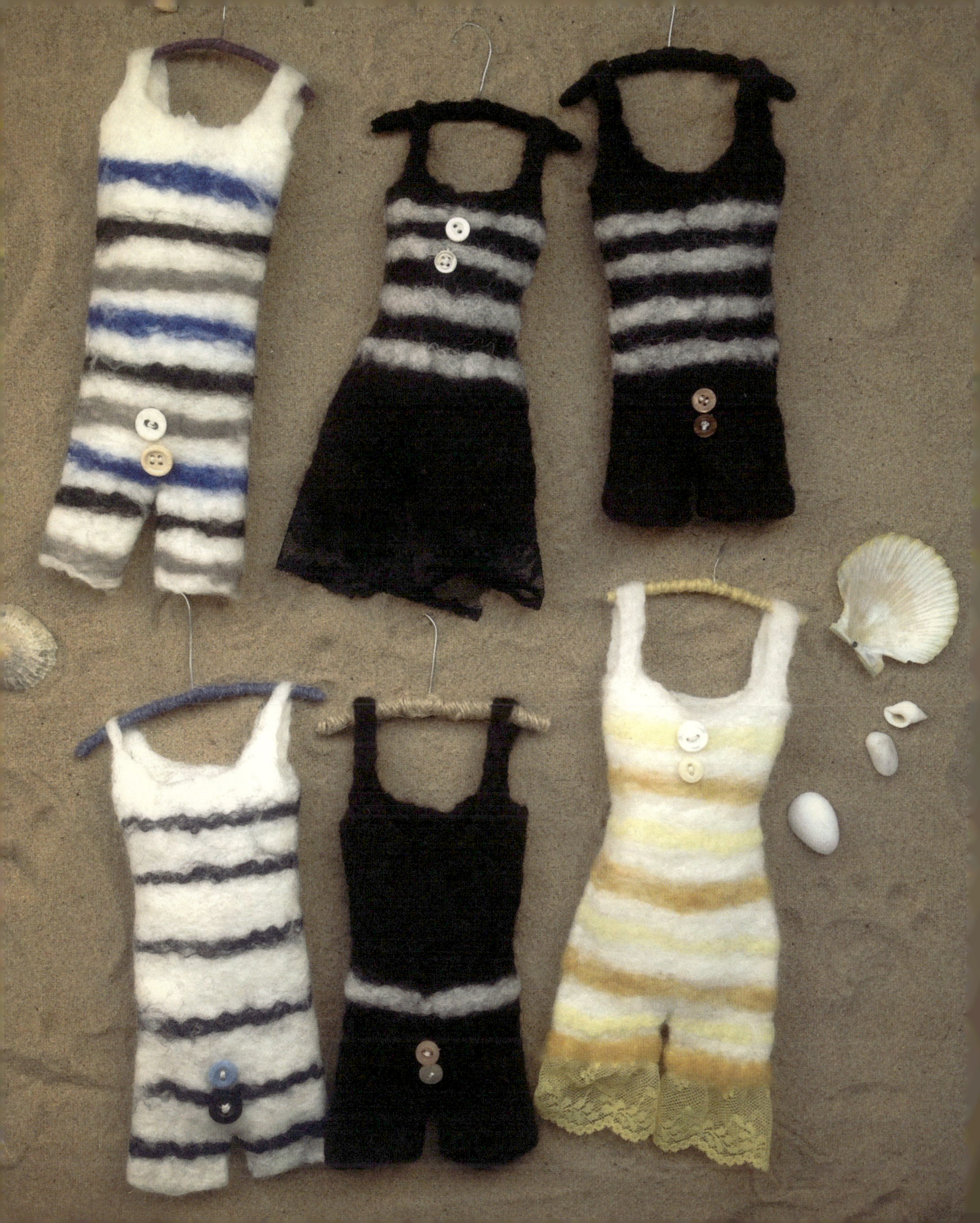

Add any surface decoration like stripes or spots, don't forget to repeat it on the back too.

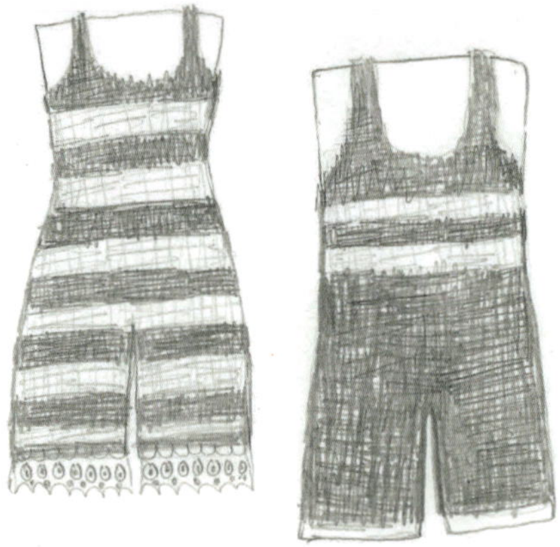

Make his swimsuit the same as her's but leave out the lace trim at the bottom.
Felt the wool. Refer to the guide below...
When dry, add some pretty buttons or stitching, pad out with a little tissue paper inside and make a tiny wire coat hanger. See page 106.

```
Ready to roll...
50 rolls each 4x directions.
100 rolls each direction, turning
wool around the resist template.
100 rolls each direction, turning
wool around the resist template.
Remove resist.
Throw 25 to 50 times.
Bamboo mat~ 25 to 50 rolls each
direction.
Rinse and blot dry.
```

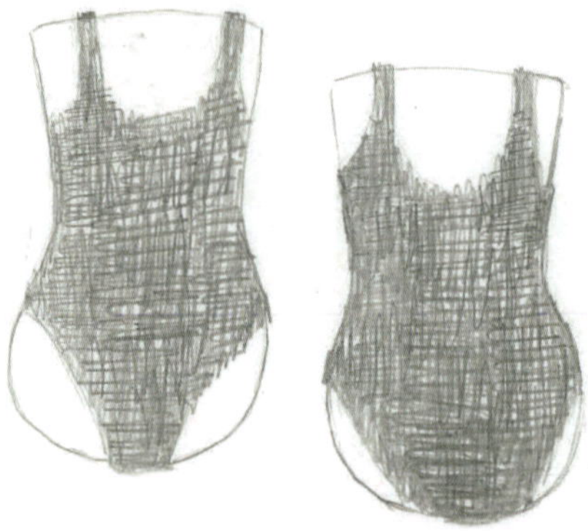

To make the Tutu

Cover the costume template in the same way as the swimsuit, but make the bottom part like knickers, instead of shorts.
Fold back the fibres for the leg opening at the front and back, as illustrated.

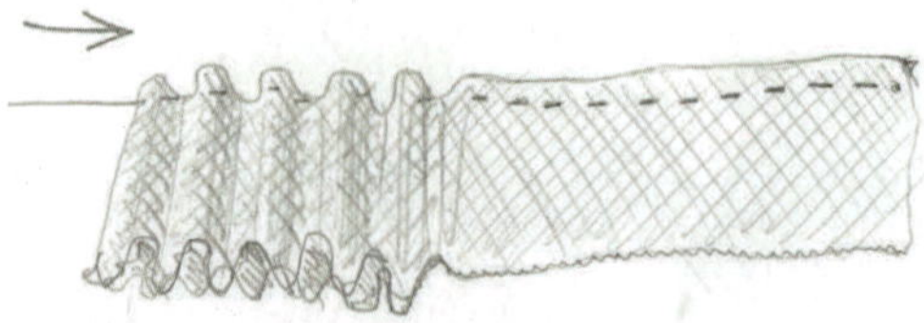

To make the tutu, cut lengths of netting about 8 cm wide, fold in half lengthways, and sew a running stitch along one edge. Pull the thread to gather the skirt, and stitch to the felt all around the hips. It helps to stuff some tissue inside the felt when stitching.
For the length required, take the hip measurement of the felt, and times it by about five. The example was made with 5x 15cm, so 75cms of netting and three layers were used, but experiment with yours.

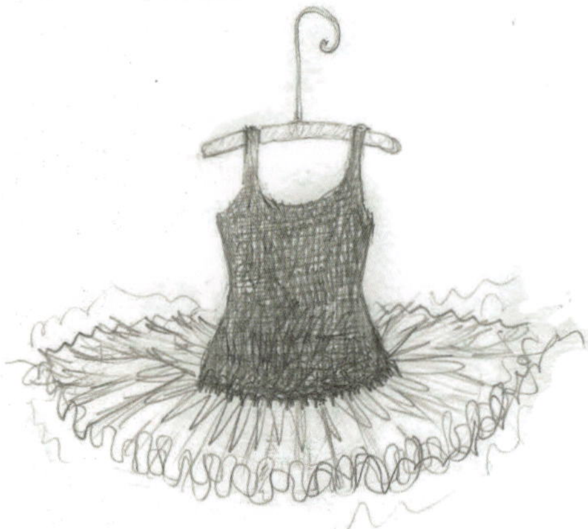

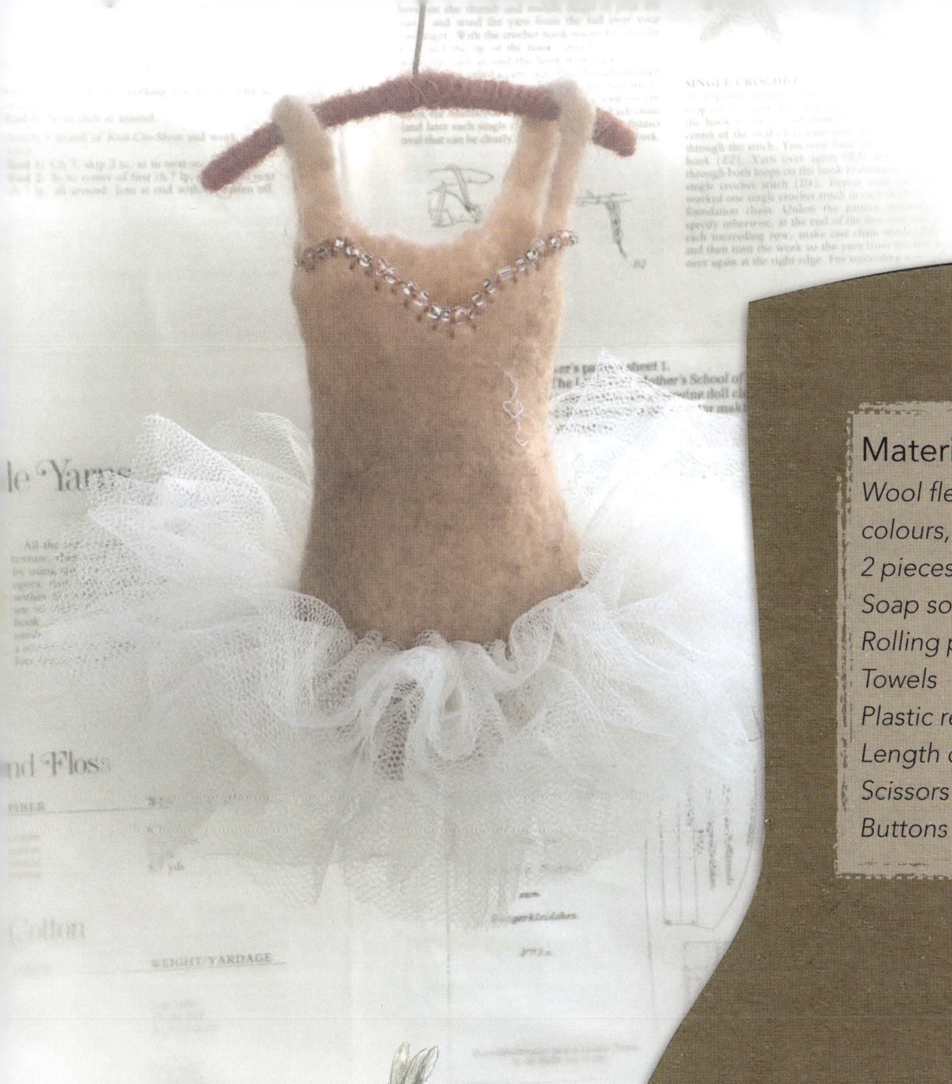

Materials and tools

Wool fleece in chosen colours, about 10 gms
2 pieces of bubble wrap
Soap solution, sprinkler
Rolling pin, Bamboo mat
Towels
Plastic resist
Length of netting or tule
Scissors
Buttons or beads

Actual size.
Tutu template should be about 18cm long.
Or make one to fit a certain character, just add about 33% for the shrinkage, or 1/3rd bigger.

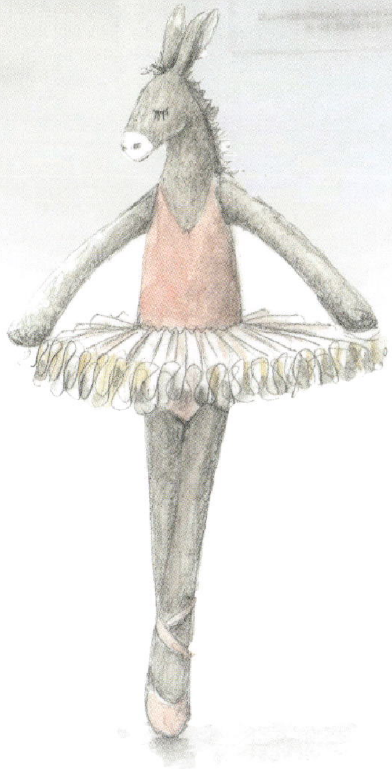

Felted Soaps

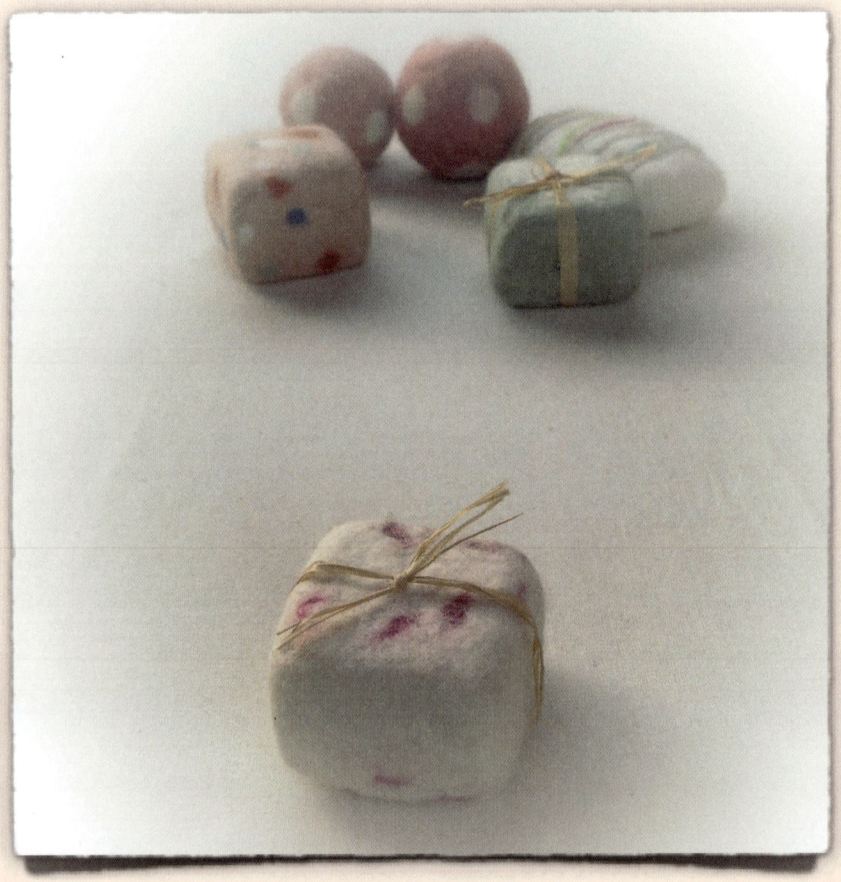

The felt covered soap is a pretty thing, the wool covering can make the soap last longer, and acts as an exfoliator. Dry the soap between use, or use simply to fragrance your drawers.. Wrap in clear cellophane and tie with a ribbon with a little instruction tag, for an unusual gift.

Materials and tools

Wool fibres, 10 to 20 gms is plenty. Choose a colour to cover, and any surface pattern colours you like.
2 pieces of bubble wrap
Soap solution, sprinkler.
Bowl of warm water
Towels
Card to make a template (optional)
Felting needles to add a surface design when dry.

Notes on technique...

Choose your favourite soap, any size or shape can be covered with a little practice. Try carving or grating the soap to adjust the shape. Keep the shavings to make more soap solution!
Add random colours for the surface, or plan a design, pattern or motif.
Needle felt a design into the surface when dry, see page 23. Use the needles horizontally into the felt, to avoid sticking into the soap.

```
Template for covering your soap.
Draw around your soap, adding
about 1 or 2cm, to make a
template.
Make up to six flat pieces of
wool to cover and overlap each
side.
2 for top and bottom,
2 for each end
2 for the surface design.
```

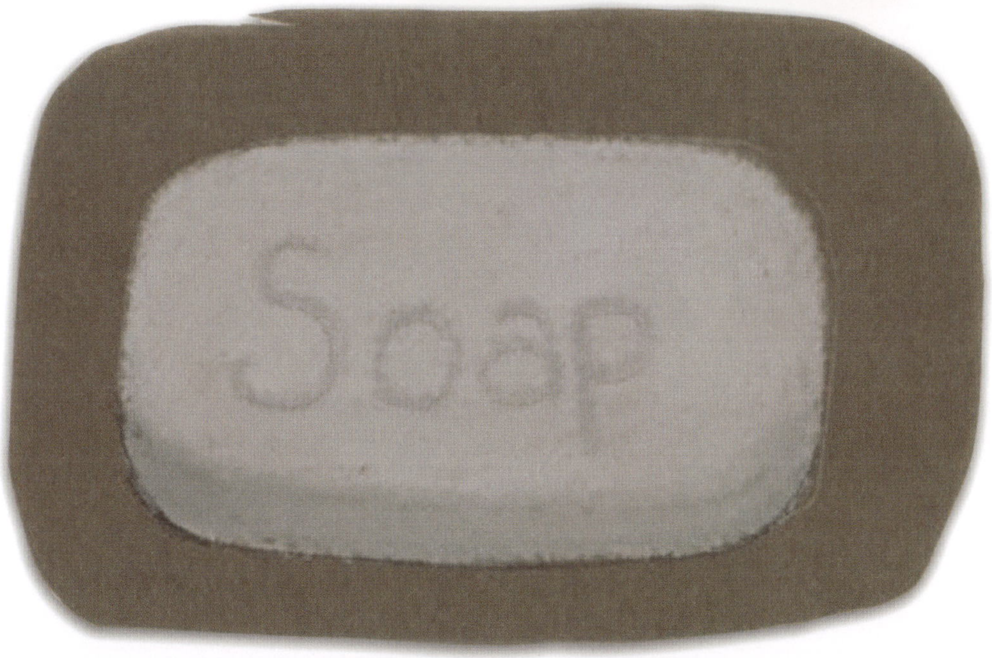

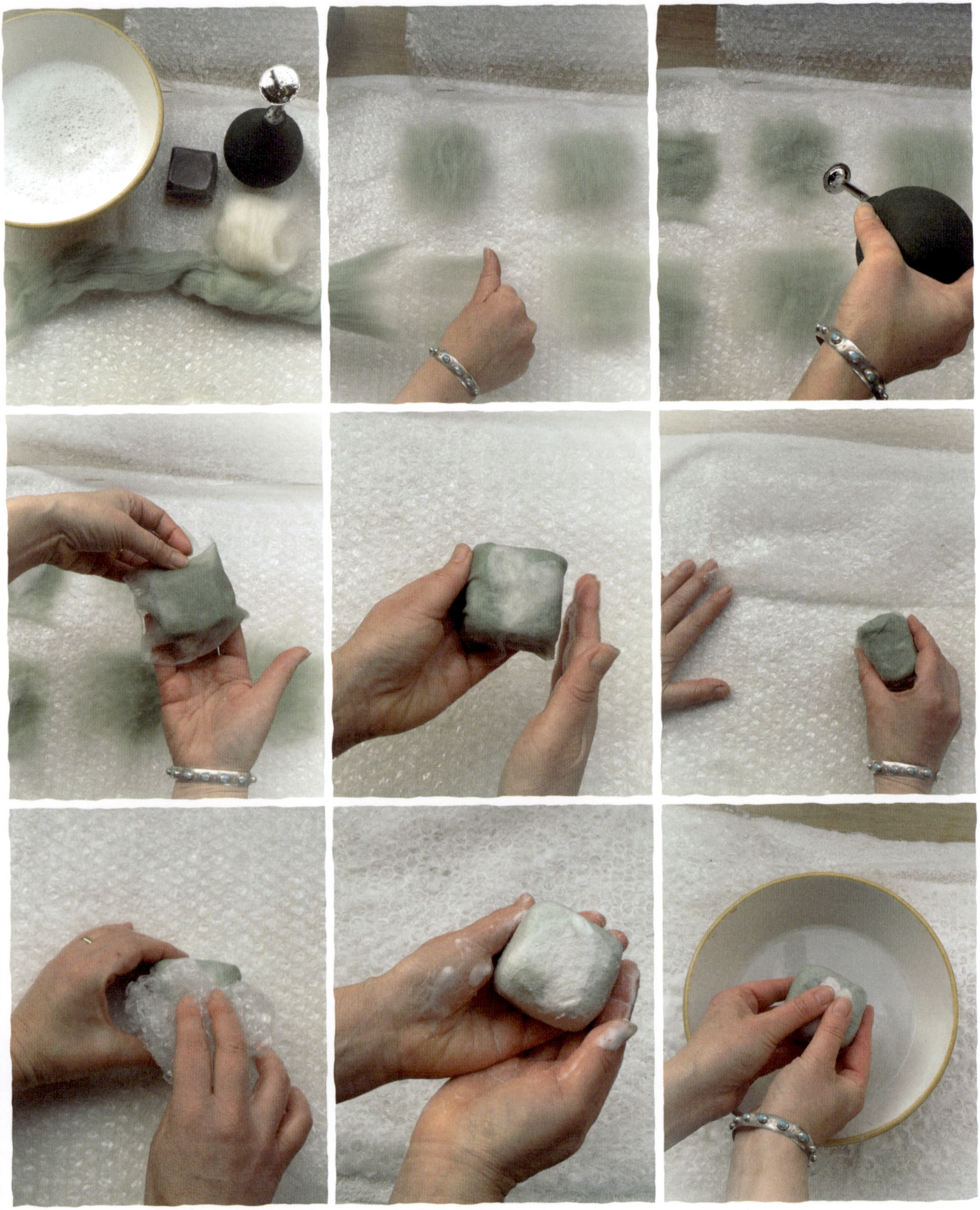

Covering your soap...

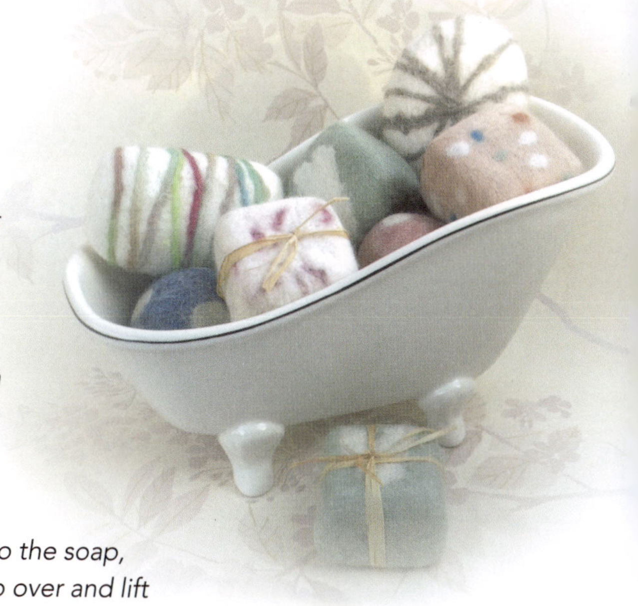

Lay out your fibres.

Place four patches of layered fibres onto the bubble wrap, enough to cover top, bottom, and both ends of the block of soap.
Lay two more patches including your chosen pattern/ colour for the outside surface.
Wet the fibres with soap solution, and press it through with bubble wrap.

Cover the soap.

Peel off the top layer of bubble wrap.
Gently lift the first patch of wet fibres, and place it onto the soap, wrapping and pressing around the form. Turn the soap over and lift the second patch of fibres onto the soap so that it overlaps. Turn the soap on its end and drop a third layer of fibres over the end. Then add the fourth, carefully wrapping the soap, and covering all surfaces . If there are any thin parts, make some more patches of fibres to cover them.

Decoration.

Now add the surface decoration, drape the patch of patterned felt over the top of the soap, turn over and drape the second.
All surfaces should now be covered and overlap all around.
You can also wrap wool yarn around the covered soap, to be felted onto the surface.

Ready to roll...

To felt the wool, gently wrap the soap inside some bubble wrap. Roll this around in your hands and rub the bubble wrap around the soap, massaging the surface to felt the wool onto the soap.
Be gentle to begin with, open up the bubble wrap to check the wool is still in place. Then continue to rub and roll around, inside the bubble wrap. The soap will create a lot of lather, so you can occasional dip the soap into a bowl of water to see how it is felting.
Keep rubbing until the wool has shrunk onto the soap and the surface is well felted. Felting may take about ten minutes or more.
Rinse and leave somewhere warm to dry.

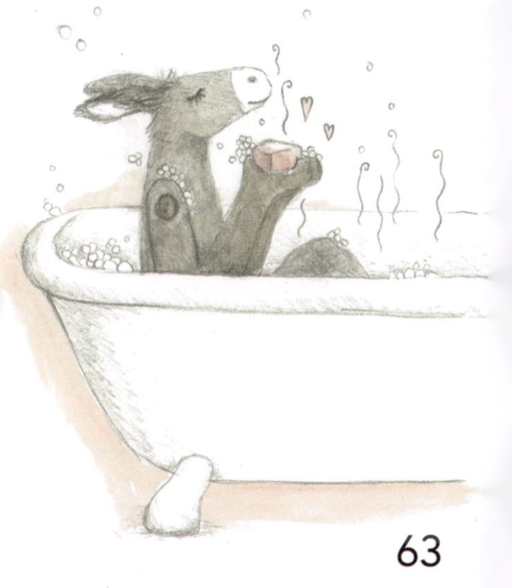

Finishing touches...

You can needle felt a design onto the wool by felting at an angle across the surface.

Mermaids

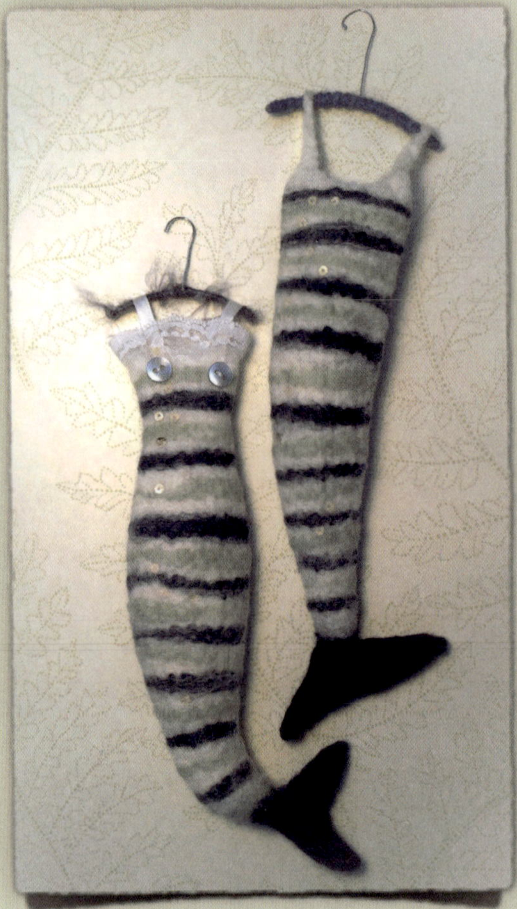

His and Her's mermaid tails.
Choose colours to match your bathroom decor, and mount them inside a lovely box frame. Fill with fragrant dried lavender.
Use vintage buttons and lace for a fairytale look.
Display with tiny wire hangers.

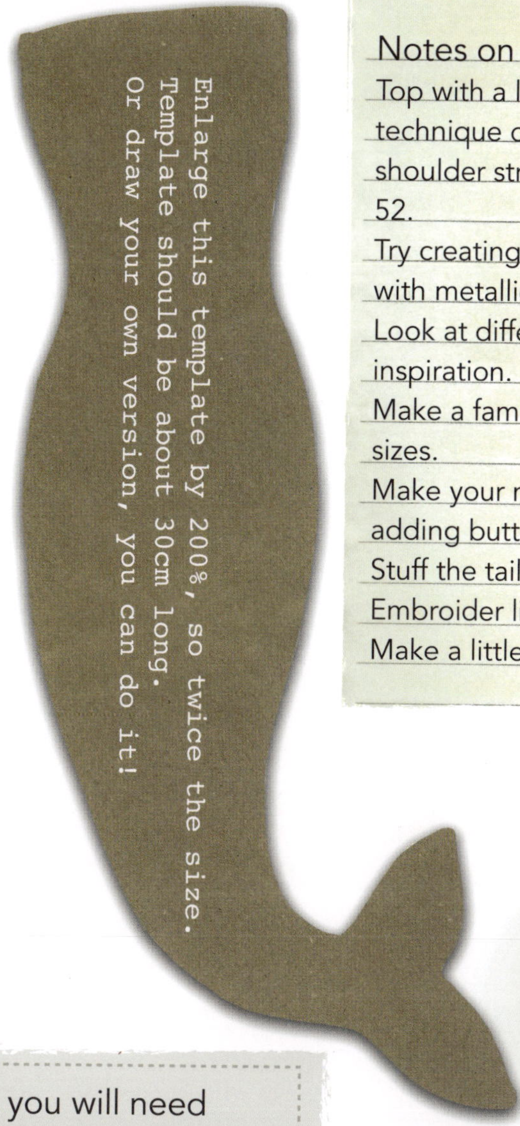

Notes on technique...

Top with a lace trim, using the nuno technique on page 28 or make with shoulder straps like the swimsuits on page 52.

Try creating patterns, scales and shimmer with metallic threads or sequins.

Look at different types of fish tails for inspiration.

Make a family of mermaids of different sizes.

Make your mermaid sparkle when finished, adding buttons and beads.

Stuff the tail with wool to make it more 3D.

Embroider lines into the tail.

Make a little wire hanger to display.

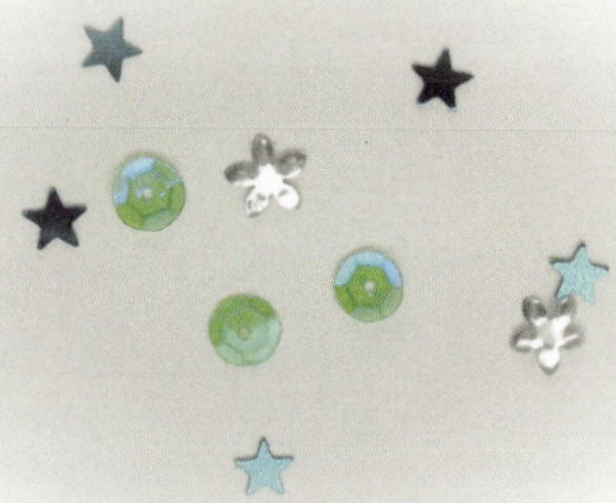

Materials you will need

Wool fleece in several chosen colours 10 gms per mermaid.
2 pieces of bubble wrap per mermaid
Soap solution, sprinkler.
Rolling pin
Bamboo mat
Towels
Plastic resist template
Length of lace or netting.
Buttons, beads, sequins, thread.

Measure the top width (front and back) of your template to give you the length of lace required.
This template uses about 15 cms of lace.

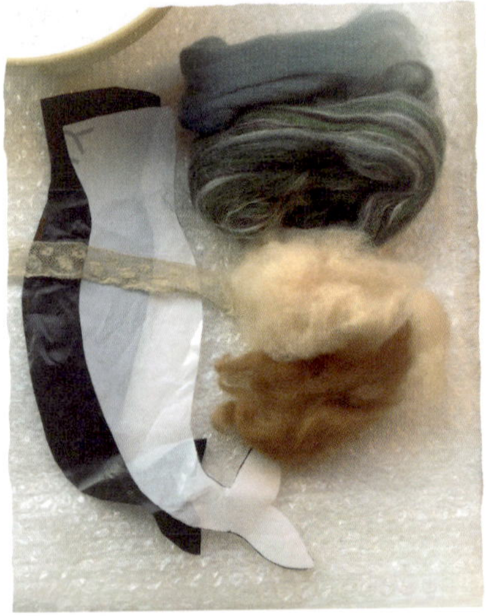
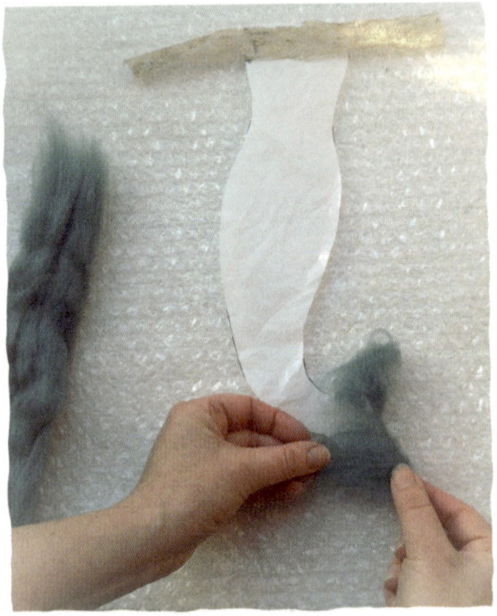
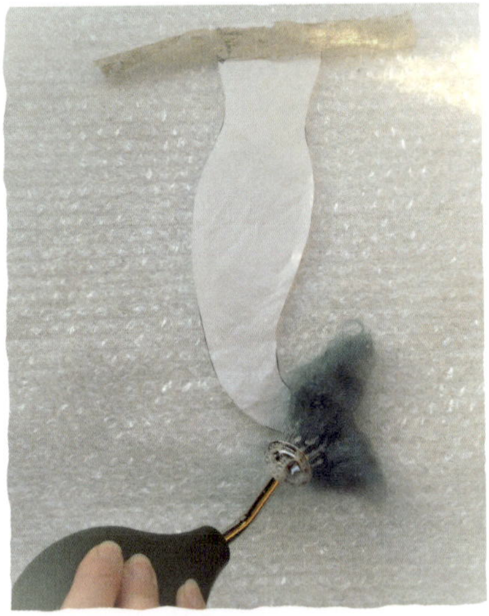
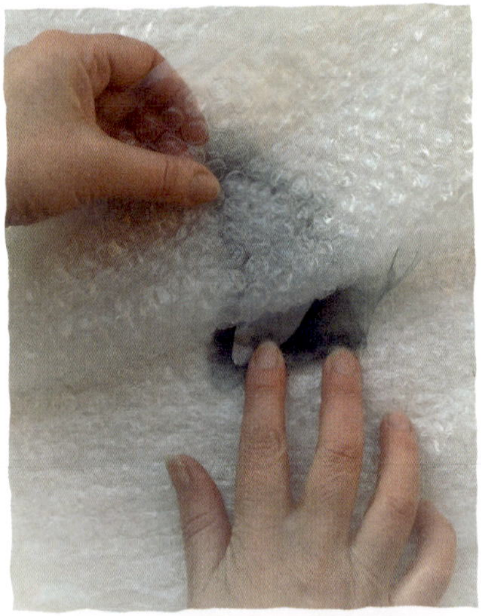
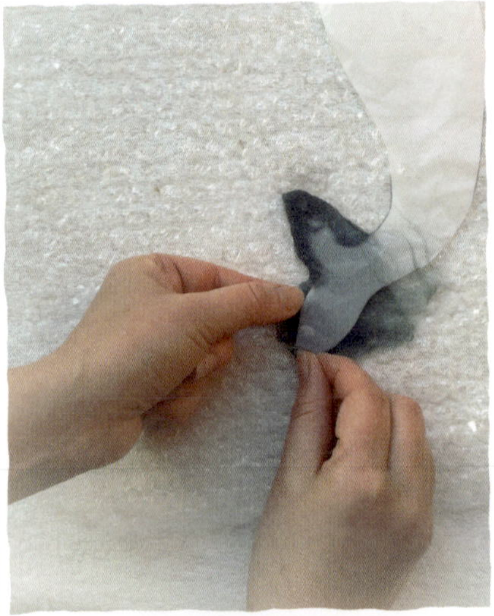
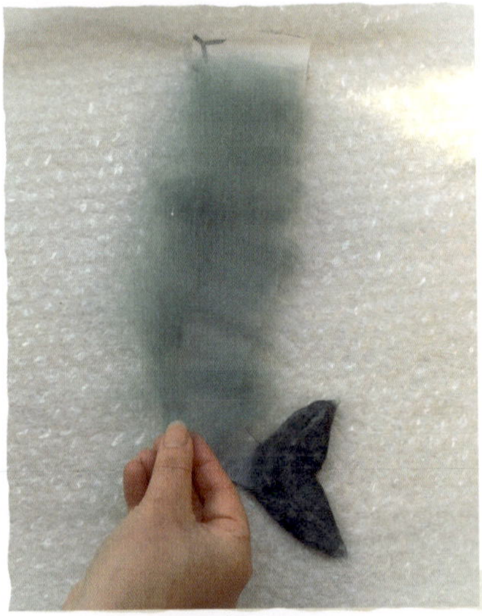
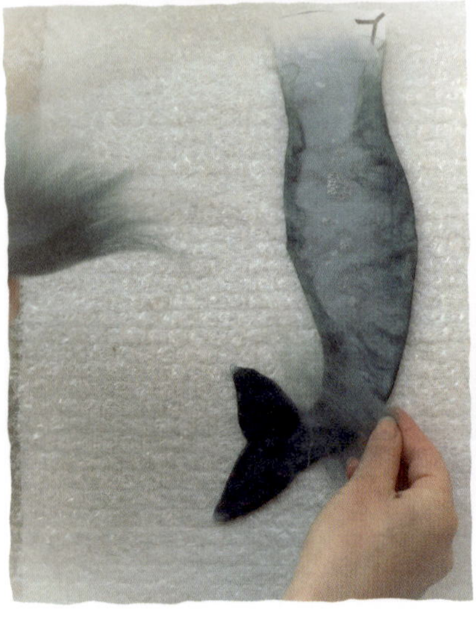
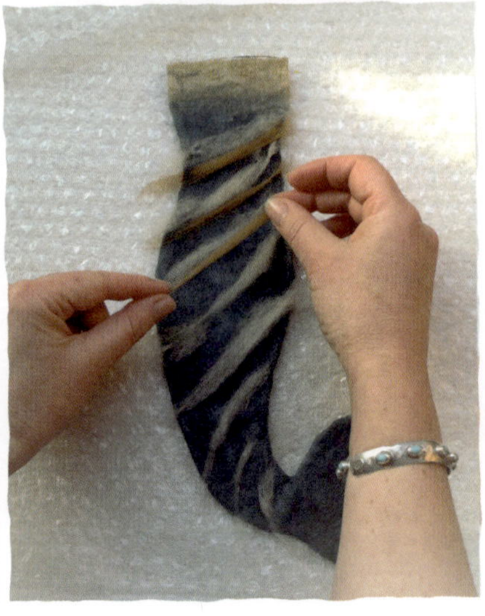
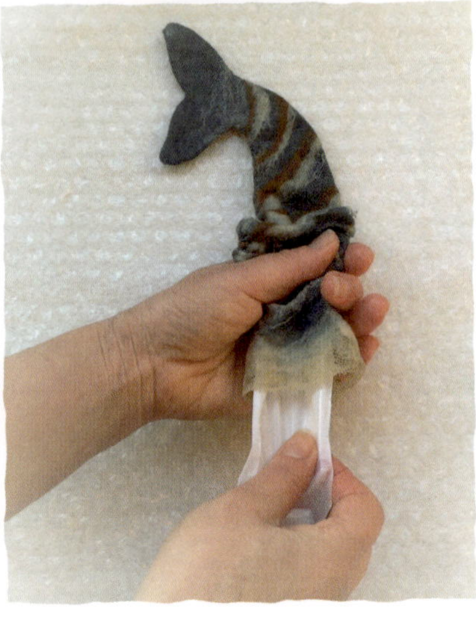

Lay out your design.

1. Front ~tail.

Start at the tail, place a fine layer of fibres over the surface of the template, overlapping the edge slightly. Stop at the edge of the tail where it joins the body, this will make it easier to fold the fibres around the corners later.

Wet the fibres with soap solution, cover with bubble wrap, and press through.

Turn the whole piece over to the back.

2. Back ~tail.

Peel off the top layer of bubble wrap.

Fold the outside fibres onto the surface of the resist. Add another fine layer over the first, overlapping the edge slightly.

Wet the fibres, cover with bubble wrap and press through.

Turn the whole piece over to the front.

3. Front

Peel off the top layer of bubble wrap. Fold the outside fibres onto the surface of the first layer of fibres. This should be enough, but check for any thin areas, and fill them in.

4. Continue to lay out fibres over the body of the template. Stop at about 2 cms from the top edge.

Wet, cover and press through, then turn everything over.

Peel back the bubble wrap, fold over the outside edges.

Fill in the centre, then add another fine layer, overlapping the edge slightly.

5. Continue to turn over and repeat the layering until the whole body is covered. Check for any thin areas, and fill them in with more fibres.

6. For the 'merman' suit, cover the template in the same way as the mermaid, then add two strips of fibres vertically, allowing the ends to overlap the fibres on the body, and the top edge of the template. Turn over, then fold the top of the fibres over the template and repeat to create the straps. You can also refer to the swimsuit workshop on page 52.

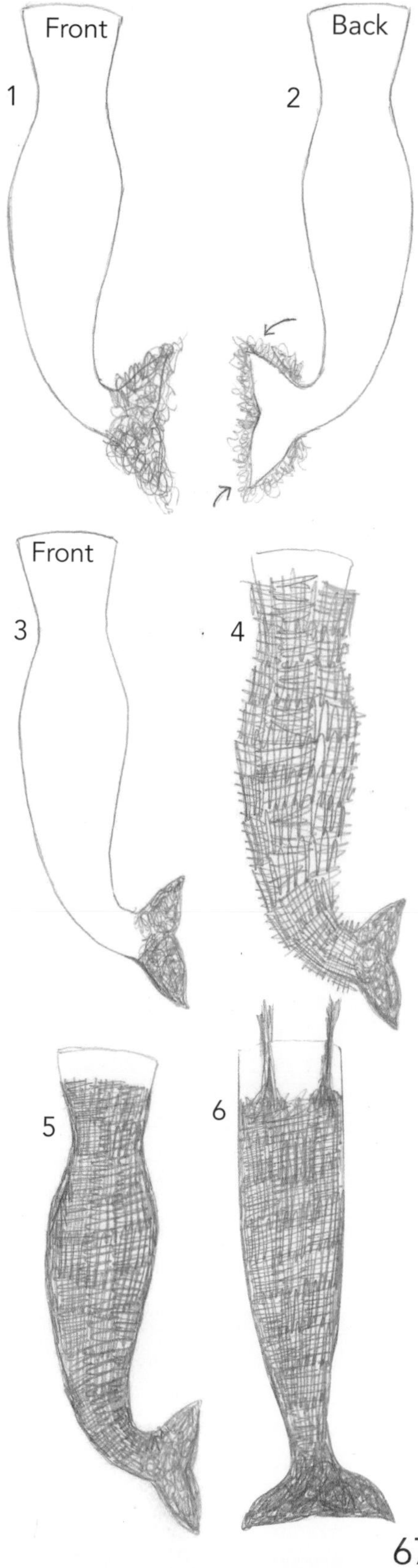

7. Lace trim ~front.
Place the strip of lace across the top edge of the mermaid, so that it just overlaps the fibres.
Place a few wisps of fibre over the bottom edge of lace, so it is sandwiched between fibres.
Cover with bubble wrap and press to wet through. Turn the whole piece over.

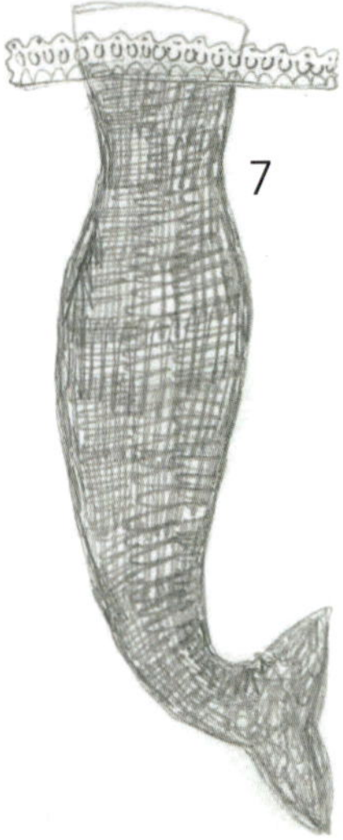
7

8. Lace trim ~back.
Peel off the top layer of bubble wrap. Fold the outside lace and fibres over onto the back. Add one more fine layer over middle of the lace.
Cover with bubble wrap and press through. Turn the whole piece back over.

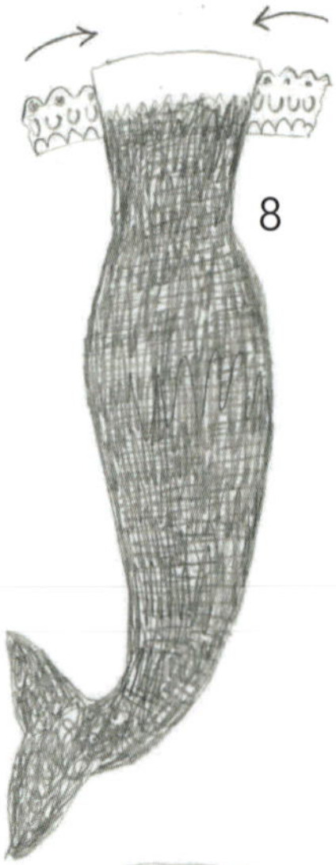
8

9. Now add any surface pattern, or decoration.
Remember if you add horizontal stripes, they can shrink more width ways, so make sure your first layer has plenty of vertically placed fibres.

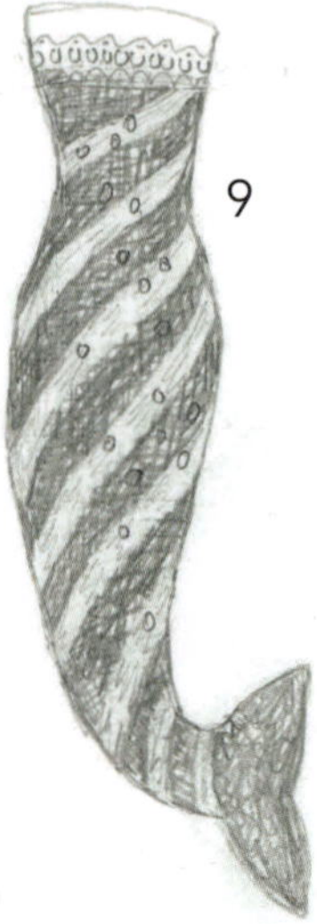
9

Felt the wool. Refer to the guide below.

Finish your mermaid tails with buttons, beads or sequins.
Stitch or glue two lengths of matching ribbon inside the top to create straps. Hang on a little wire coat hanger as on page 106.

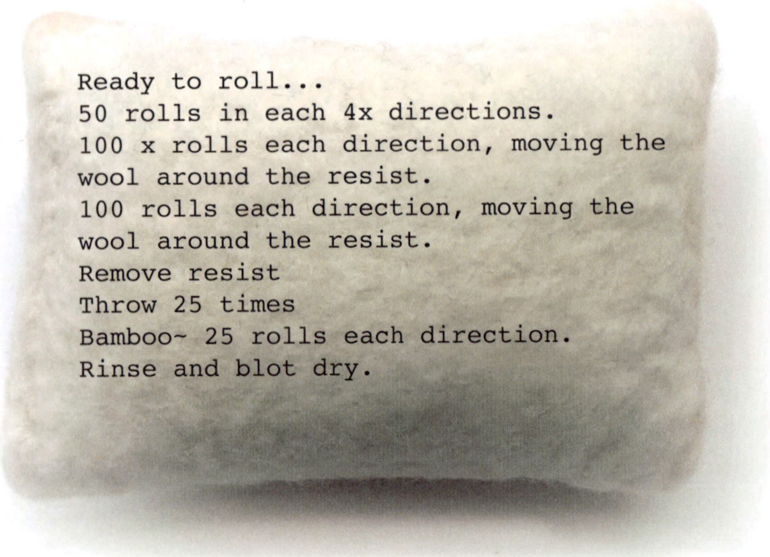

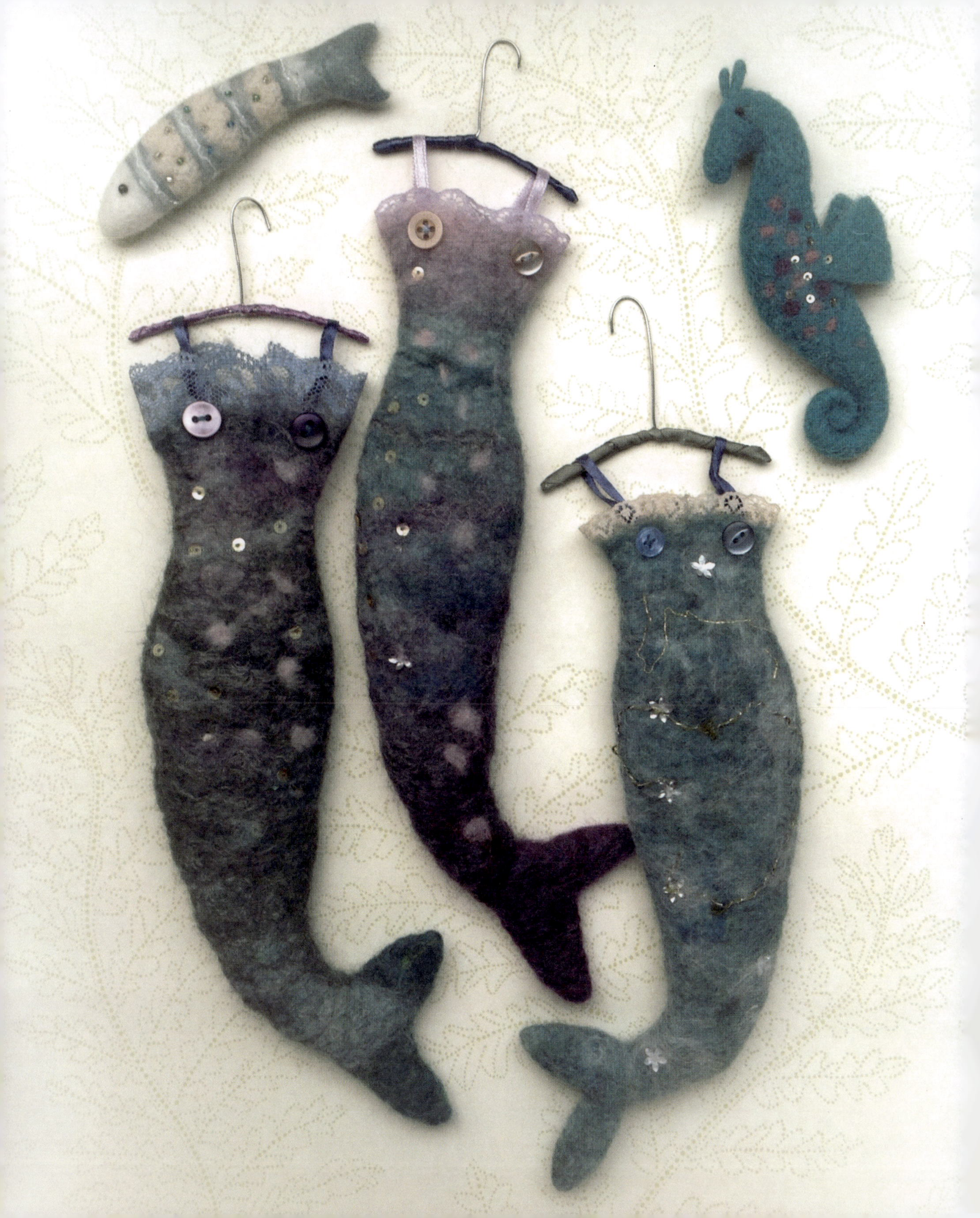

Slippers and Booties

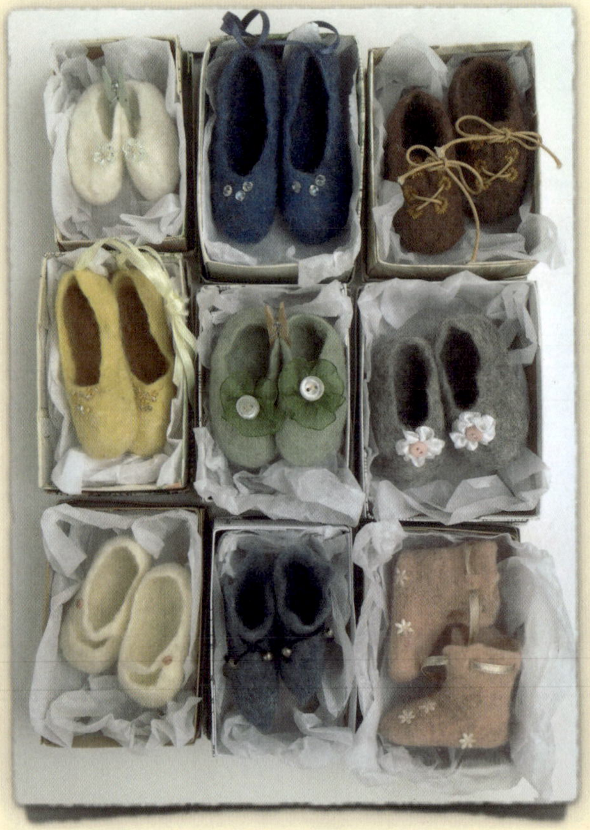

Tiny bootie decorations to celebrate a new baby, or ballet slippers for a dancer, wellies for a gardener, or elf shoes for a festive tree...Make a mini shoe box to present them in, see page108.

Here are several ways of making different styles, using the plastic resist method, or by forming them over perfectly shaped pebbles from the beach. Make a template to fit a favourite doll. They can even be scaled up and made to wear, using lots more wool, a resist template and a shoe last, or mouldered over real soapy feet.

Materials and tools

Wool fleece in your chosen colours 10gms per pair.
Several sheets of bubble wrap
Soap solution, sprinkler, bowl
Rolling pin
Bamboo mat
Towels
Plastic resist template
Or shoe-shaped pebbles.
Scissors
Tissue paper
Buttons or beads
Ribbon, string or yarn
Sewing needles and threads

Notes on technique...

This workshop shows three different techniques...
~Resist method ~slippers, making sole and upper shape.
~Two-sided to make booties.
~Shaping over a form, by covering small pebbles.
Try different colours of wool for the insoles, or soles, or different layers for insides and outsides.
Lots of rubbing and shaping at the fulling stage will really enhance the 3D quality.
Use your fingertips and bubble wrap to massage into shape.

Decorate your slippers with buttons and beads and embroidery.
Add a mini peg and ribbon to hang them as decorations

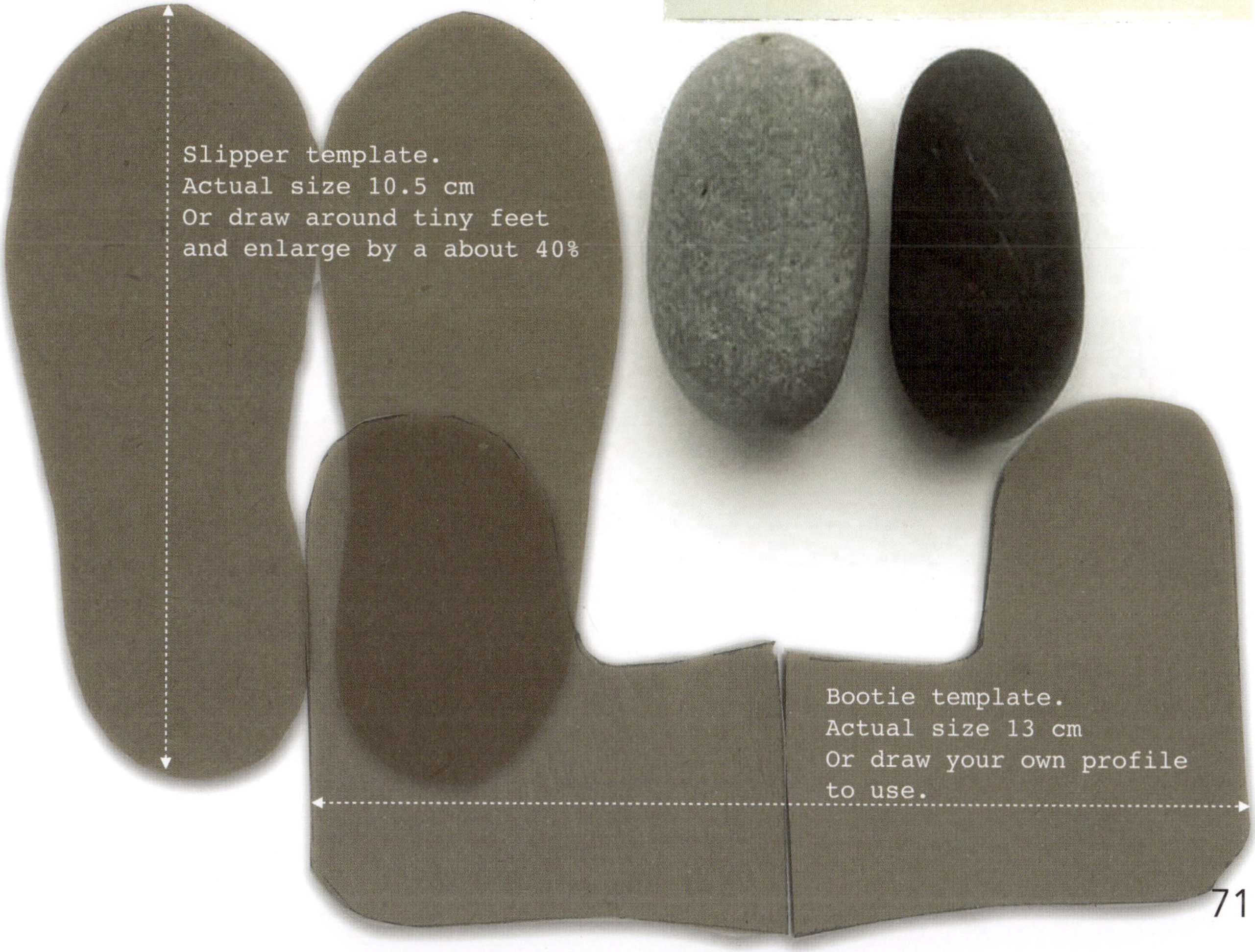

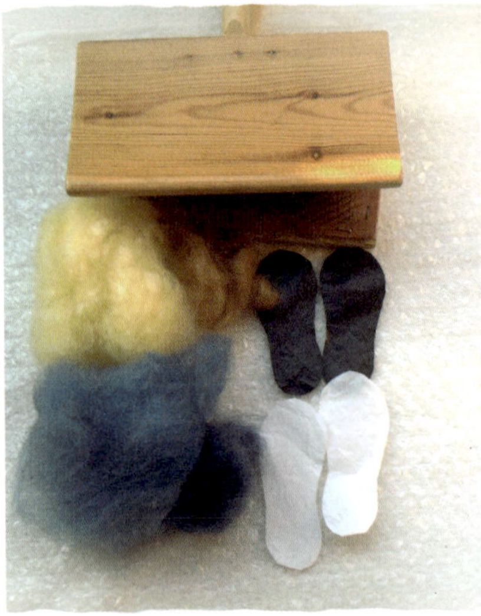
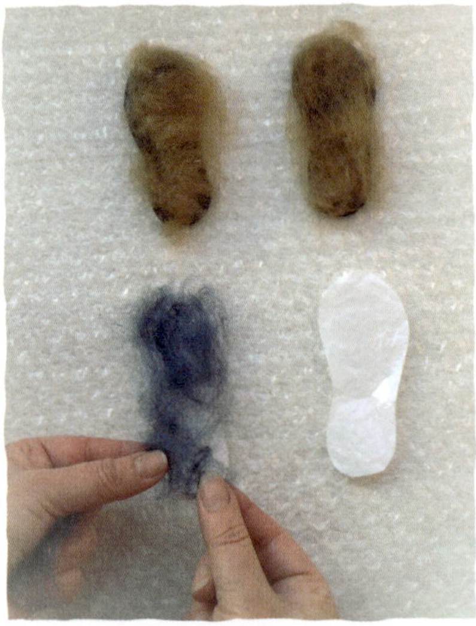
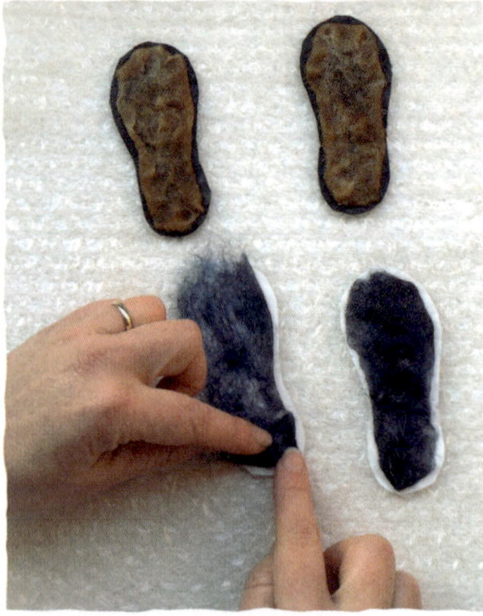
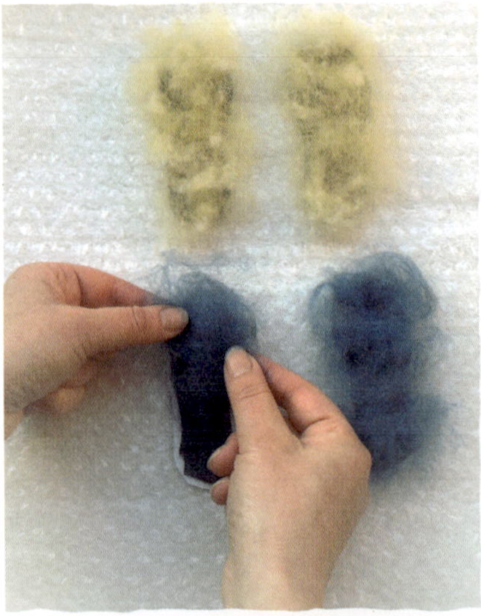
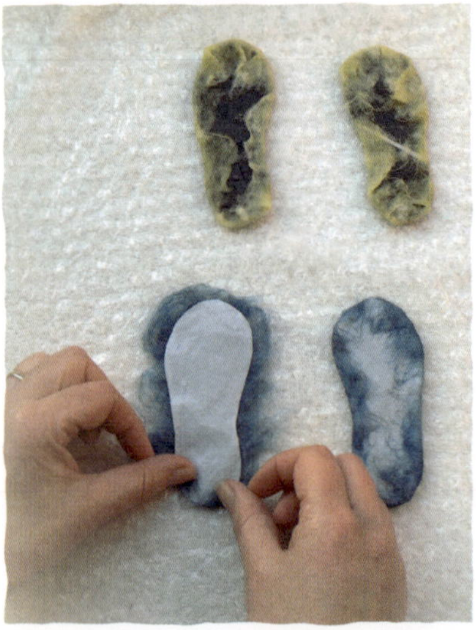
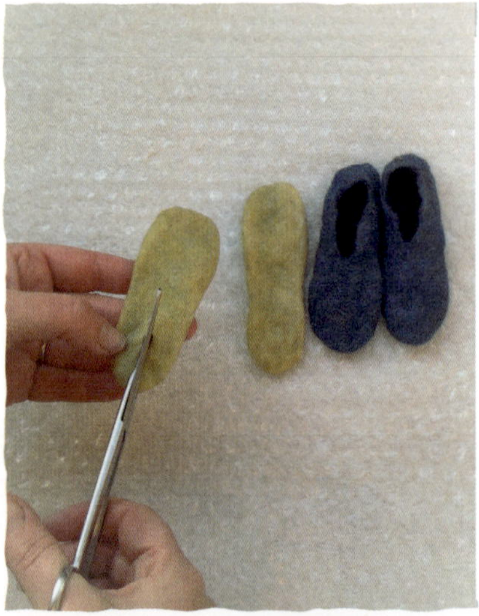
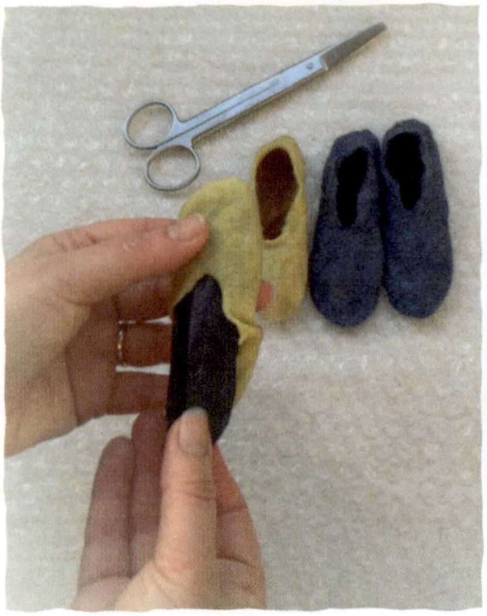
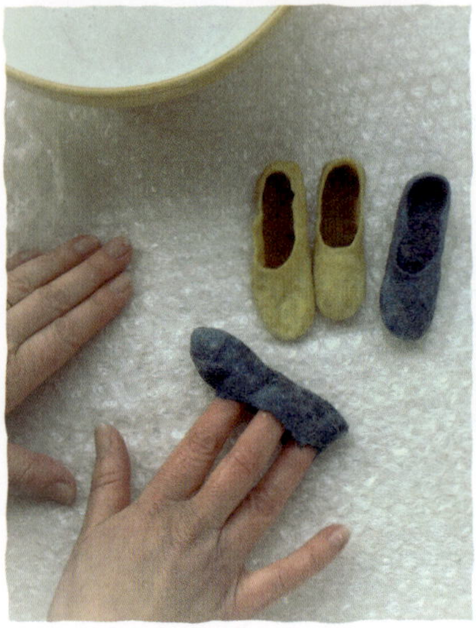
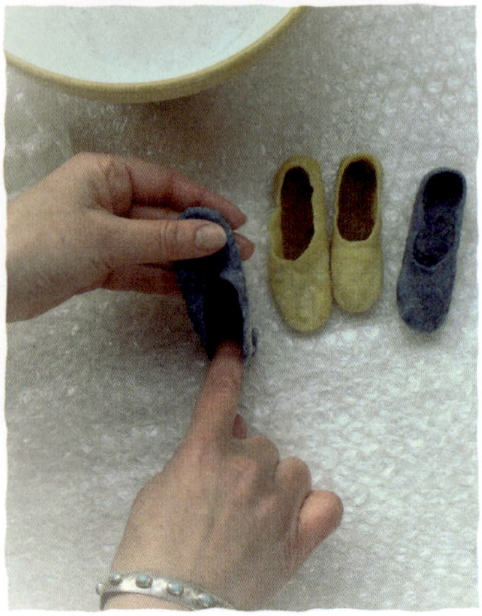

Making slippers with a resist template .

1. Lay out your design. *(See pictures opposite)*
You can work on the pair together.
To make slippers with a coloured insole, first lay a small amount of contrasting fibres onto one side of the template, but not overlapping the edges.
Then using your chosen slipper colour, place a fine layer of fibres over the surface of each slipper template, covering the insole layer and overlapping the edge slightly. You may like to place a tiny amount of the insole colour on the surface, so you can tell which side is top and bottom.
Wet the fibres with soap solution, cover with bubble wrap, and press through.
Turn the whole piece over.

Peel off the top layer of bubble wrap. Fold the outside fibres onto the surface of the resist. Fill in the gap with a fine layer of fibres. Add another fine layer over the first, overlapping the edge slightly. (middle row, left and centre)
Wet the fibres, cover with bubble wrap and press through.
Turn the whole piece over.

Peel off the top bubble wrap. Fold the outside fibres onto the surface of the first layer of fibres. This should be enough, but check for any thin areas, and fill them in.
Add any other surface pattern or details.

Felt the wool*.. refer to the guide below, cutting and removing the template, then massaging the slipper into shape, as shown opposite.*

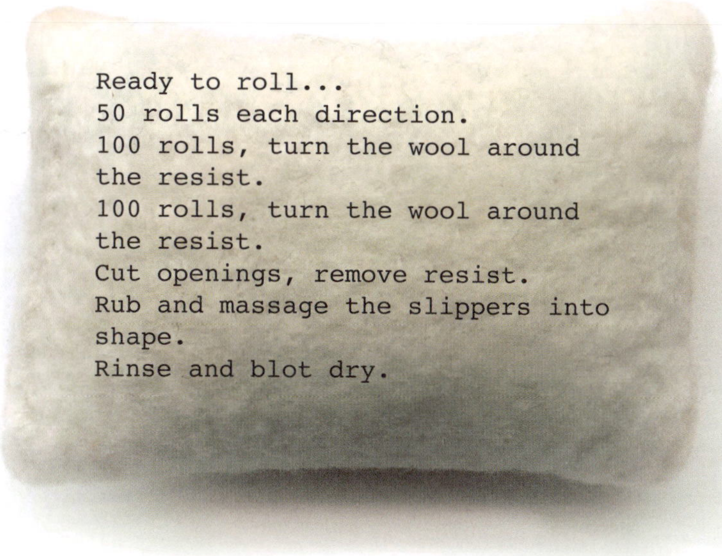

Rinse out the soap and blot dry,
Reshape the slippers, then stuff the insides with tissue paper to hold the form as they dry.

Finishing touches...
Embellish with buttons, beads or laces, fastenings of your choice.
Sew a ribbon at the heels or use a tiny clothes peg to hang.

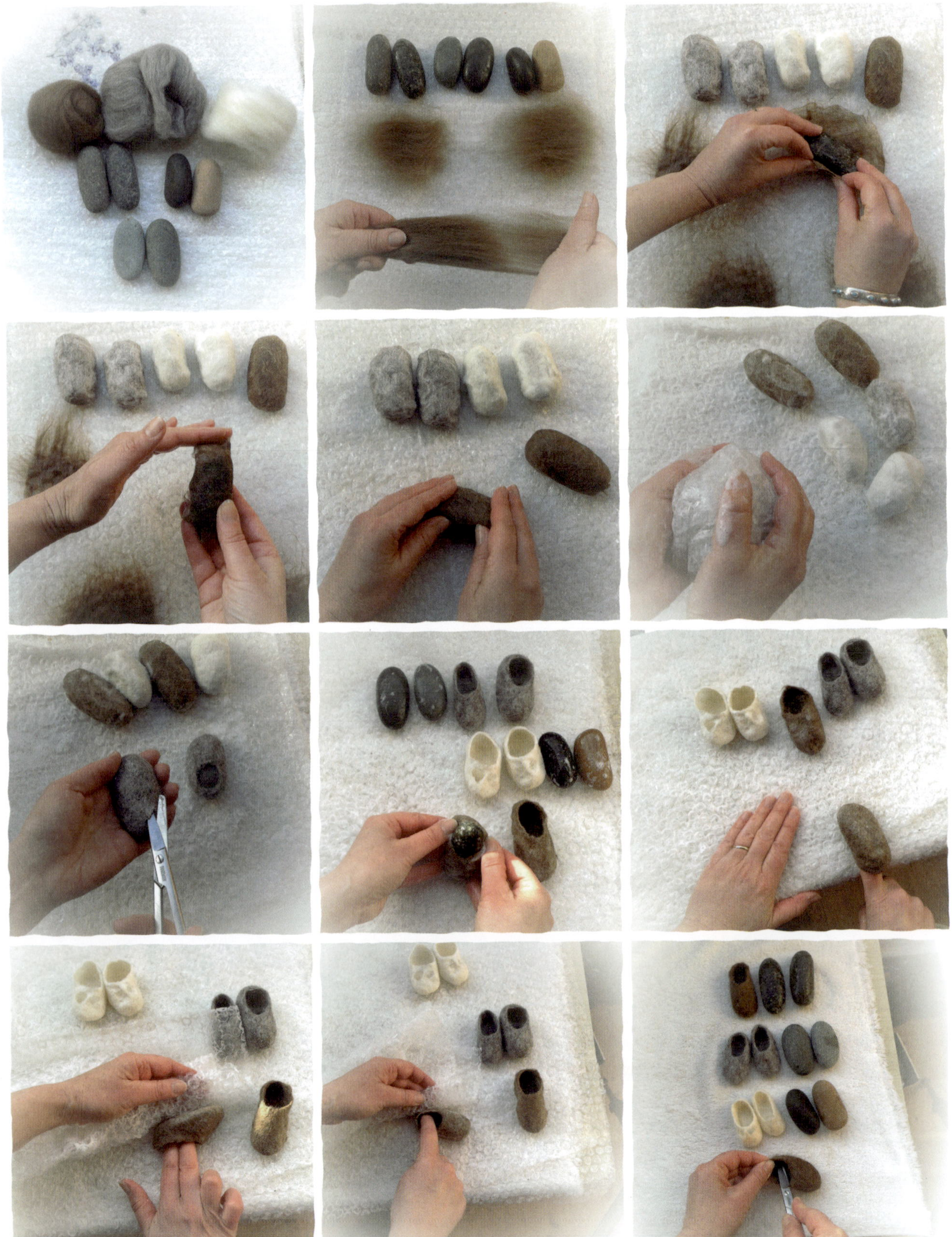

Making slippers with a pebble form

These slippers are created in a similar way to the covered soap and rattle, so you can refer to the techniques on pages 32 and 60 but this time you will remove the pebbles.
If you can match up a pair of pebbles that's great, if not you can always make one slipper after the other, using the same pebble. Just prepare your patches of felt at the same time, so they will be a similar thickness.
Use much smaller amounts of wool to cover each pebble.

*1. Lay out your fibres. (Top row opposite)
Two patches each, slightly larger than the pebble should be enough.*

*2. Wet the wool and one at a time, gently wrap and cover the pebbles.
Gently roll the pebble around, and roll inside bubble wrap to begin the felting slowly. (Second row)*

*3. When the wool has felted onto the surface, cut your opening, and remove the pebbles.
(3rd row)*

*4. Use your fingertips and bubble wrap to massage the felt into a 3D shape. Continue rubbing until the wool firms up and a nice shape is formed.
You can trim the opening of the slippers and rub the edges smooth.
Rinse and reshape, then stuff with tissue until dry, to hold the form.
Add your finishing touches. If your slippers are a gift, you can make a smart shoe box to present them in. See page 108.*

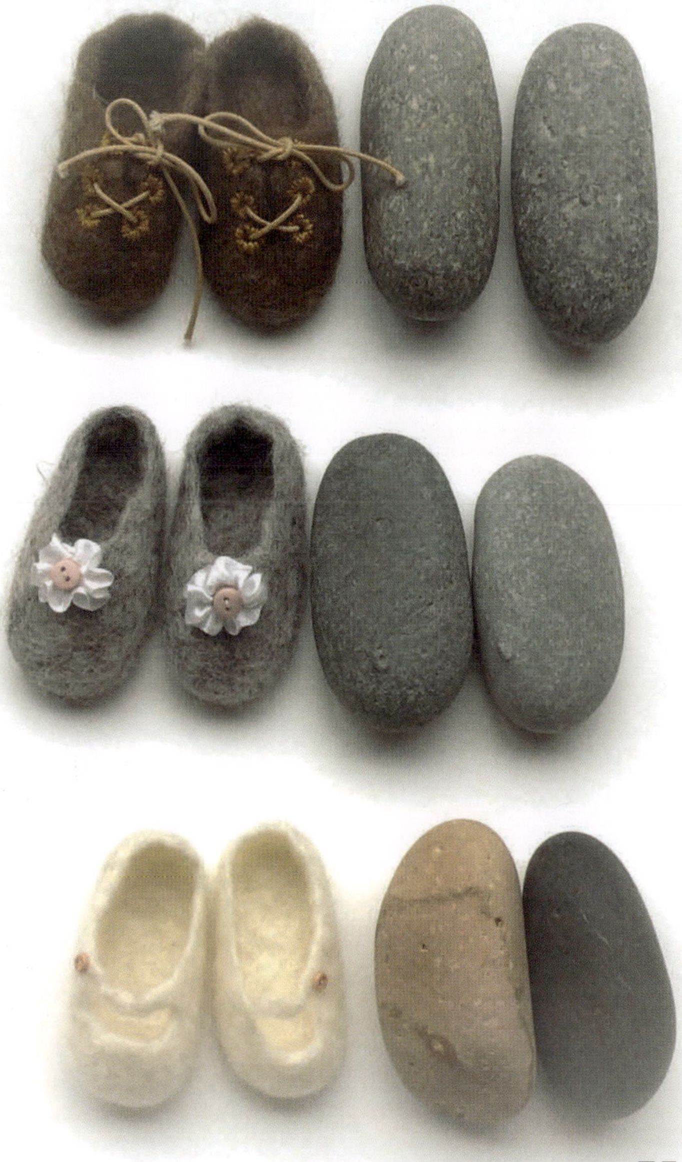

Making Booties with a resist template

This template makes both booties together.
Refer to the resist technique shown on page 27. Cover both sides with a fine layer of fibres, fold over the edges and add any surface decoration.
Begin the felting process, refer to the guide on the right.
Cut the wool and the template in half to separate the pair, as shown below and trim the opening to your desired shape.
Remove the template and use your fingertips and bubble wrap to massage them into a 3D shape. Rub the bottom across the bubble wrap to flatten the sole of the bootie.
Rinse, blot in a towel, reshape, and stuff with tissue until dry.
Add your tiny finishing touches of buttons, beads, bells or laces.

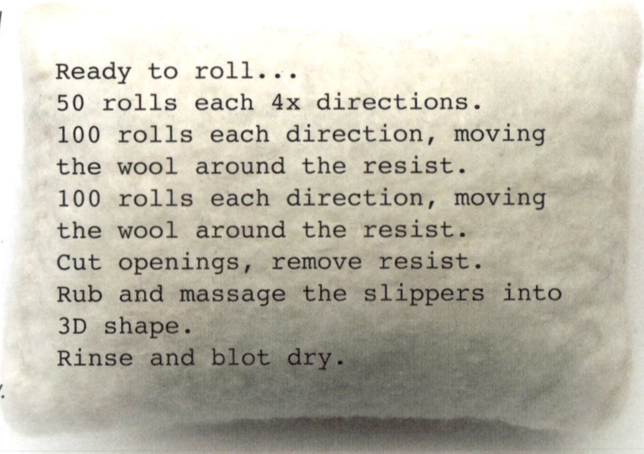

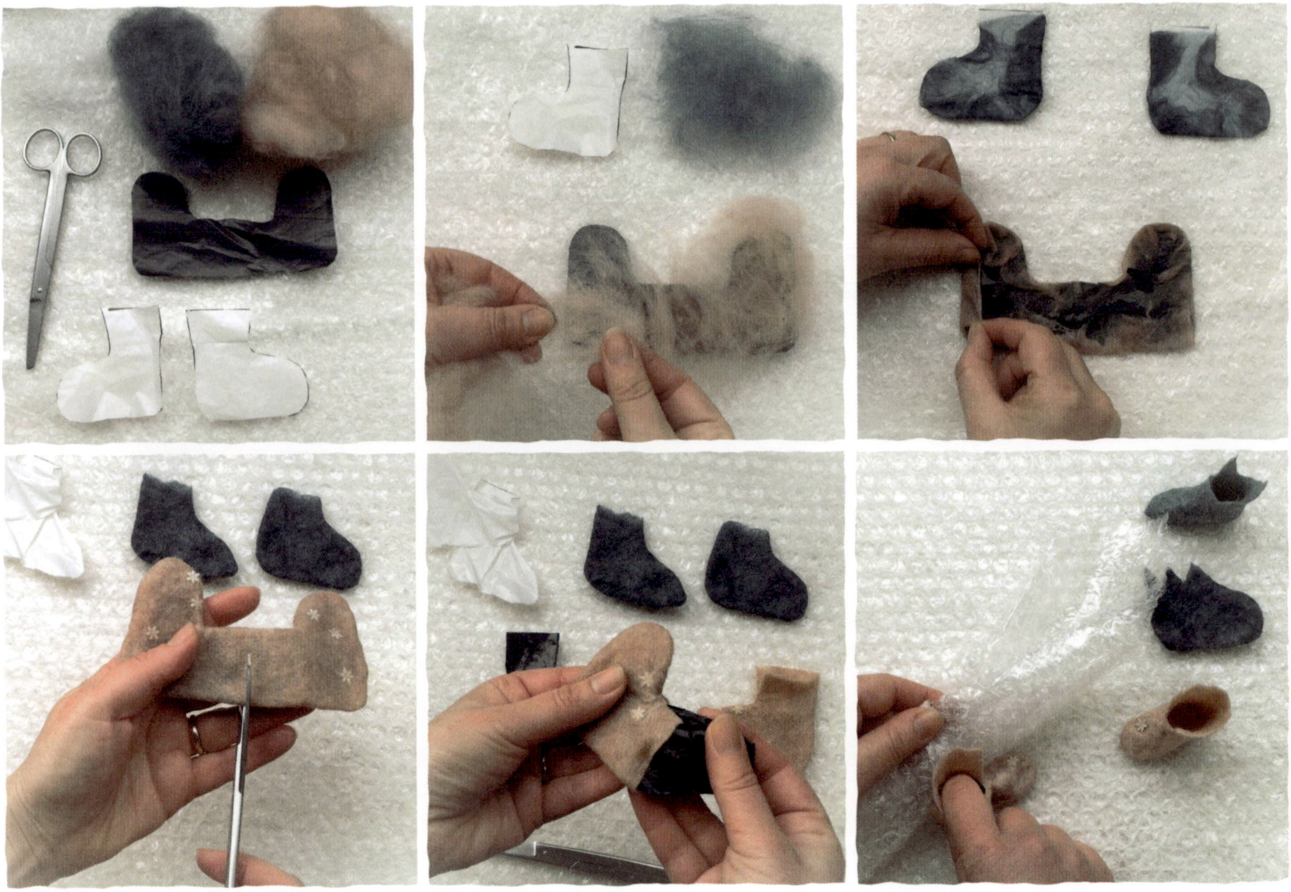

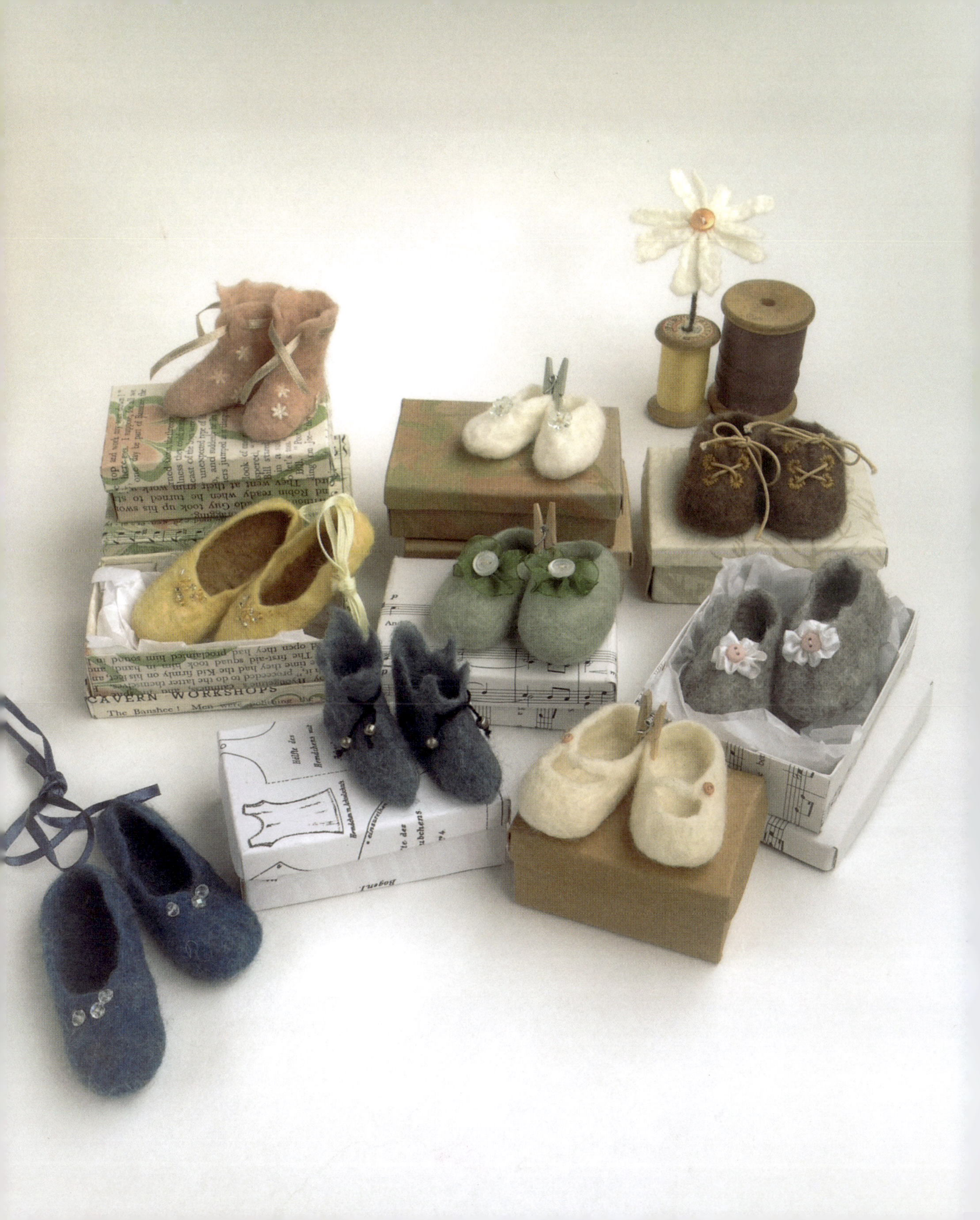
CAVERN WORKSHOPS

Onesies

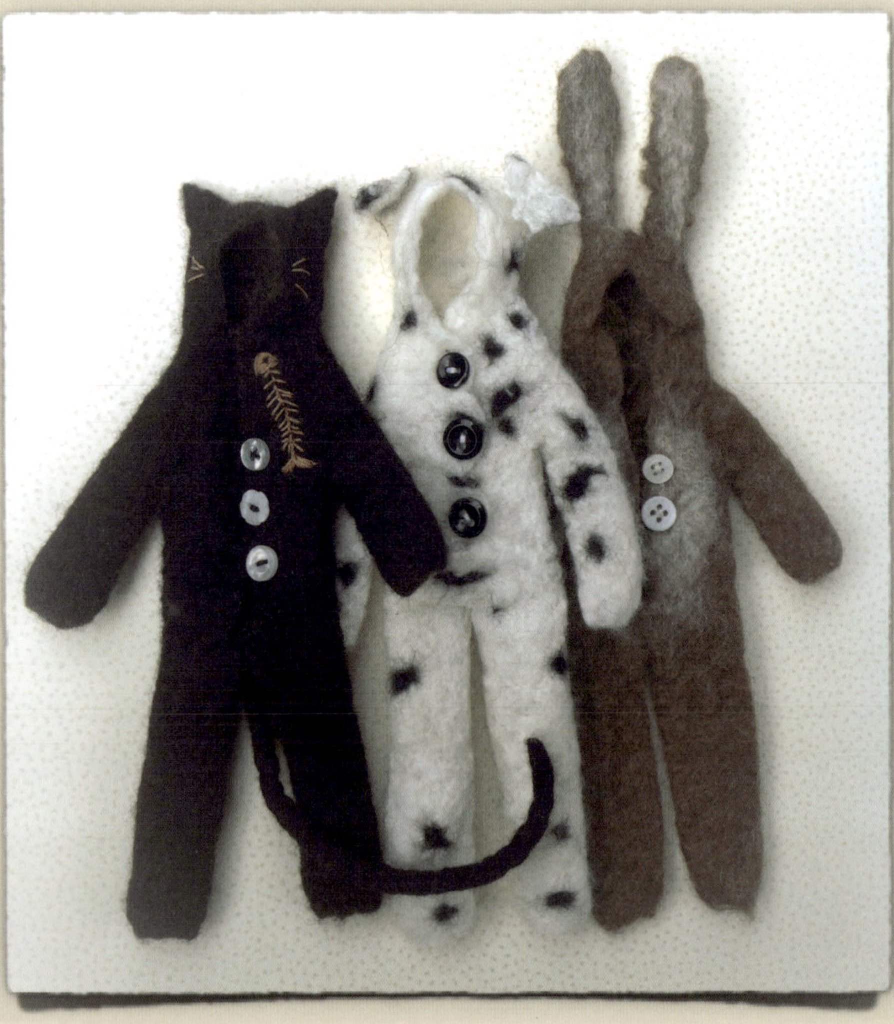

Have fun with this one, it could be a custom~made onesie inspired by someone's favourite animal, just plan the colours, and add ears and tail.
You can make the onesie to fit a particular doll or figure, just draw around the doll and enlarge between 30 and 40%

Materials and tools

Wool fleece in chosen colours at least 10 gms
2 pieces of bubble wrap
Rolling pin
Bamboo mat
Soap solution, sprinkler
Towels
Plastic resist cut from enlarged template opposite (or design your own)
Scissors
Buttons or beads or thread for decoration.

Enlarge the template by 200%
Template should be 25cm in length, so twice the size shown.
Or make your own pattern from a doll...simply draw around the doll and add about 30 to 40%

Notes on technique..

This workshop shows how to make the cat onesie, and the page of photographs show how to make the hare or rabbit.
Cover your template first, then add the ears. Be sure that some fibres from the ears overlap the front and back.
Add the tail before felting, but if you forget, you can always needle felt it in position later, see page 104.
The finished cat and dog onesies are about 21cm long, and the hare onesie is about 25cm

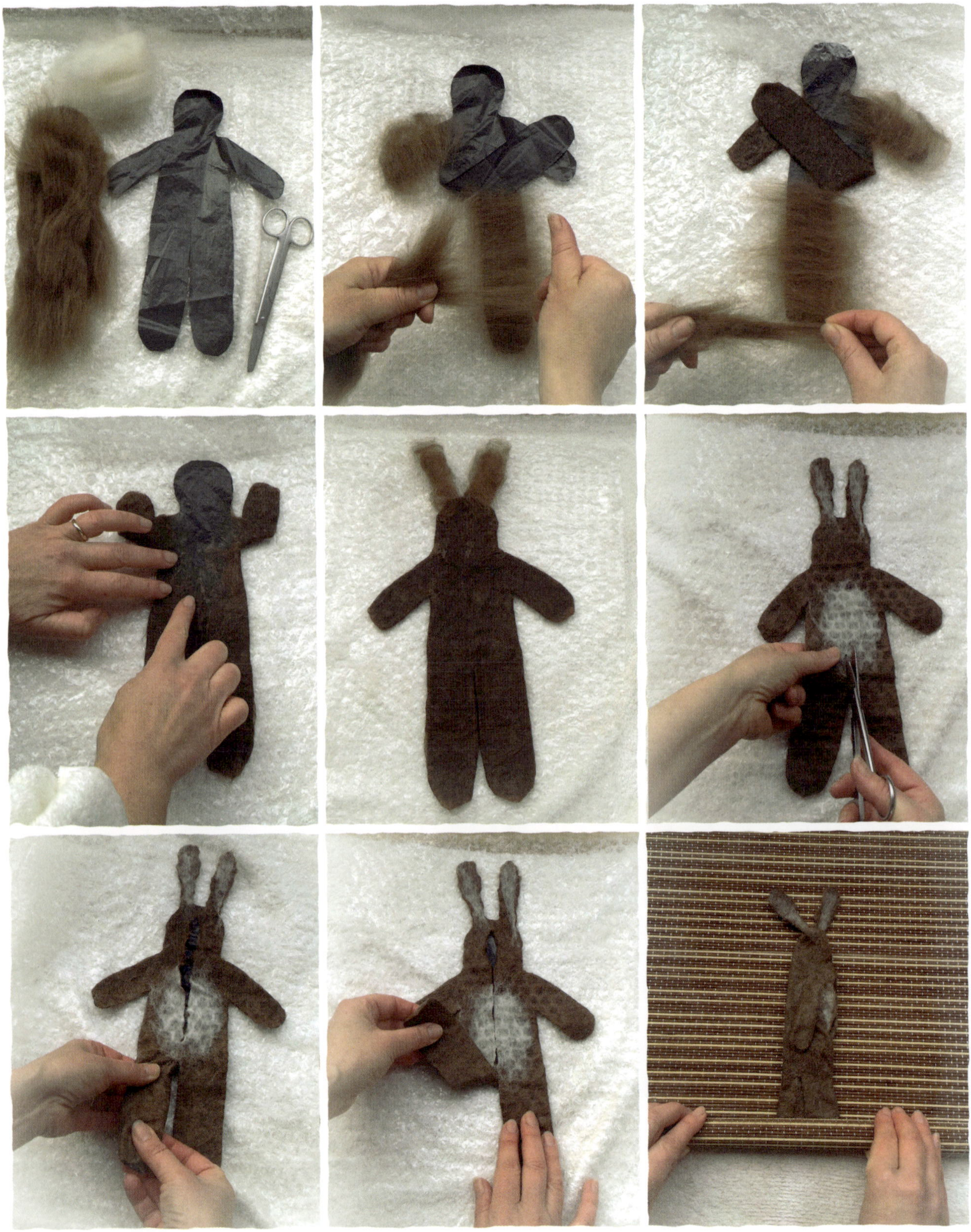

Lay out your design.

1. Fold the left leg of the template up and across the body, out of the way.
Place a fine layer of fibres over the surface of the right leg, covering and overlapping the edge slightly. Also cover the left arm.
Wet the fibres, cover with bubble wrap, and press through.
Turn the whole piece over to the back.

2. Peel off the top layer of bubble wrap.
Fold the outside fibres onto the surface of the resist.

3. Fill in the centre with a fine layer of fibres. Add another fine layer over the first, overlapping the edge slightly. Do this for both the arm and the leg.
Wet the fibres, cover with bubble wrap and press through.
Turn the whole piece over to the front

4. Peel off the top layer of bubble wrap. Fold the outside fibres onto the surface of the first layer. Add one more fine layer over the middle of the first. This should be enough, but check for any thin areas, and fill them in.

5. Unfold the left leg back down onto the bubble wrap. Then fold the covered leg up and across the body, out of the way.
It helps to place a piece of plastic between the covered arm and leg, so the fibres don't join together.

6. Repeat the layering of fibres so that all the limbs are covered.

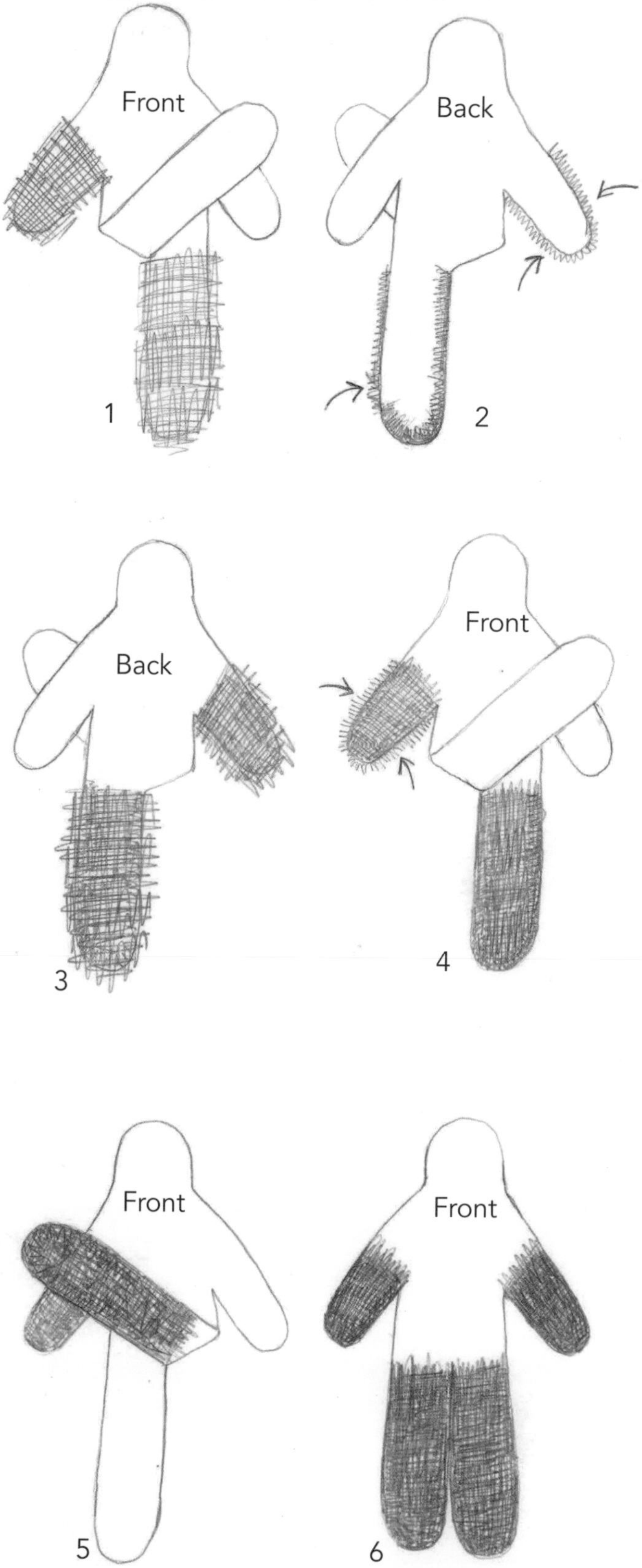

7. Fold both covered arms of the template up and out of the way. Place a fine layer of fibres over the surface of the body, from the under arms down to the legs, covering and overlapping the edge slightly.

8. Repeat the layering of fibres as before, so both sides are covered.

9. Shoulders and hood.
Fold the covered arms back down.
Repeat the layering of fibres so that all of the template is covered front and back. This should be enough, but check for any thin areas, and fill them in.

10. Ears.
Place some fibres so that they overlap the top of the hood. Fold over the edges to create your chosen ear shape. Repeat this on the back so the fibres overlap both sides.
You can now add any surface decoration, or shading.

11. Tail. (Refer to the technique on page30)
Take a length of fibres about 18cms and wet one end. Roll between your palms to felt the wool. Keep the top end of the tail dry.
Open out the dry fibres and position the tail on the back of the onesie.
It may help to place a piece of plastic beneath the rest of the tail to prevent it merging.
Cover with net, and give the ear and tail joins a little soapy rub, to encourage the fibres to merge.
Felt the wool. Refer to the felting guide below.
12. After the first 4x 50 rolls, cut the openings.
When the onesie is dry, add some extra detail with stitching, buttons or beads, and try for size.

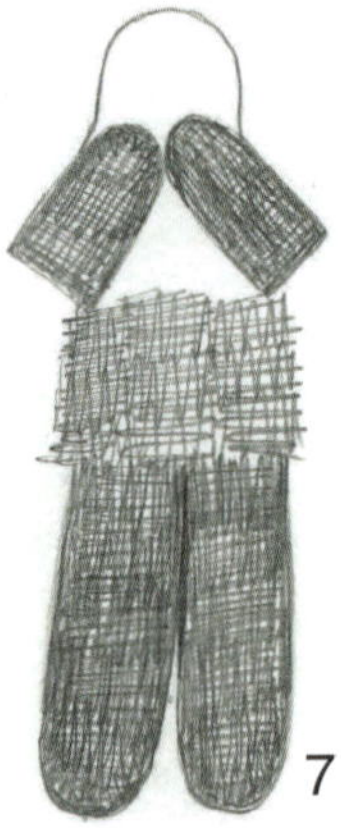
7

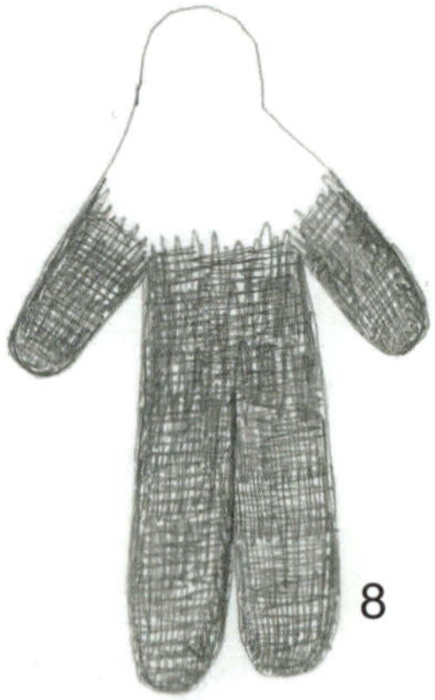
8

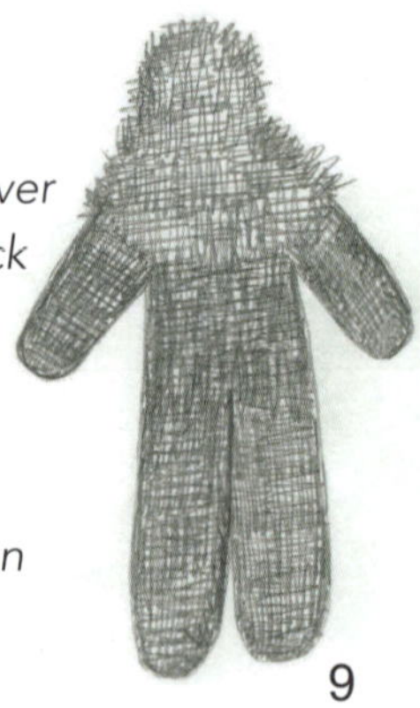
9

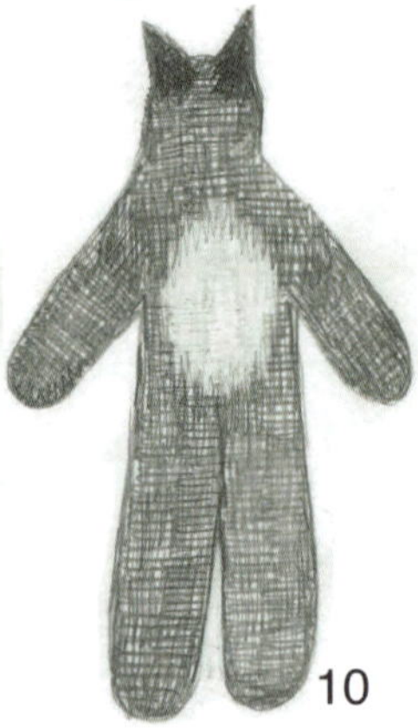
10

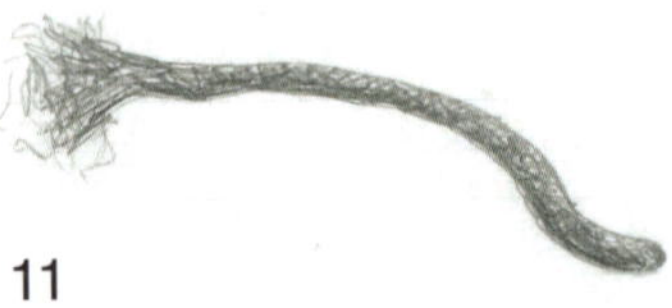
11

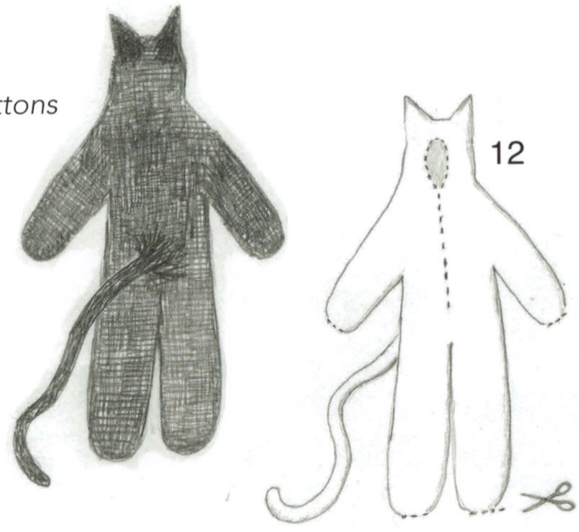
12

Ready to roll...
50 rolls each 4x directions.
Cut openings.
100 rolls each direction, turning wool around the resist template.
100 turns each direction, turning wool around the resist template.
Remove resist
Throw 25 to 50 times.
Bamboo mat~ 25 to 50 rolls each direction.
Rinse and blot dry.

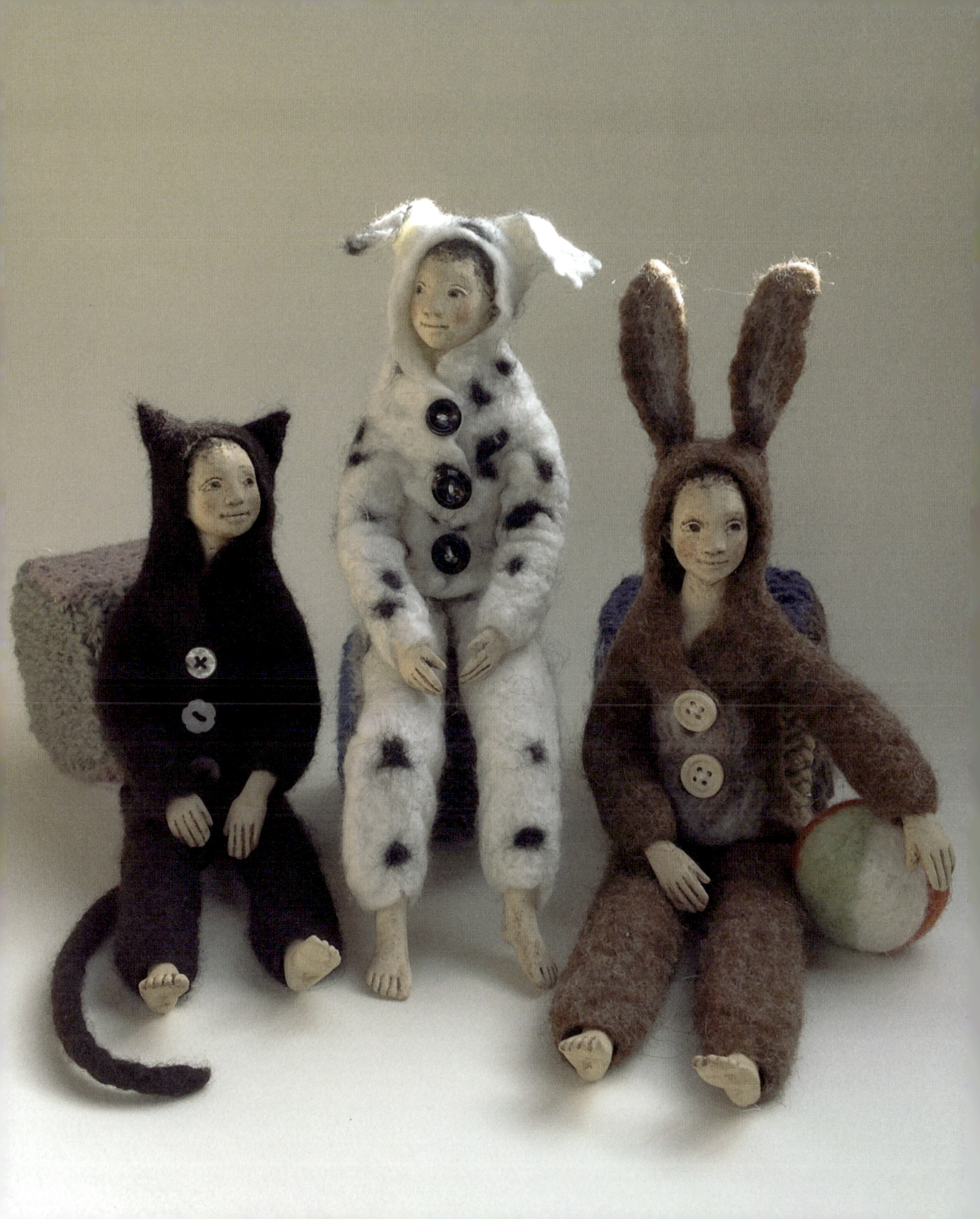

Gloves

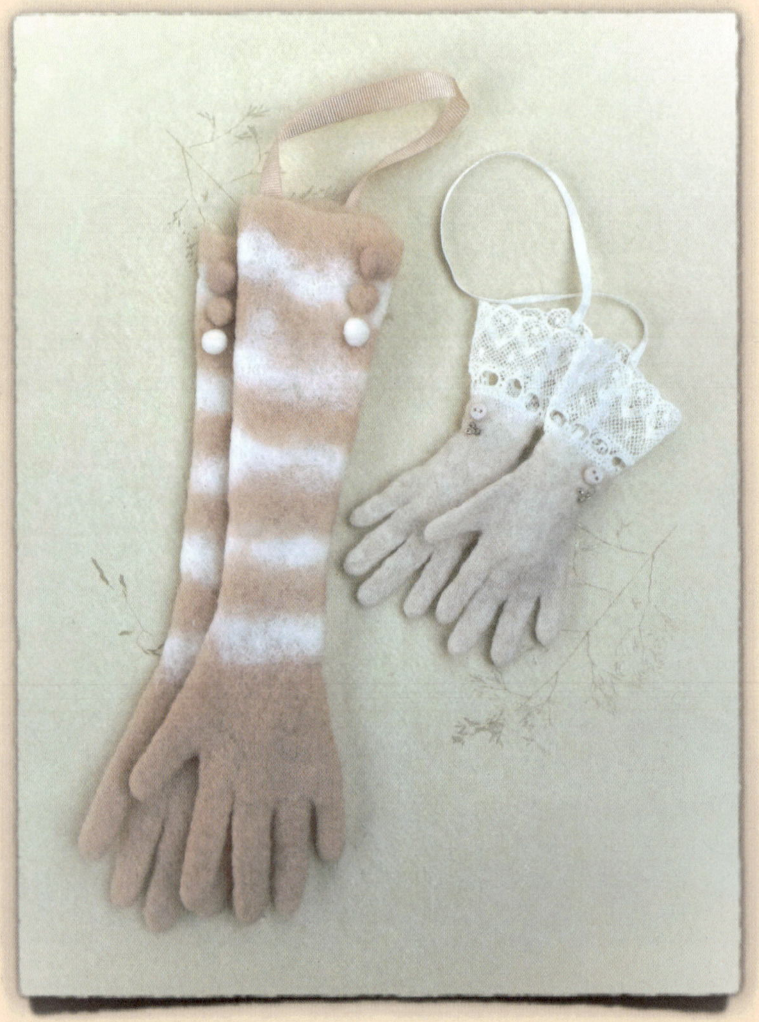

Special occasion gloves, finished with delicate buttons and beads. These would be perfect for wedding favours, a new baby gift, or mounted in a deep box frame. Join together with a length of ribbon and you'll never lose one.

Materials and tools

Wool fleece in your chosen colours
10 to 20 gms will be plenty. Cashmere or lambswool is ideal as the fibres are quite short, easy to fold around the fingers of the resist!
2 pieces of bubble wrap per pair
Soap solution, sprinkler, bowl, Rolling pin
Bamboo mat, Towels
Plastic resist
Lace for cuffs
Ribbon or lace to join gloves together
Scissors
Buttons or beads
Sewing needle and threads

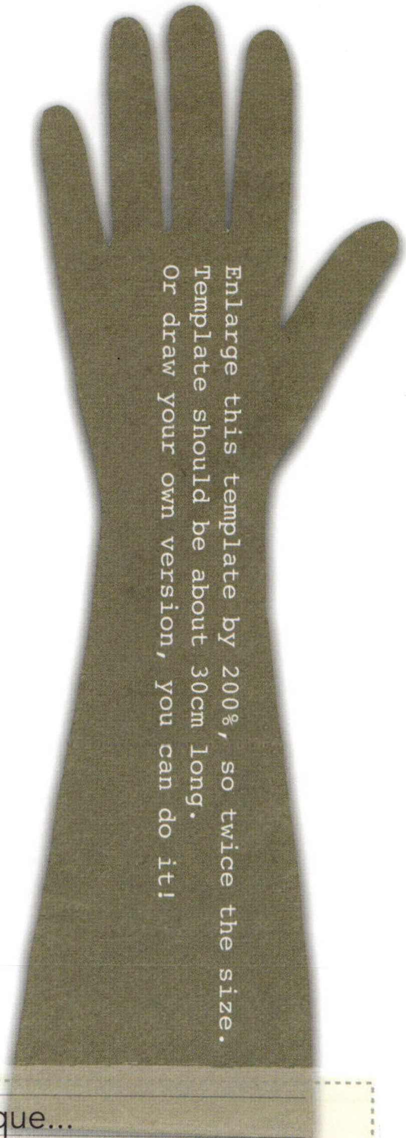

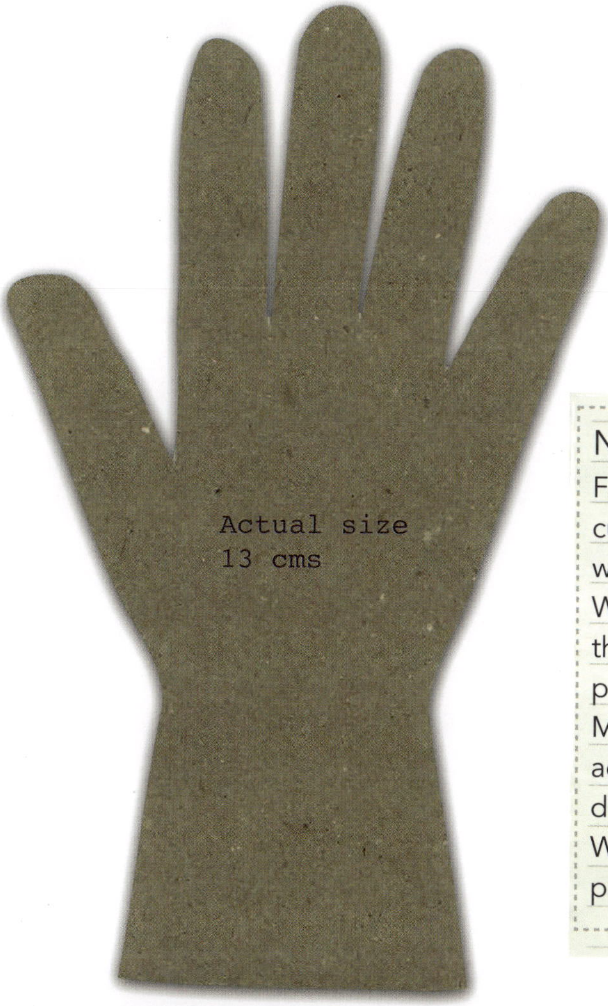

Notes on technique...

For the short gloves, measure the width of the cuff, and double it, for the length of lace you will need.
When wetting the fibres, be careful not to flood the wool, you shouldn't need to add much, just press it through each time you add more wool.
Make sure your fibres are random, not just across the width, or it will shrink unevenly and distort.
When complete, use pretty ribbon to keep the pair together.

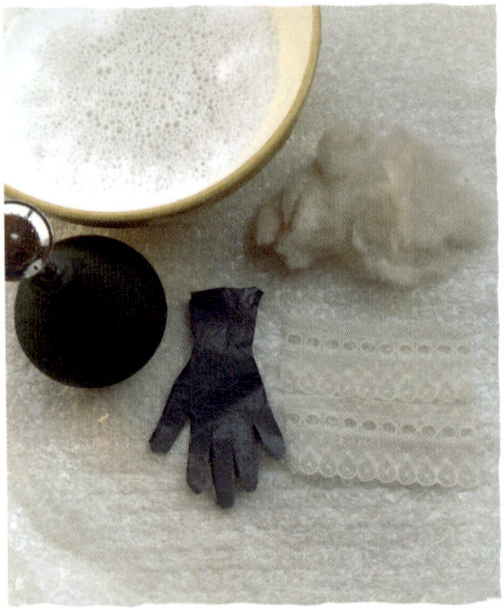
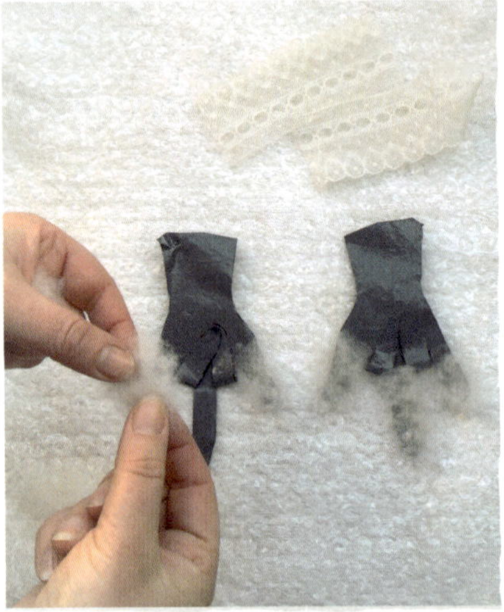
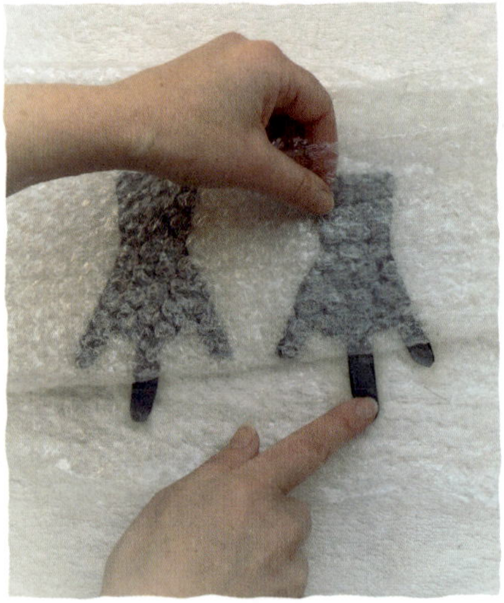
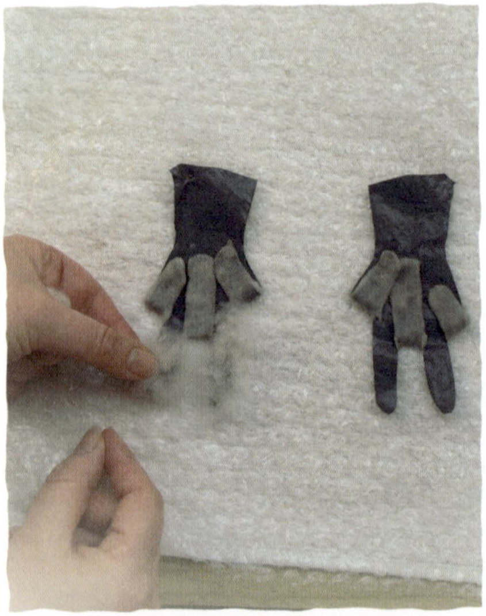
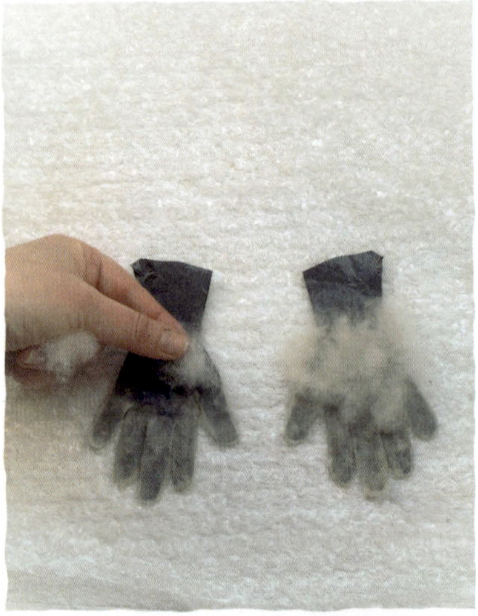
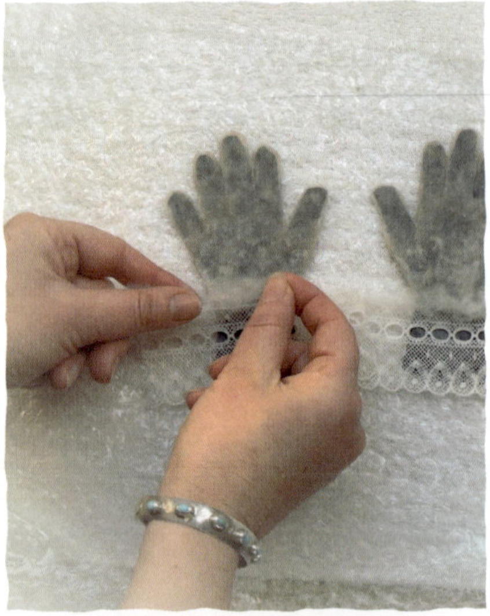
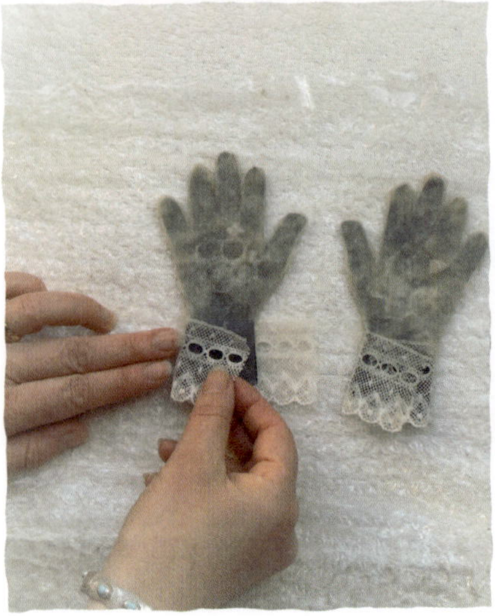
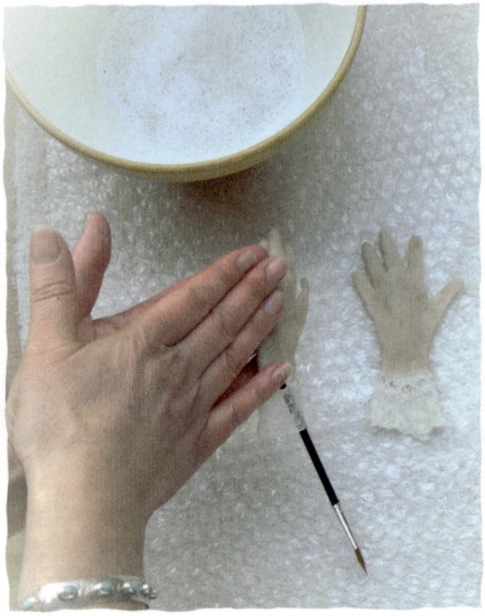
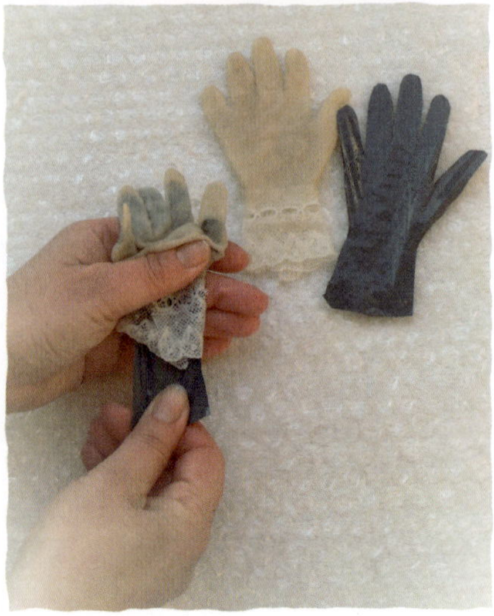

Lay out your design

Make both gloves together.
(Illustration shows just one hand)

1. (Palm) Place your template on the bubble wrap and fold the first and third fingers of the template upwards so they are out of the way.

2. Place a very fine layer of fibres over the thumb, middle and little finger of the template, overlapping the edge slightly.
Gently wet the fibres, cover with bubble wrap and press through.
Turn the whole piece over.

3. (Back) Peel off the top layer of bubble wrap.
Start at the finger tips, fold the outside fibres onto the surface of the resist. Fold them on each digit.

4. Add another fine layer over the first, overlapping the edge slightly.
Wet, cover with bubble wrap and press through.
Turn the whole piece over.

5. (Palm) Peel off the top layer of bubble wrap. Fold the outside fibres onto the surface of the first layer of fibres.
This should be enough, but check for any thin areas, and fill them in.

6. Fold back down the first and third fingers of the resist.

7. Fold back the covered thumb, middle and little fingers onto the hand, out of the way.

8. As before, cover the bare fingers with fibres, fold over the edges, and cover both sides.
Make sure you cover the thumb right down to where it joins the hand.

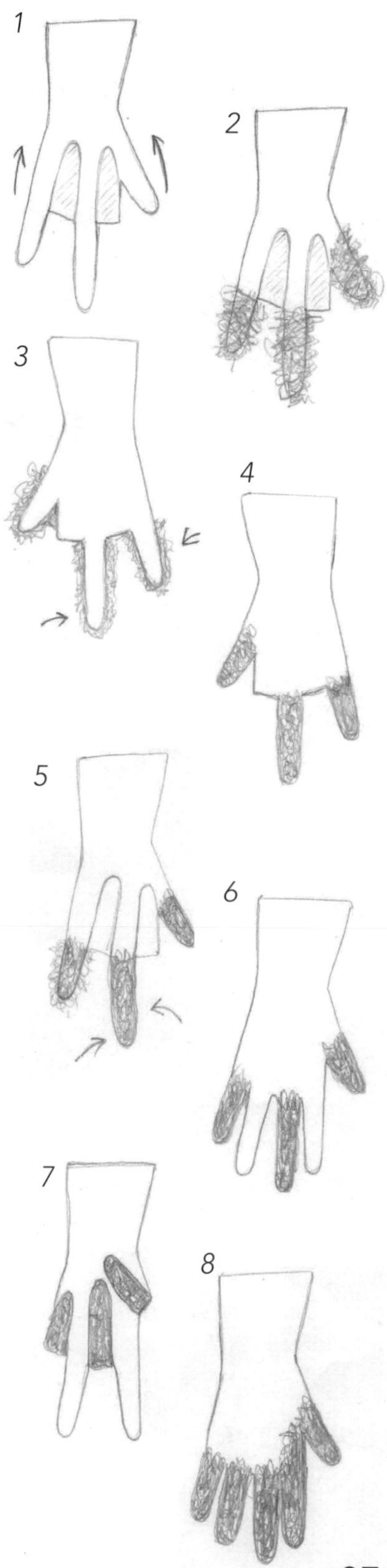

9. (Palm) Now you can fill in the palm and wrist of the template. Starting from the base of each finger and thumb, continue to add a fine layer of fibres over the exposed resist. Allow the fibres to overlap the edge slightly. Stop about 2 cms from the end .Wet, cover and press through.

10. (Back) As before, fold over the outside edges of fibre onto the surface of the resist.
Continue to fill in the palm and wrist and fold over the edges until the template is covered.
This should be enough, but check for any thin areas and add small amounts of fibre to fill them in.

9 10

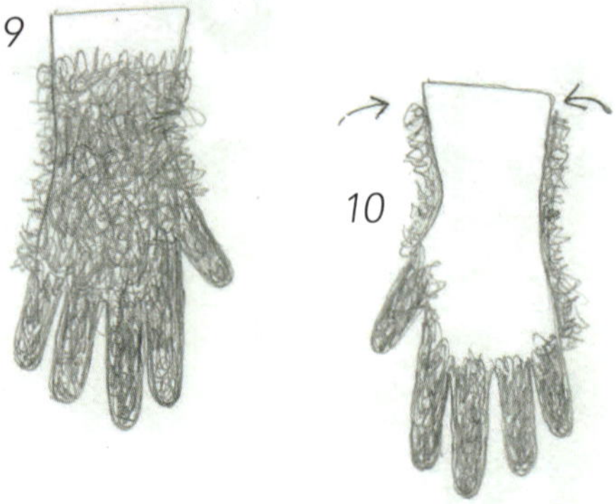

(For the lace edged gloves)
11. Place the length of lace over the edge of the fibres on the back of the glove.
Add a small wisp of fibre over the edge, so the lace is sandwiched between fibres. Wet, cover, and press through.
Turn the whole piece over.

12. Peel back the bubble wrap.
Fold the lace and fibres over onto the edge of the fibres on the wrist. Add a small wisp of fibre to cover the edge of the lace where it meets the wool.
Cover and press through.
Turn the whole piece over.
***Felt the wool**. (Refer to the guide, right)*

11 12

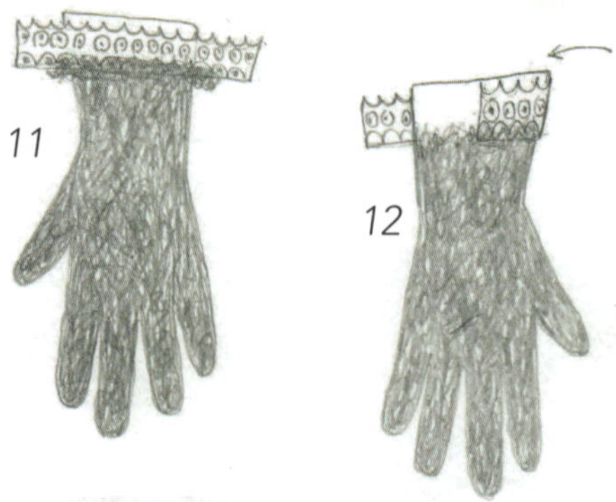

13. (For the long gloves)
Continue from step 9 adding the fibres right down the sleeve, just leave a gap at the end.

13

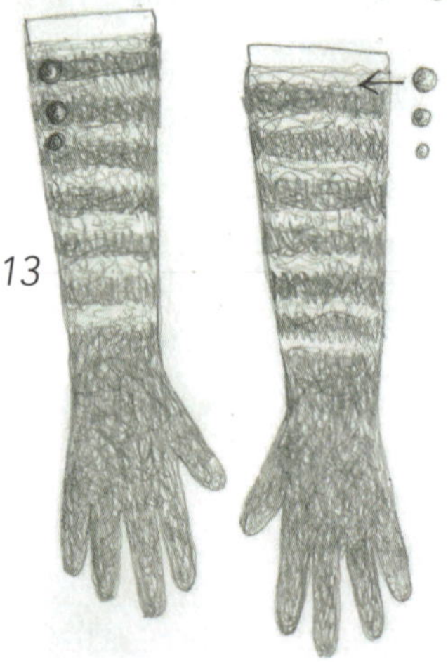

***Felt the wool**. (Refer to the guide on the right)*

Extra tips...
Insert a long paintbrush into each finger of the gloves and roll in your palms to harden the felt.
Make some little felt beads for the long gloves, as directed on page 30 and attach with few stitches for a finishing touch.

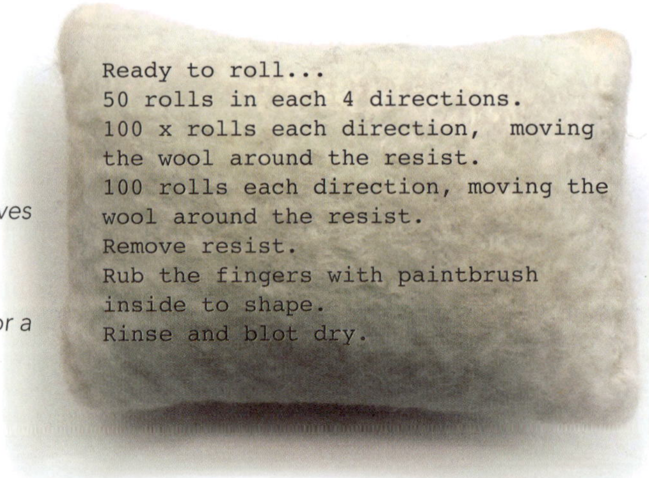

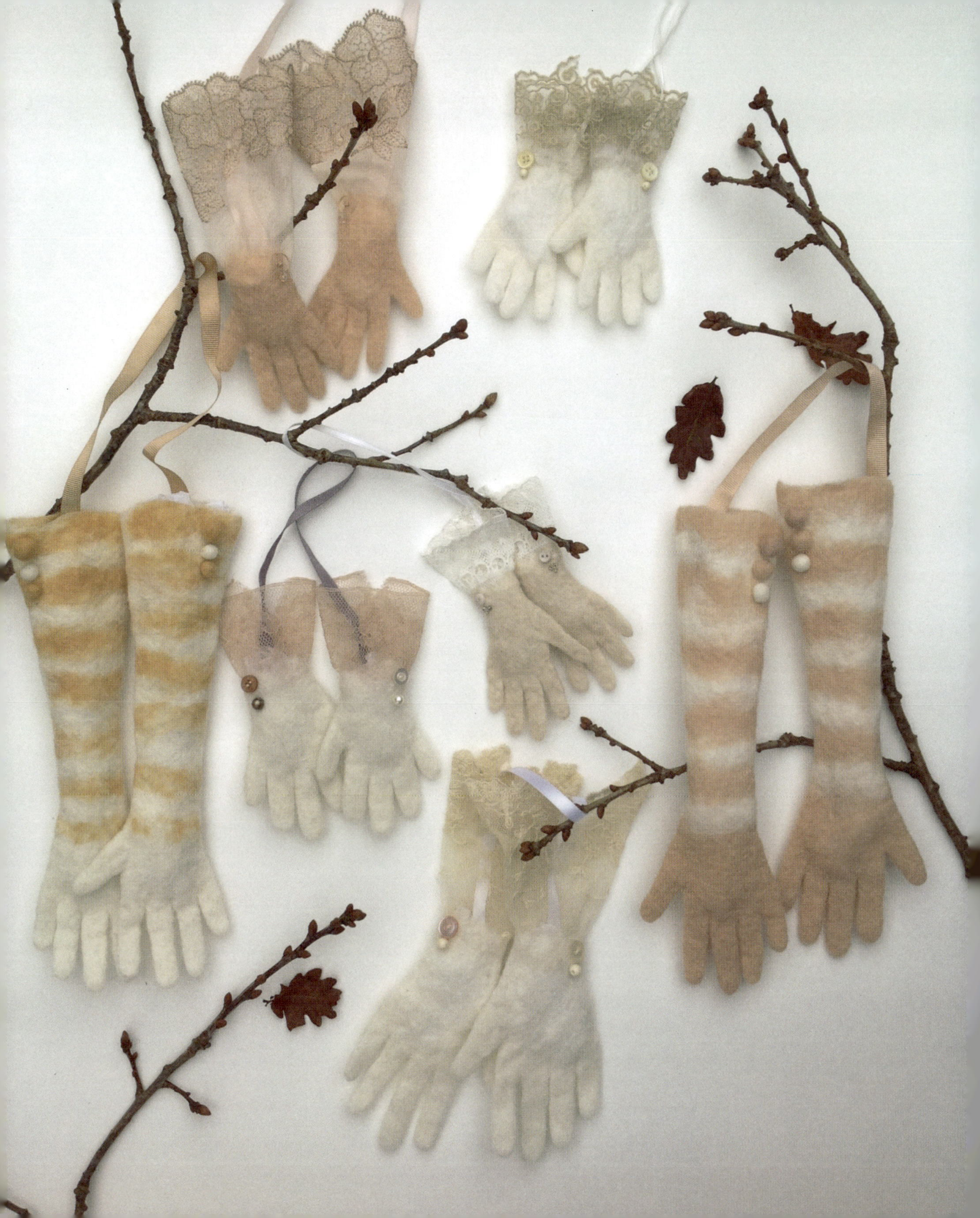

Coats and Dresses

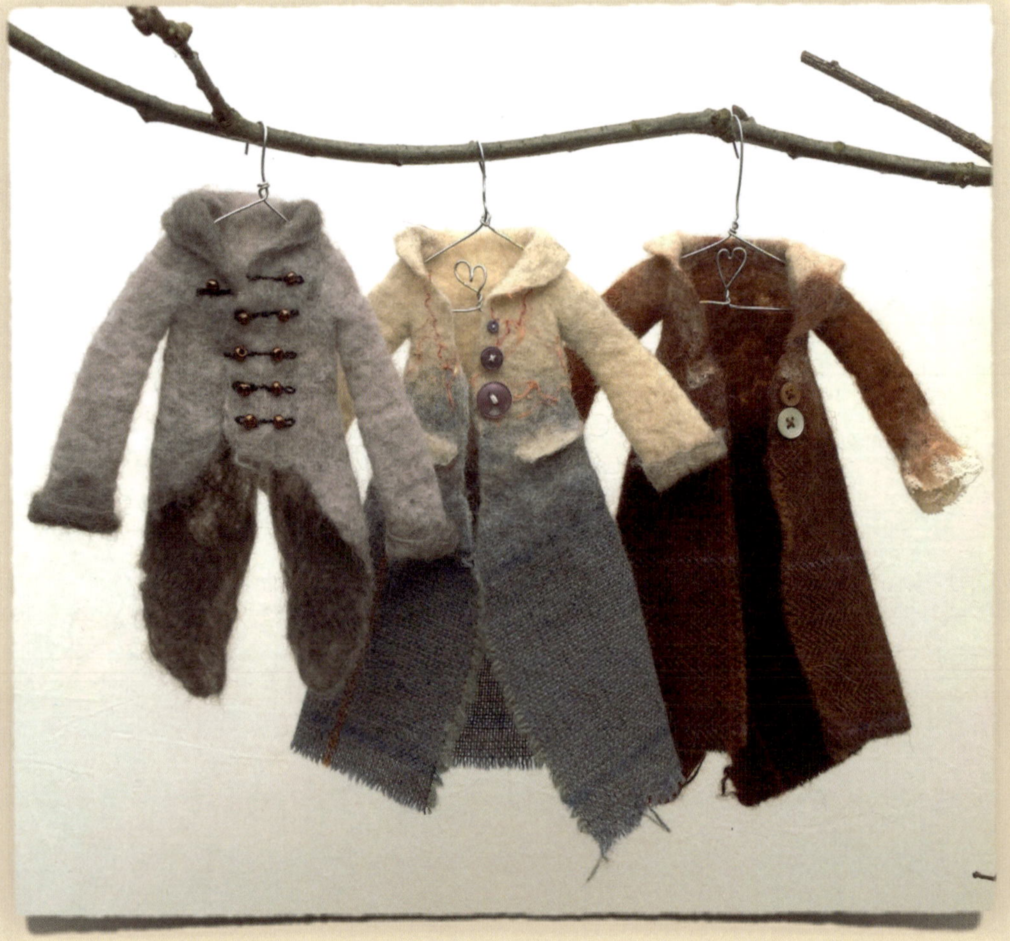

Miniature coats and dresses. Use fabric remnants to create coat tails and skirts, embedded into the design.
Add a hood, collar, cuffs, a belt and buttons and beads
Finish with tiny wire hangers.

Materials and tools

Wool fibres in your chosen colours
About 10gms per garment
2 pieces of bubble wrap per garment
Soap solution, sprinkler
Rolling pin
Bamboo mat
Towels
plastic resist
Some fabric to include
Iron
Buttons or beads
Sewing needle and threads

Notes on technique...

This workshop uses the nuno technique.
Refer to the tips on page 28.
You can also make them just with wool, leave out the fabric and experiment with longer lengths, different sleeves and collars.
Embellish with tiny buttons and beads and some hand stitching.
Display on a little wire hanger, see page107
This template will make a garment to fit the donkey doll on page 98. Or adjust the dimensions to fit your own if needed.

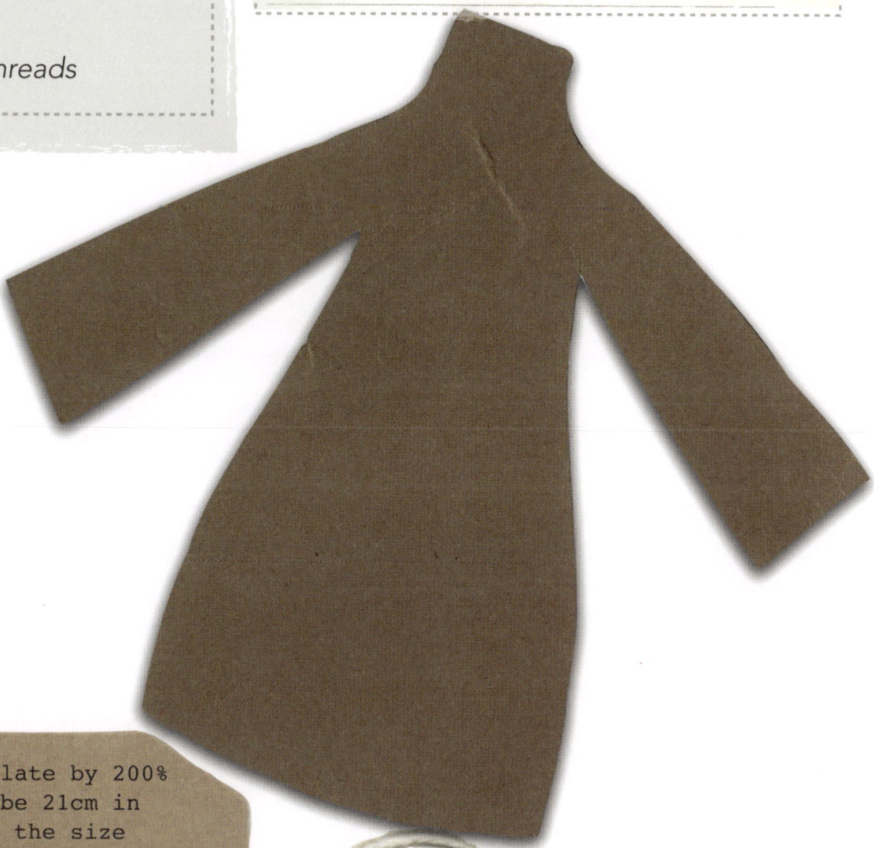

Enlarge the template by 200%
Template should be 21cm in length, so twice the size shown.
Or make your own pattern from a doll...simply draw around the doll and add your estimated shrinkage, e.g. 33%

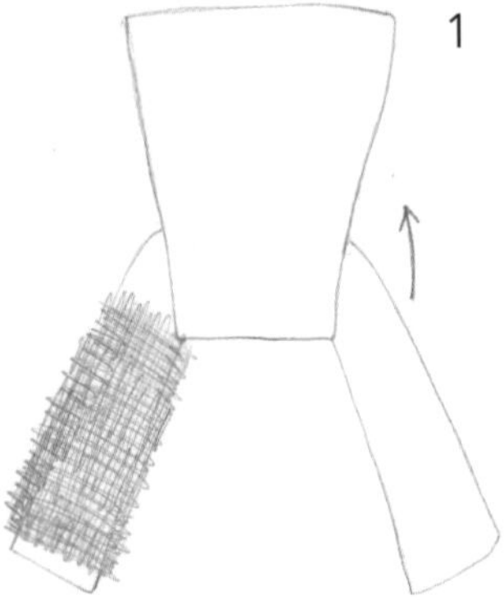
1

Lay out your design.
Start with the sleeves

1. Front.
Place your template on the bubble wrap and fold the body part of the template upwards, so it's out of the way. Place a fine layer of fibres over each arm, overlapping the edge slightly.
Wet the fibres, cover with bubble wrap, and press through. Turn the whole piece over to the back.

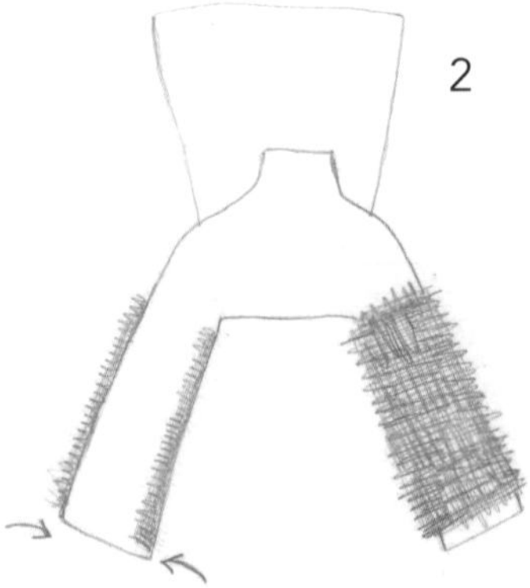
2

2. Back.
Peel off the top layer of bubble wrap. Fold the outside fibres onto the surface of the resist on each sleeve. (See left sleeve) Fill in the gap with a fine layer of fibres. Add another fine layer over the first, overlapping the edge slightly. (See right sleeve)
Wet the fibres, cover with bubble wrap and press through. Turn the whole piece over to the front

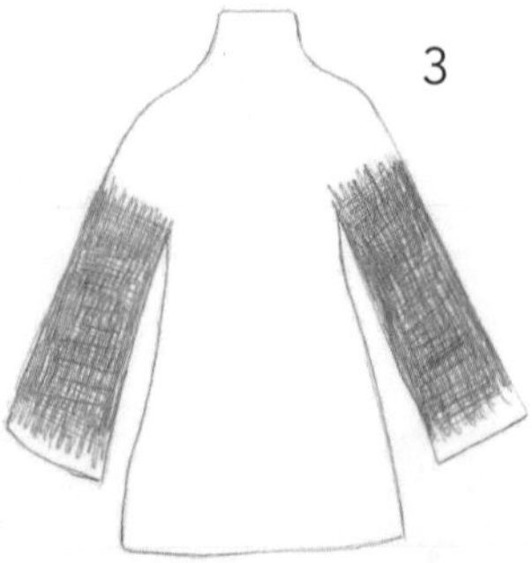
3

3. Front
Peel off the top layer of bubble wrap. Fold the outside fibres onto the surface of the first layer of fibres. Add one more fine layer over middle of the first. This should be enough, but check for any thin areas, and fill them in.
If you wish to have lacy cuffs, refer to the stocking workshop on page 46. Place the strip of lace over the bottom edge of the sleeves. Place a thin wisp of fibres over the top of the edge of lace, so it's trapped.
Fold down the body of the template as in picture

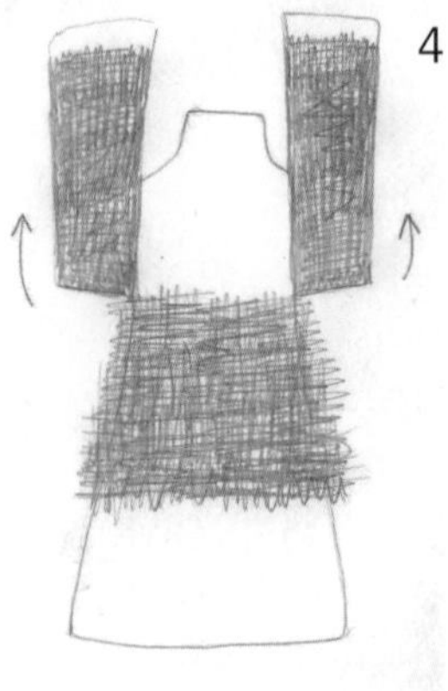
4

4. Front body.
Fold both covered arms up out of the way.
Starting from underneath the arms, continue to add a fine layer of fibres over the body of the dress. Allow the fibres to overlap the edge slightly. Stop just below the point you wish to add the fabric, so they will overlap.
Wet, cover and press through.

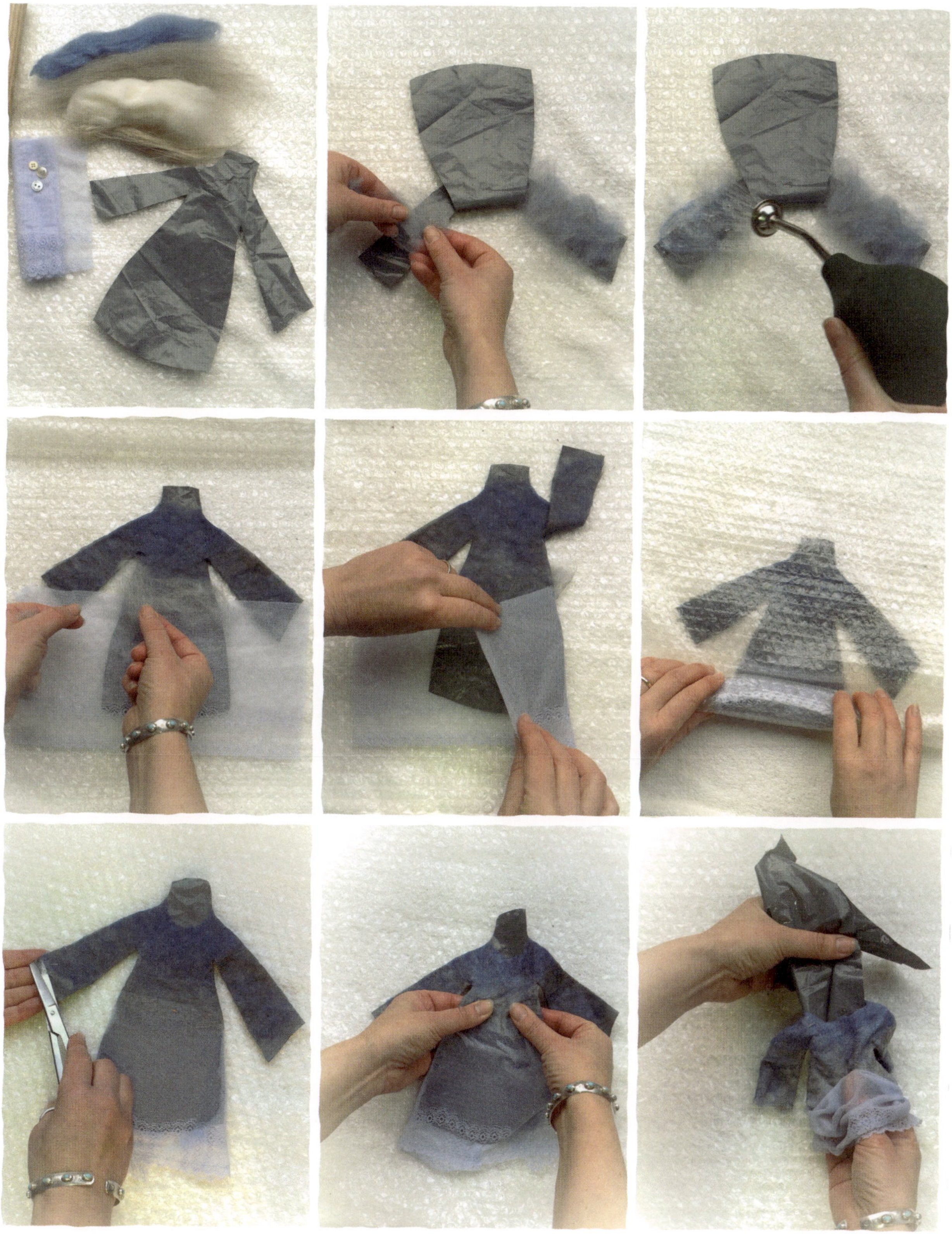

5. Back body
Peel off the bubble wrap. Fold over the outside edges of fibres onto the resist.
As before, fill in the centre with fibres. Add another fine layer of fibres, allowing them to overlap the edge of the template.
Wet, cover, press through.
Turn whole piece back over to front.

6. Front
Peel back the bubble wrap.
Fold over the outside fibres onto the surface of the first layer. Place one more fine layer over the middle of the shape, and check for any thin areas.
Fold down the sleeves as in the drawing.

7. Front, shoulders and neck
Decide on the type of neckline you would like.
You can create a scoop neckline, or continue up the neck of the template to create a fold-down collar, or even include a hood. (refer to the onesie workshop on page 78)
Continue to cover the rest of the template with more fibres, overlapping the edge slightly.
Repeat the above steps to complete the dress.

8. Adding the fabric.
Decide if you would like the edges of the material at the front or the back. This page shows the opening at the front, so turn the template over and start on the back. For the opening at the back, start with the front.
Either way, fold the covered arms up and out of the way.
Place the strip of material over the bottom edge of the fibres. Place some fibres over the top of the edge of the cloth, so it is sandwiched between layers of wool.
Cover with bubble wrap and press through. Turn the whole piece over.

5

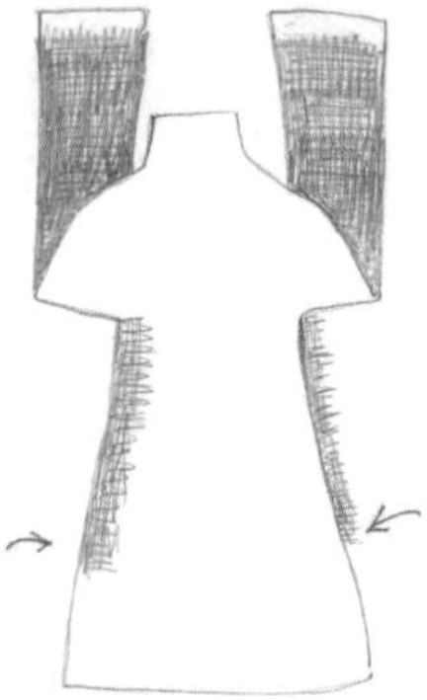

6

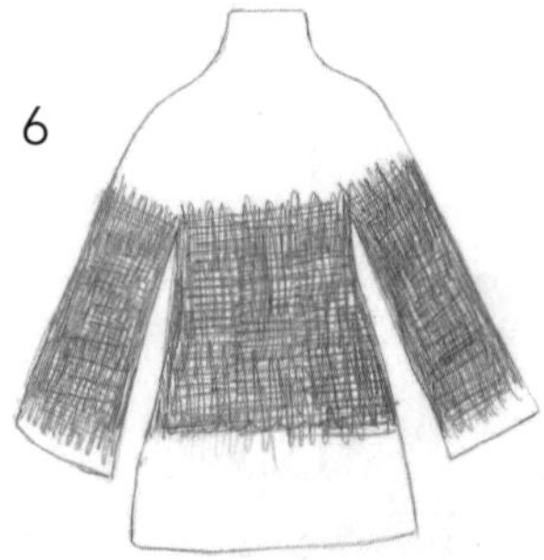

7

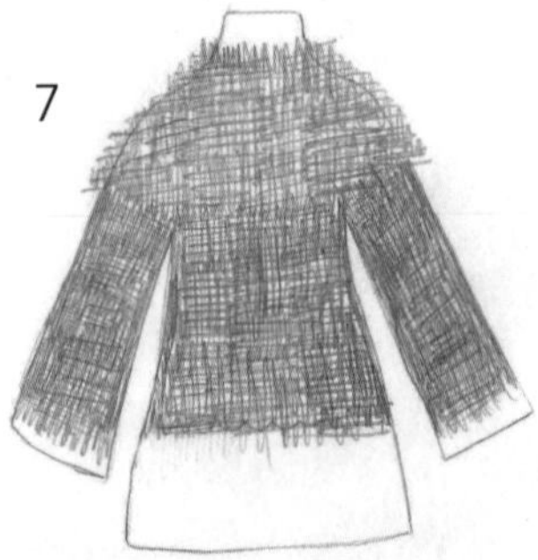

8

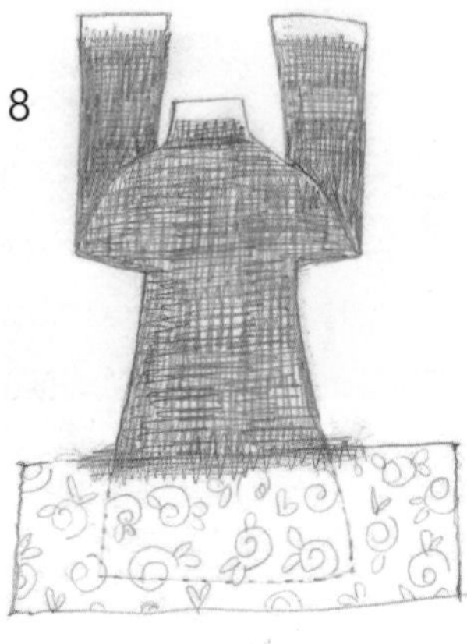

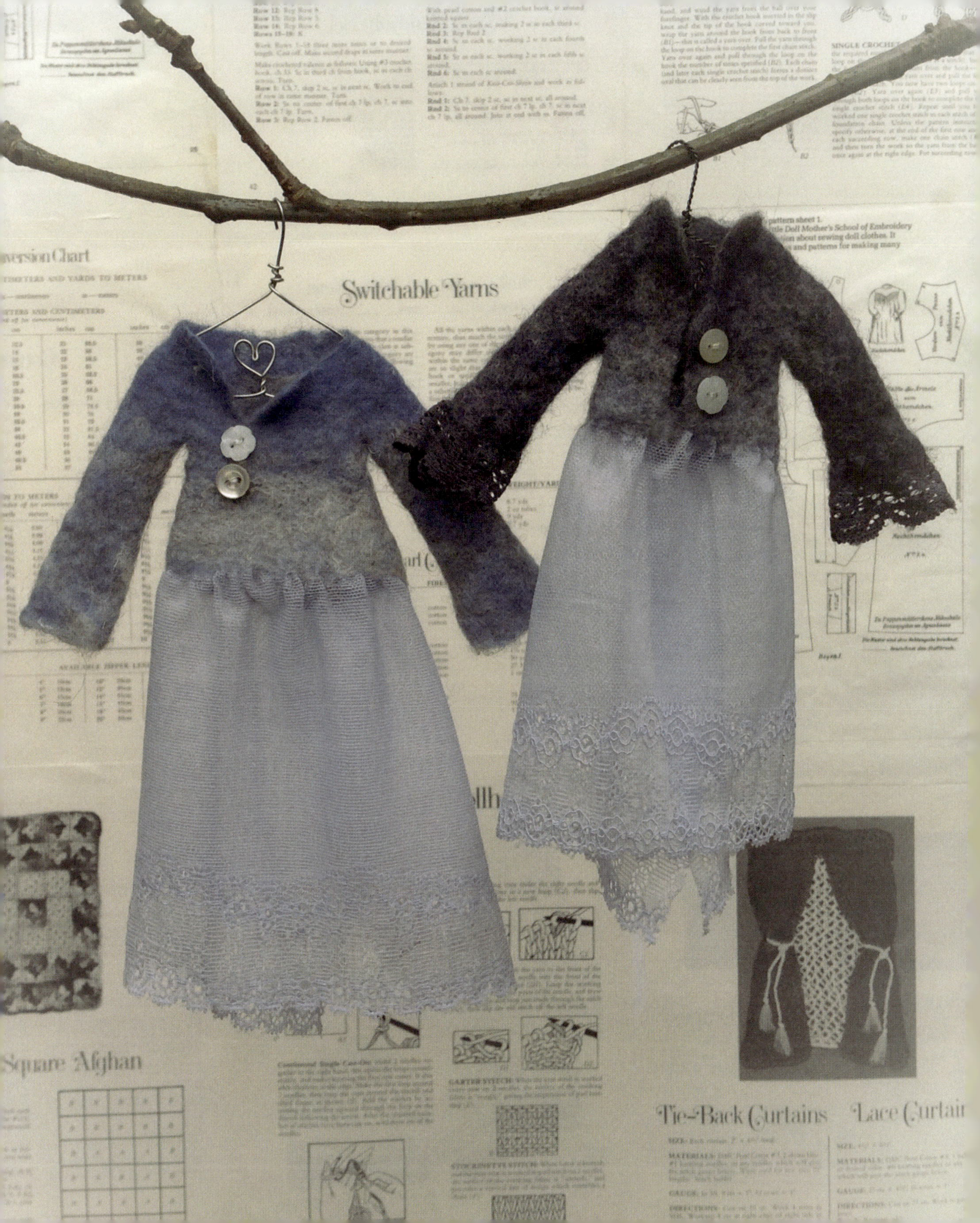
Switchable Yarns
Square Afghan
Tie-Back Curtains
Lace Curtai

9. Back
Peel back the bubble wrap.
Fold the cloth and fires over onto the front of the template onto the bottom edge of fibres. Add more fibres to cover the edge of the cloth where it meets the wool.
Cover and press through.
Turn the whole piece over and fold the outside edges over again.
Decide if you wish to add any more surface detail .

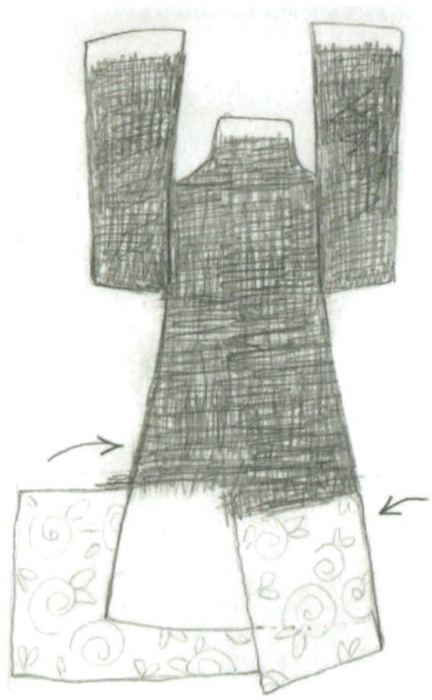

Felt the wool. Refer to the guide below.
During the felting, you can rub inside of the surface or the fabric with a small piece of bubble wrap, or a gloved hand to encourage the fibres through the cloth.
Continue to roll until fully felted, but at intervals, turn the felt around the template to avoid lumpy seams.

Ready to roll...
50 rolls each 4x directions.
Cut openings.
100 rolls each direction, turning wool around the resist template.
100 turns each direction, turning wool around the resist template.
Remove resist.
Throw 25 to 50 times.
Bamboo mat~ 25 to 50 rolls each direction.
Rinse and blot dry.

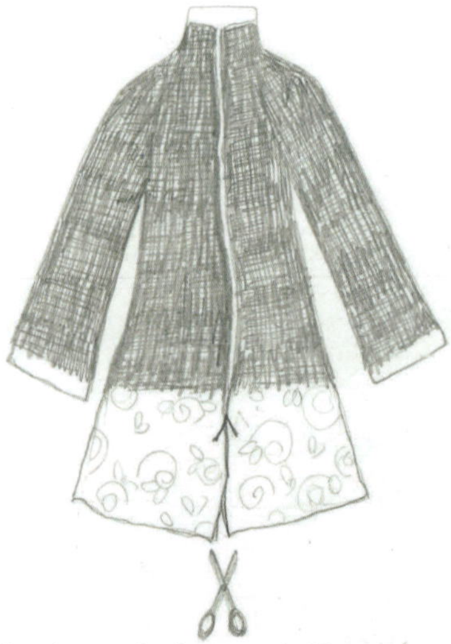

To make the coat.

For the coat, make in the same way as for the dress, but cut right through the wool. (See pictures opposite)
You can do this after the first 4 x 50 rolls of felting, or experiment with cutting at a later stage for different edges.
Starting at the natural edge of the cloth at the font, cut through the felt to the neck to create the opening.
Experiment with the seam to one side, or a cut in a wavy or diagonal line.

Use an iron to steam the coat dry, and press the fabric.
Choose buttons and beads and any stitching to embellish your exquisite design.
Try for size, or display on a tiny handmade wire hanger, more details on pages 106 and 107.
Make a whole collection of elf couture!

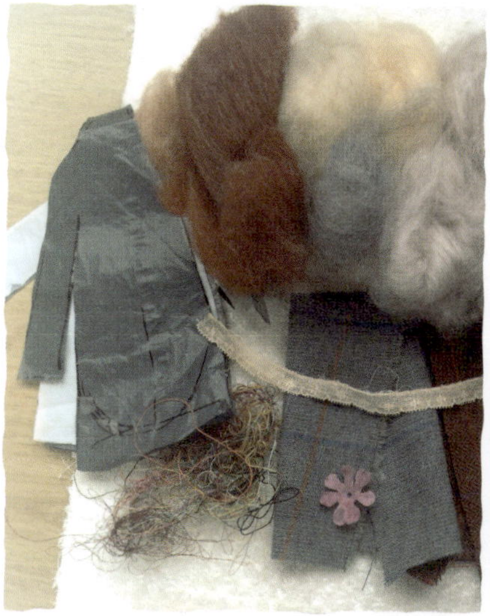
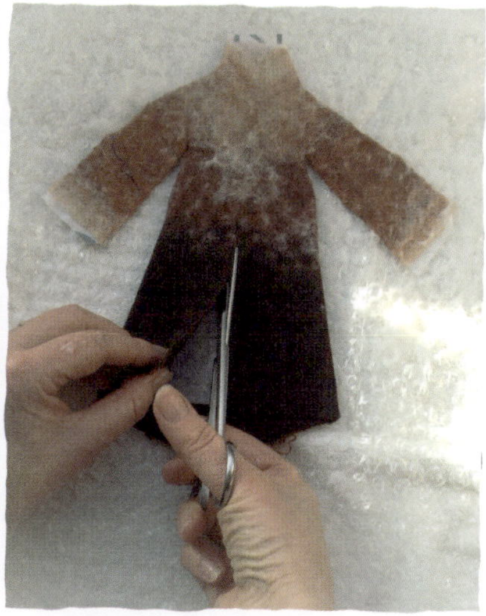
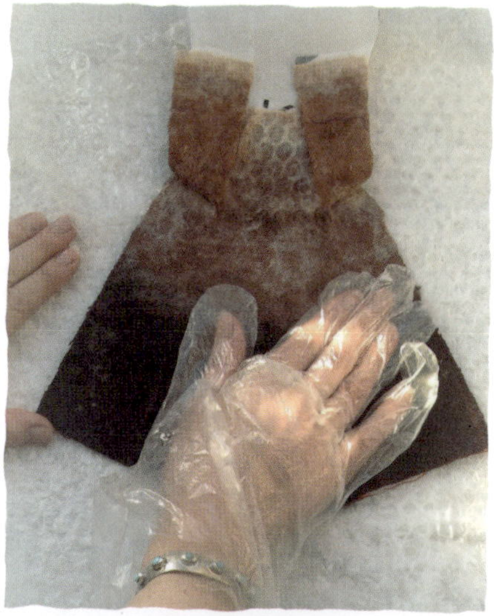
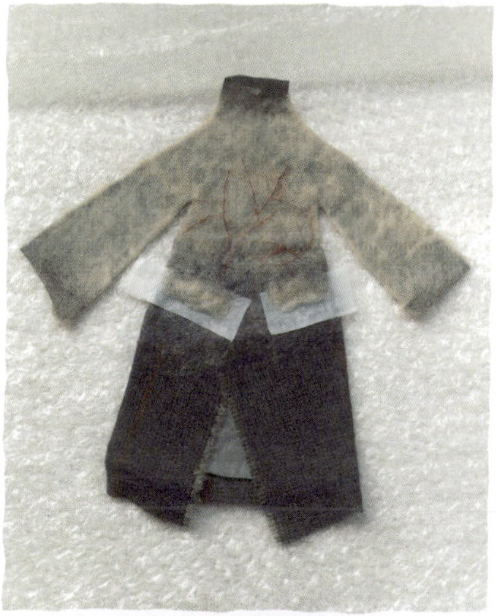
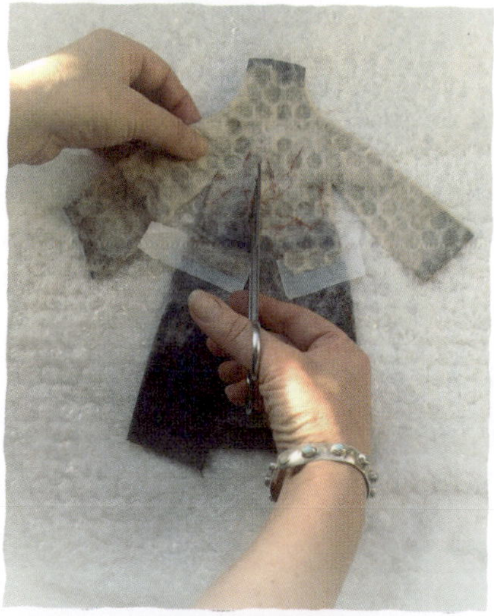
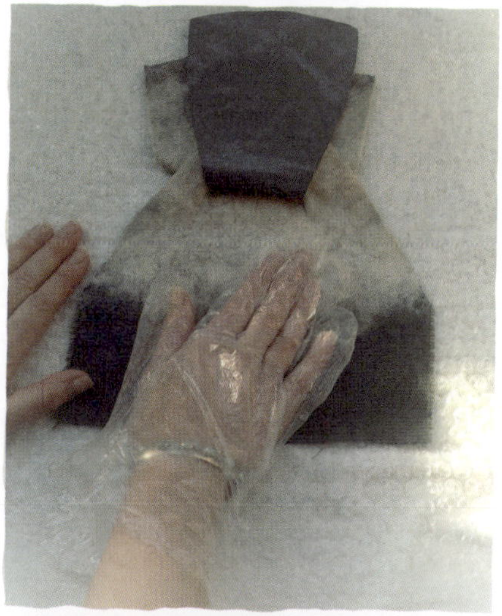
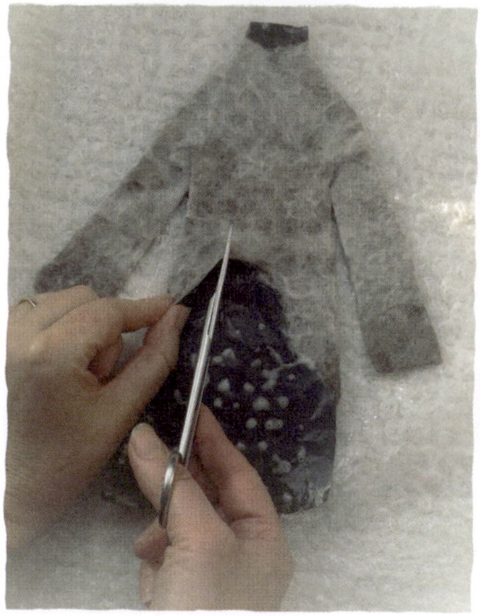
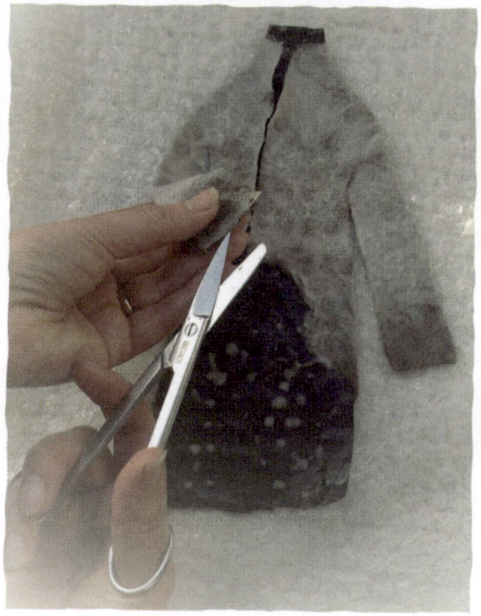
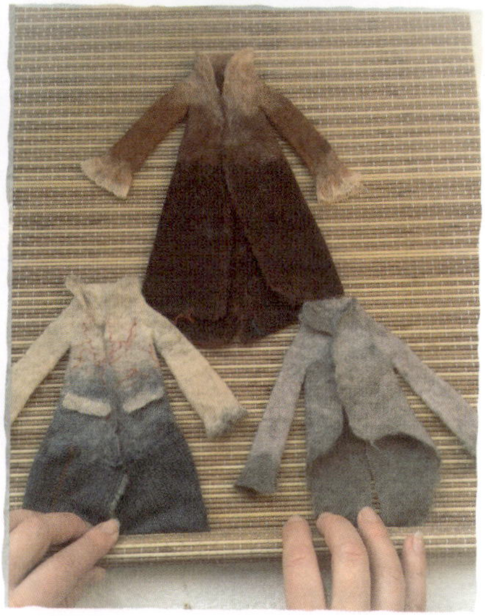

Dolls

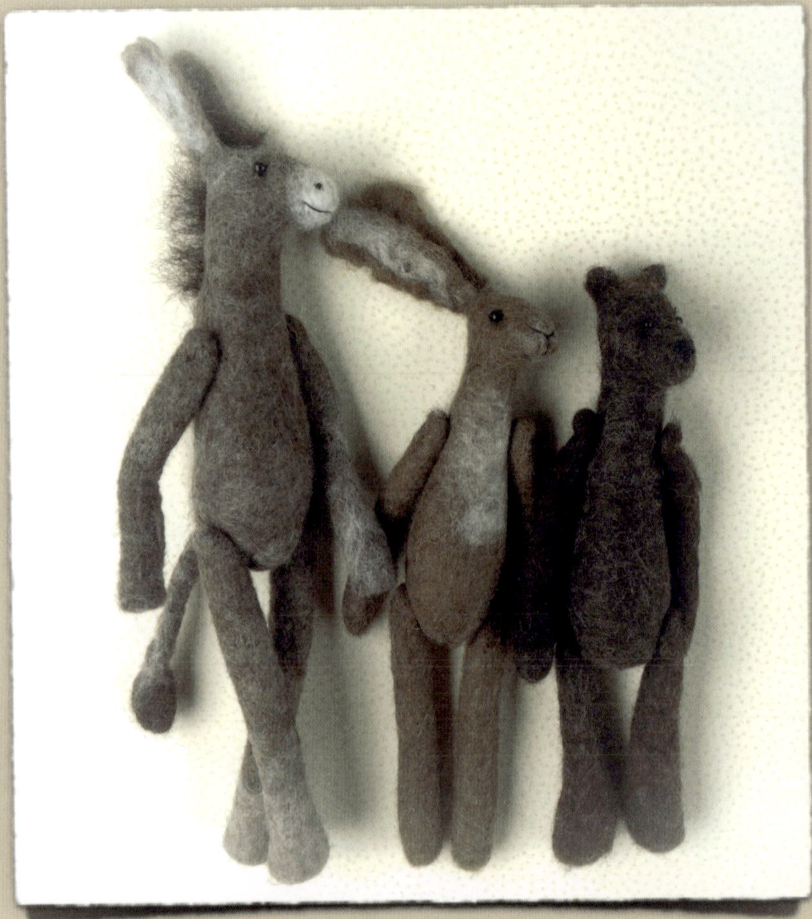

Charming characters that you can dress with the some of the little garments in this book, or design your own outfits. Adjust the shape of the head, and ears to make other animals, like a pointed face for a mole or mouse and black and white stripes to make a badger.

Materials and tools

Wool fibres in natural colours and wool for stuffing 25 to 30 gms in total
2 pieces of bubble wrap
Rolling pin
Bamboo mat
Soap solution, Sprinkler
Bowl,Towels
Plastic resist, cut from the template below
Pipe cleaners or wire
Sewing needles
Strong thread
2mm or 3mm black beads
Buttons for joints (optional)
Scissors
Felting needles

Notes on technique...

This workshop shows how to make the donkey doll. There are also templates for the bear and hare/rabbit on page 103.

When making the ears, try placing the ear template beneath the bubble wrap as a guide.

Where the ears and tail join the body, give the wool a good rub, through some netting to encourage the fibres to merge.

Vary the scale of the templates to make a family ~small for baby, medium, and large, also change colours to make them varied.

Use shiny beads, buttons and thread for the details.

Try adding other stuffings for a different feel, like rice or dried, fragrant flowers.

When you make the legs and arms, don't worry if they don't quite match, you can always needle felt them at the ends.

Make them with wire pipe cleaners inside, so they can bend at the elbows and knees.

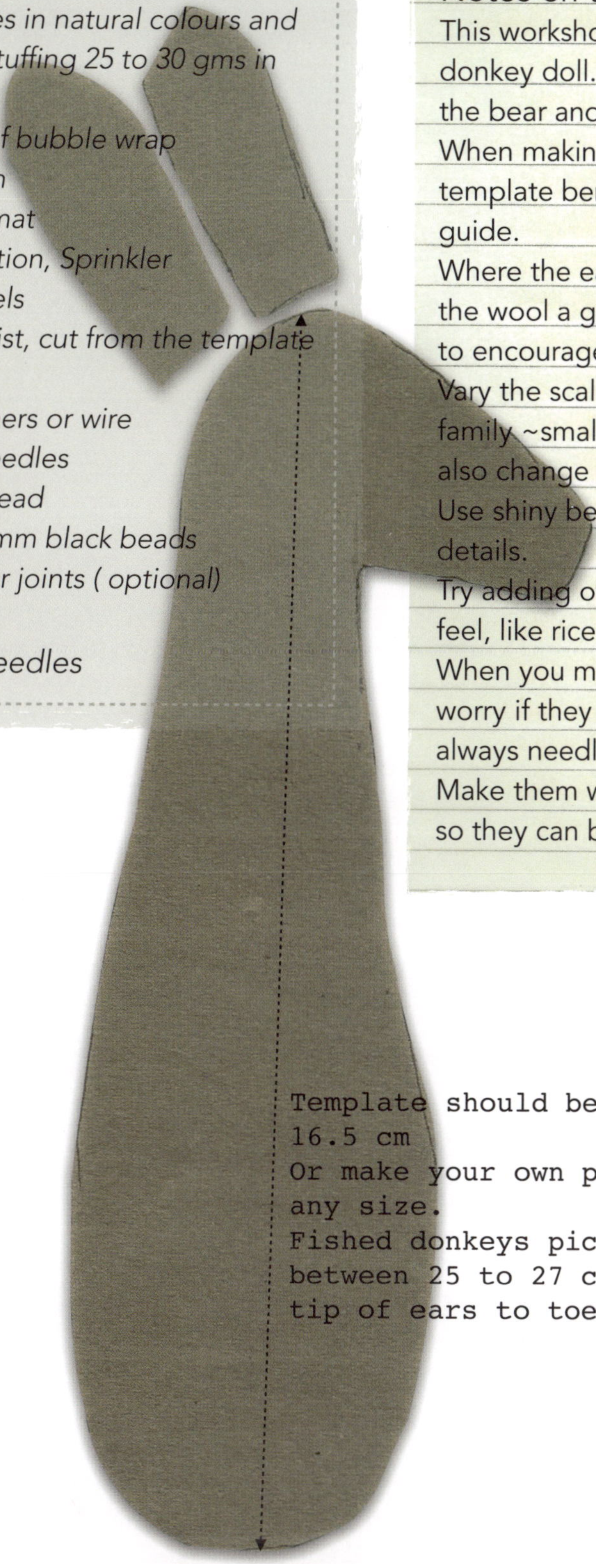

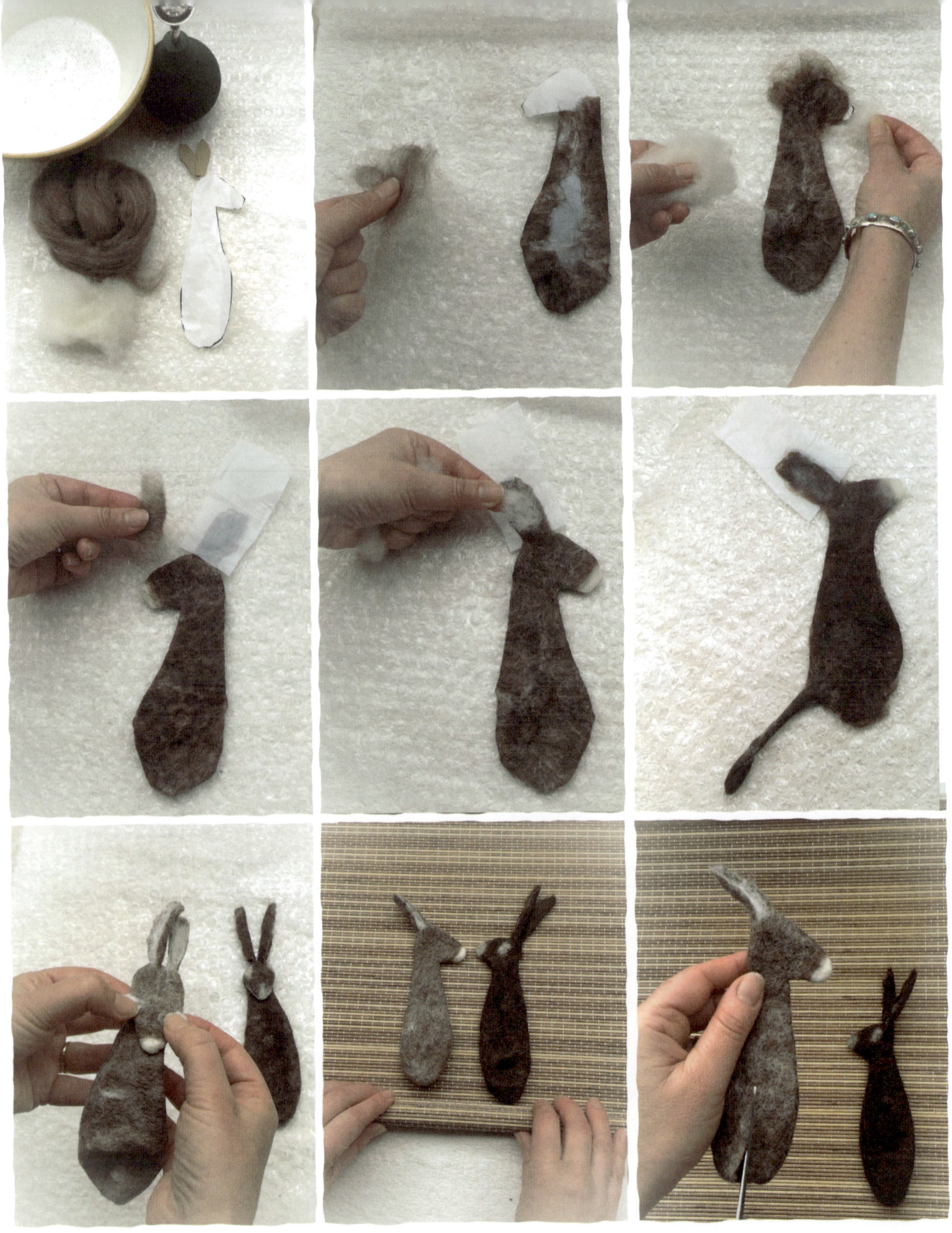

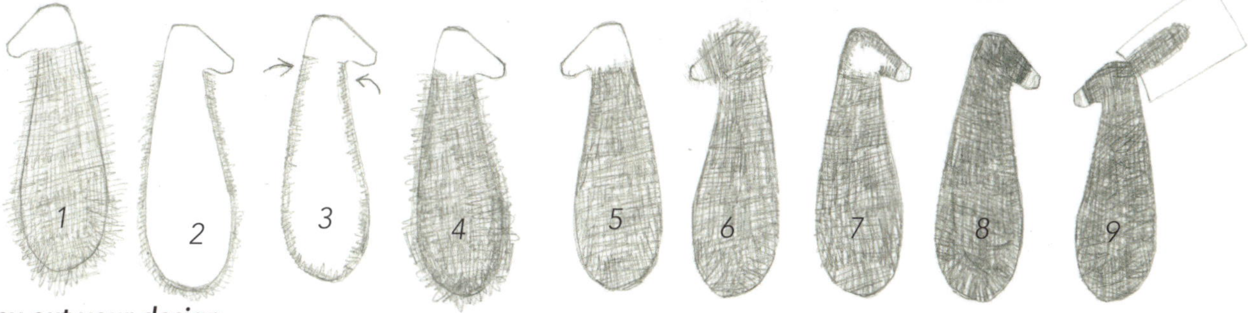

Lay out your design.

1. Place a fine layer fibres over the surface of the body up to the neck, covering and overlapping the edge slightly.

Wet the fibres, cover with bubble wrap, and press through.

2. Turn the whole piece over to the other side. Peel off the top layer of bubble wrap.

3. Fold the outside fibres onto the surface of the resist.

4. Fill in the centre with a fine layer of fibres. Add another very fine layer over the first, overlapping the edge slightly.

Wet the fibres, cover with bubble wrap and press through.

5. Turn the whole piece over.

Peel off the top layer of bubble wrap. Fold the outside fibres onto the surface of the first layer. Add one more fine layer over the middle of the first. This should be enough, but check for any thin areas, and fill them in.

6. Cover the head of the template, leaving the nose. Place some white fibres over the end of the nose. Cover, press through and turn over.

7. Fold over the edges.

8. Fill in the rest of the head and add white nose.

9. Add ears. Place a small piece of plastic resist in between to keep the two ears from joining together, but be sure some fibres overlap and join to the top of the head. Wet through and turn over as before. Repeat this on the back to form the second ear. Fold any edges over to make a nice shape to each ear.

10. Tail. (Refer to the techniques on page 30. You can add the tail at this stage, wet felting it to the body, or if you forget just needle felt it on later, when you add the legs, see page 104)

Take a length of fibres and wet one end. Roll between your palms to felt the wool. Keep one end of the tail dry.

For the tip of the tail, add some darker fibres and roll to create a thick end.

Open out the dry fibres and 'pin the tail on the donkey.'

Cover with net, and give the tail and ears where they join the body a good soapy rub, to encourage the fibres to merge

Felt the wool...see the guide right.

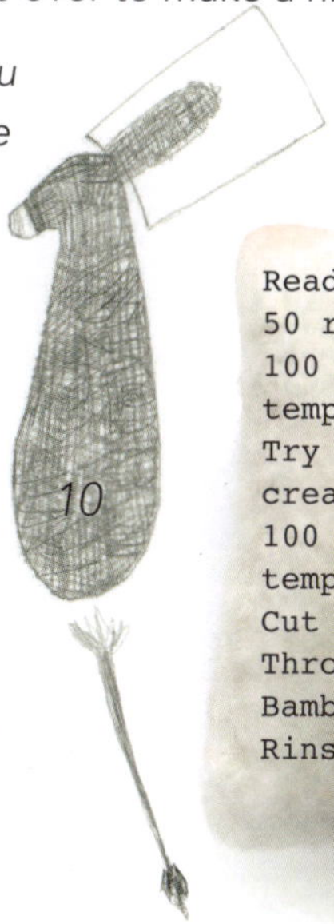

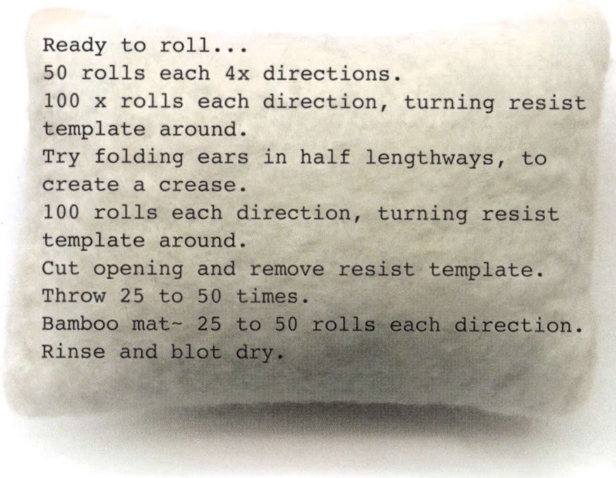

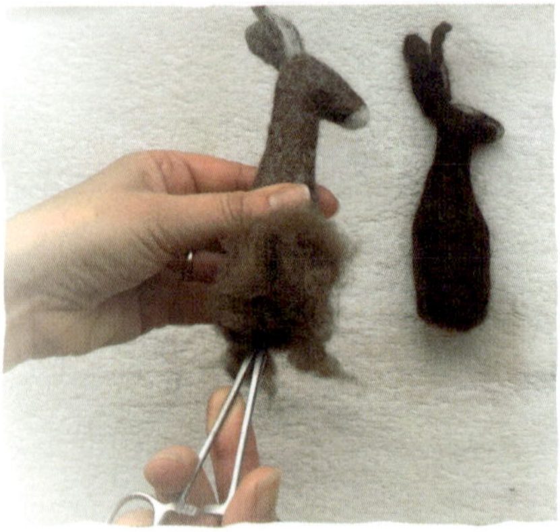
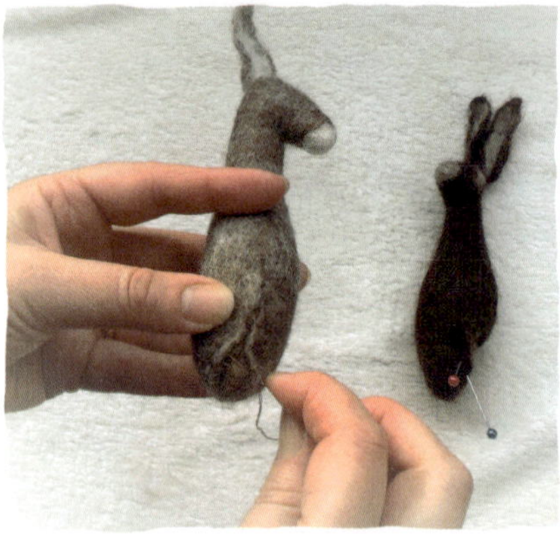
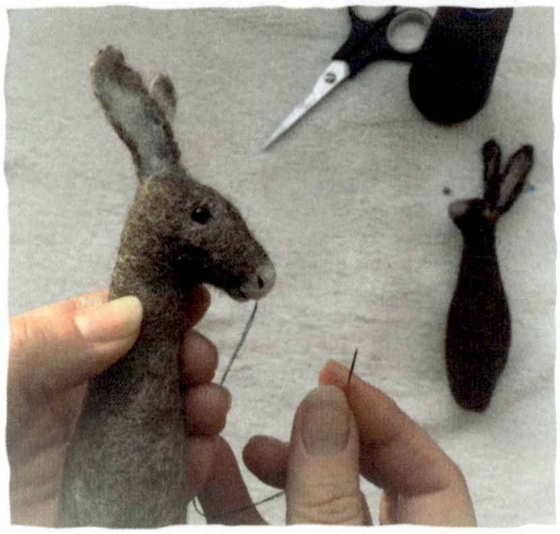
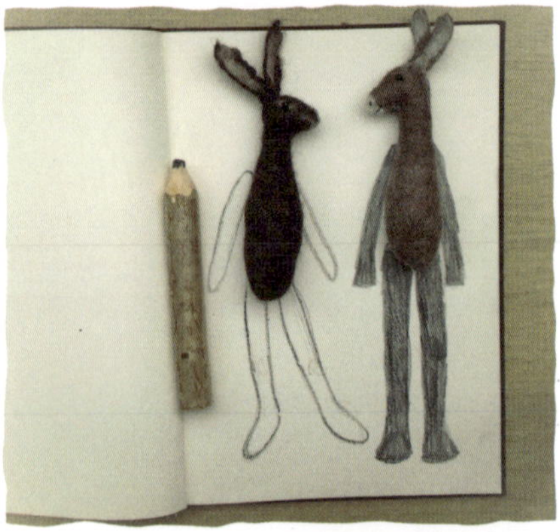
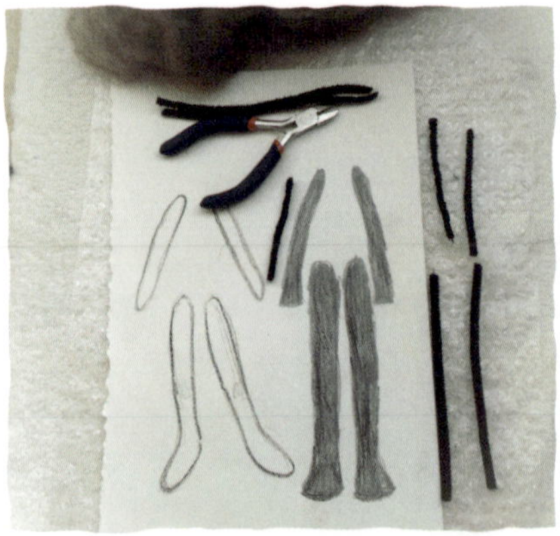
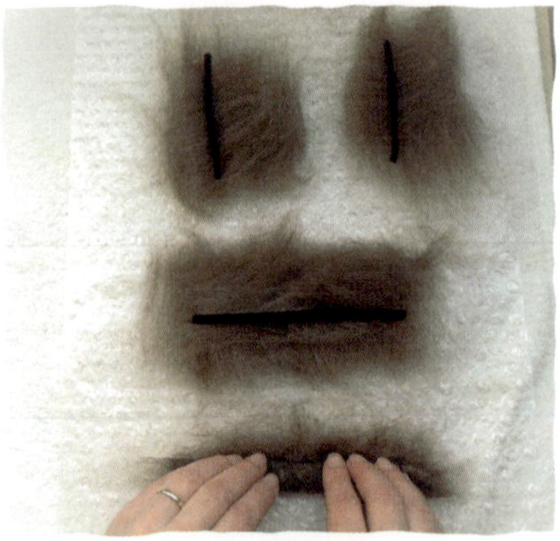
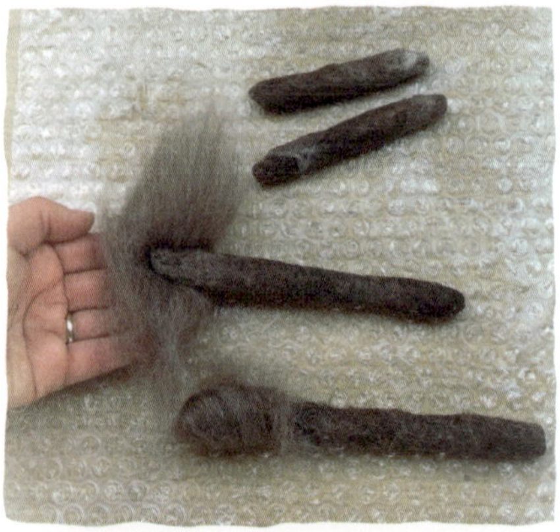
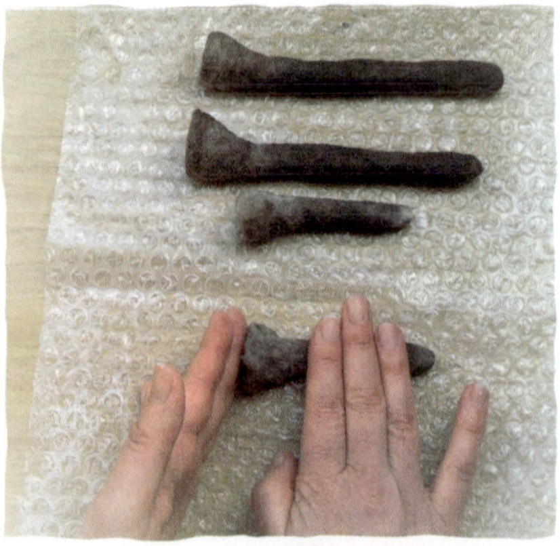
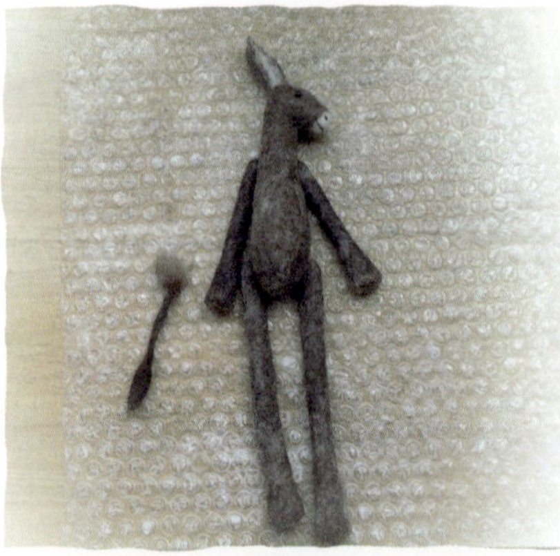
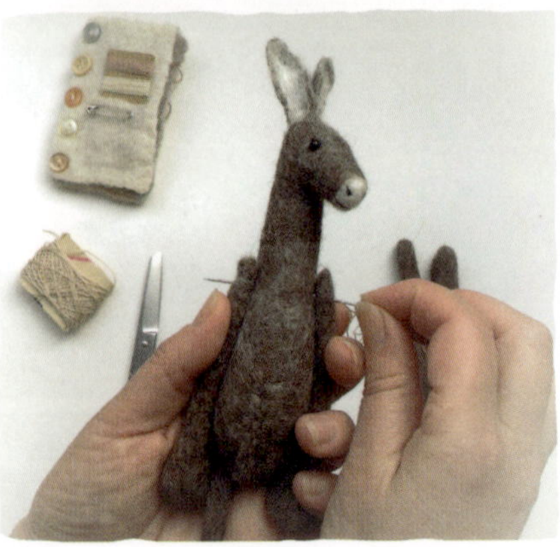
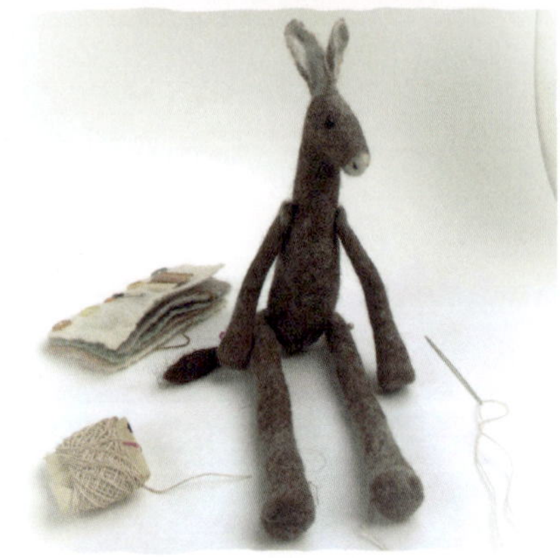
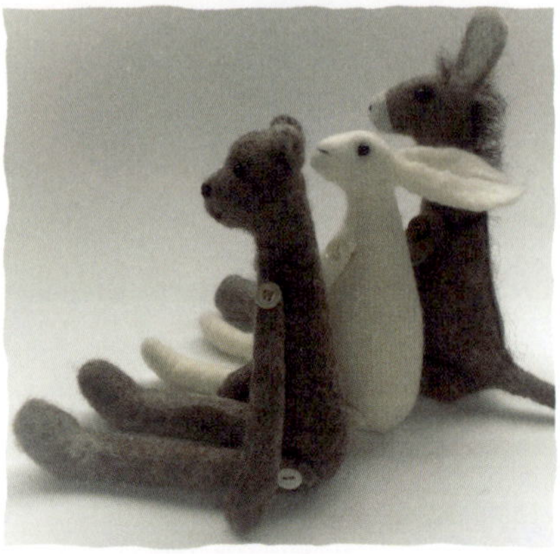

Stuffing.

When the body is dry, fill with your chosen stuffing. Pack the nose and head quite firm, and squeeze into shape with your fingers. Stitch the opening closed.

Arms and Legs.

Refer to the techniques on page 30 and see pictures opposite.
Make the arms and legs as long or short as you like, depending on the size of the body.
Place the body onto a flat piece of paper or card and draw the arms and legs as you would like them to look.
Cut some pipe cleaner to the length, bend the sharp ends over.
Experiment with different amounts of wool, the more wool you use, the thicker the limbs will be. Have equal amounts prepared so the two legs/arms will match.
Roll each pipe cleaner up inside each wool. Wet the wool with soap solution and gently roll the limb a little.
Add more wool to one end to create thickness for the feet or hands/hoofs.
If the limbs become a little thin, roll more wool fibres around the length to thicken.
Continue to roll and shape the limbs until they are well felted and firm, about 15 minutes for each pair should do it.

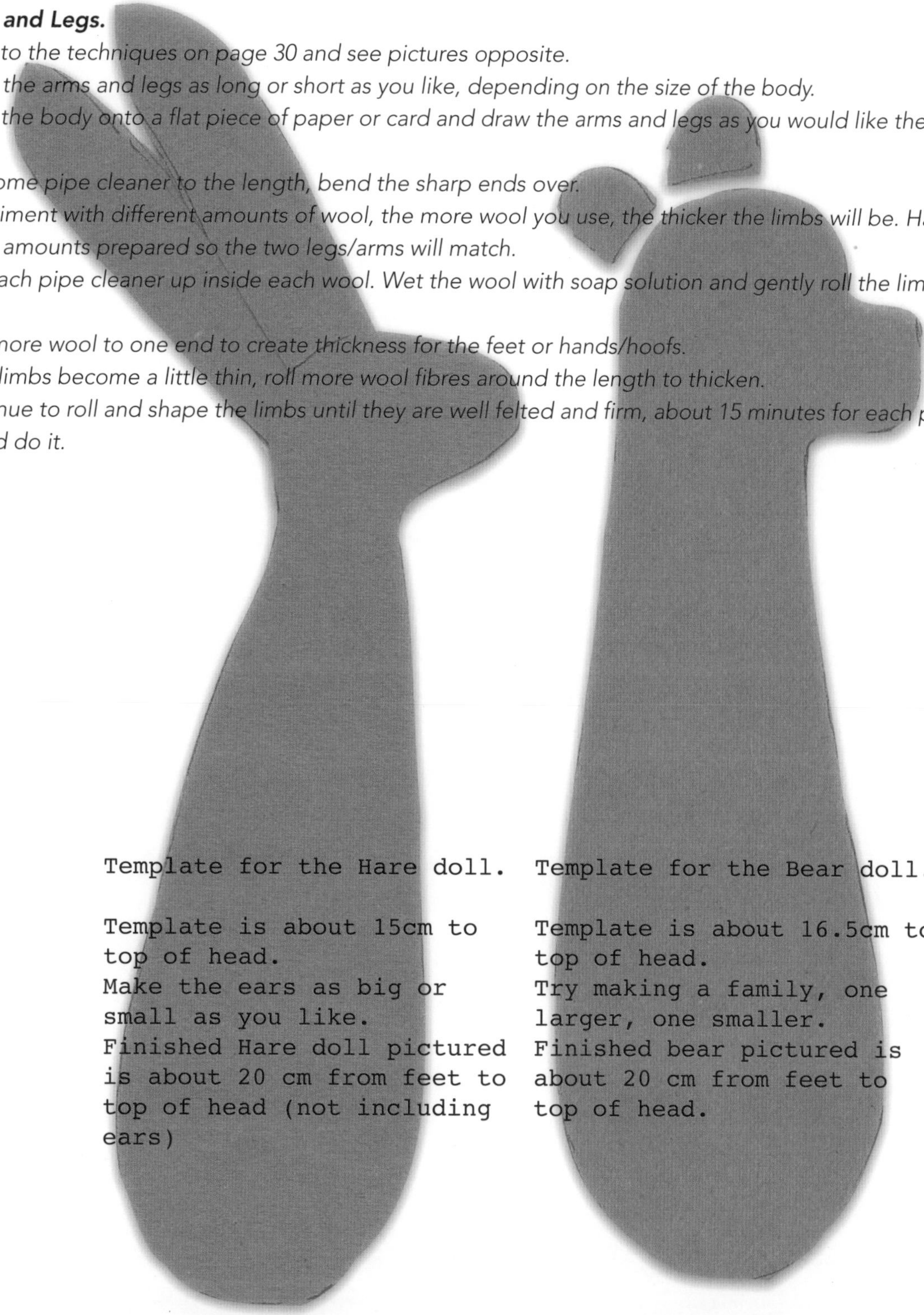

Template for the Hare doll.

Template is about 15cm to top of head.
Make the ears as big or small as you like.
Finished Hare doll pictured is about 20 cm from feet to top of head (not including ears)

Template for the Bear doll.

Template is about 16.5cm to top of head.
Try making a family, one larger, one smaller.
Finished bear pictured is about 20 cm from feet to top of head.

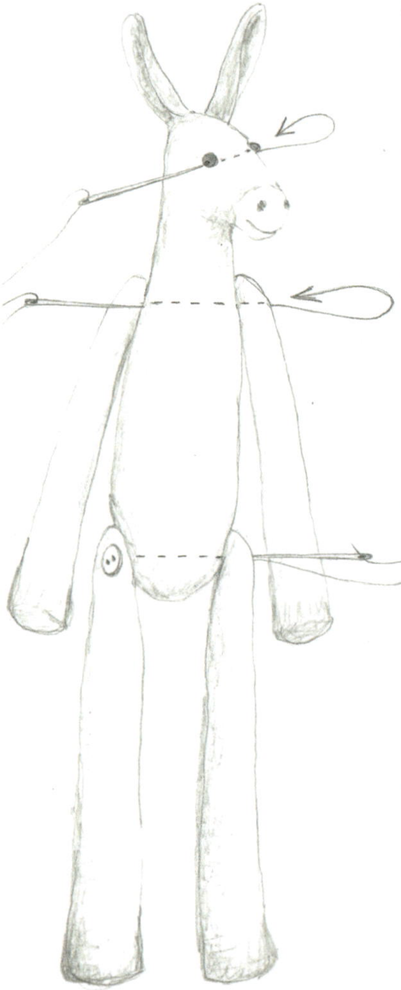

Stitching the eyes, nose and limbs in place.

Eyes.

Pin the beads onto the face to find the best location. Knot your thread and stitch into the wool, just behind the bead. Sew through to the other bead. Thread the bead onto the needle and sew back through the head to the beginning. Sew through the second bead and back through the head and repeat to secure the eyes in position.

Nose and mouth.

With the same thread, sew through to the white nose and stitch two nostrils. You can also add a couple of stitches below to create a smiling mouth. (These details can also be needle felted) Stitch back through the nostrils several times to finish, then cut the thread.

Arms.

Pin the arms into position at the shoulders.

Knot a strong thread and sew into the body where the arm is pinned. Stitch straight through the body, and out through the other arm at the shoulder. Stitch back into the shoulder and straight through the body and out through the other shoulder. Repeat several times. Make a couple of extra stitches, just through the body to secure the thread, and cut.

Legs.

Pin the legs in place at the hips. Check the position, then repeat the stitching as for the arms.

Dress your lovely doll in some handmade felt clothes made from the other workshops in the book. To make a template from your doll, try drawing around it, draw the dress shape and increase by about 33% or your own estimated shrinkage rate.

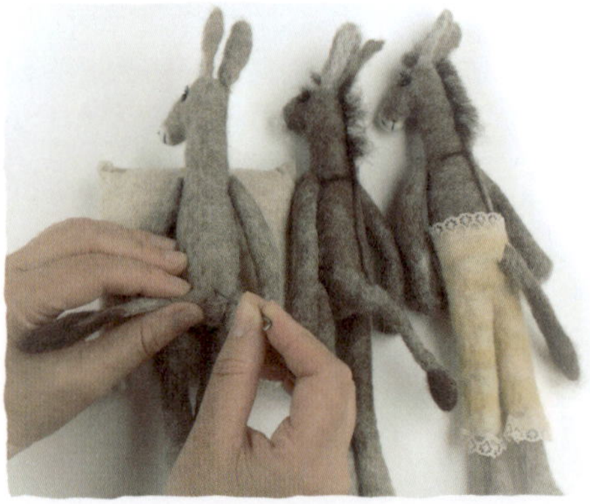

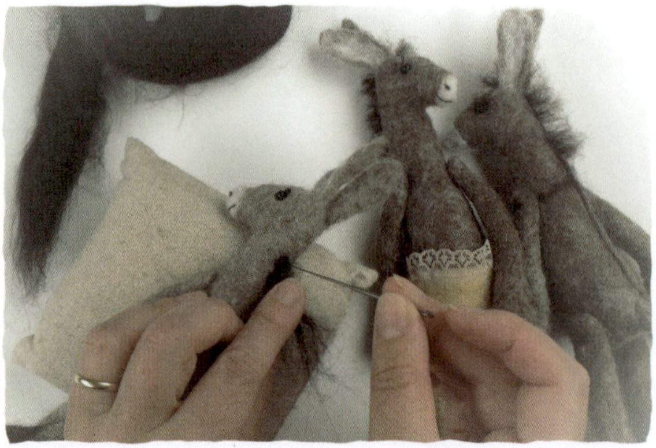

Needle felting the tail into place, and extra details.

If like me, you forgot to add the tail when making the body, you can needle felt it into place. Open out the dry loose fibres at the top of the tail. Hold the tail in position and needle felt the fibres into the body, by repeatedly poking into the wool all around. If necessary, add a few extra fibres and needle felt those too.

You can also needle felt some detail into the hands/hoofs and feet, as above.

Add some wiry fibres to the back of the neck to create the mane, and the cross on his back.

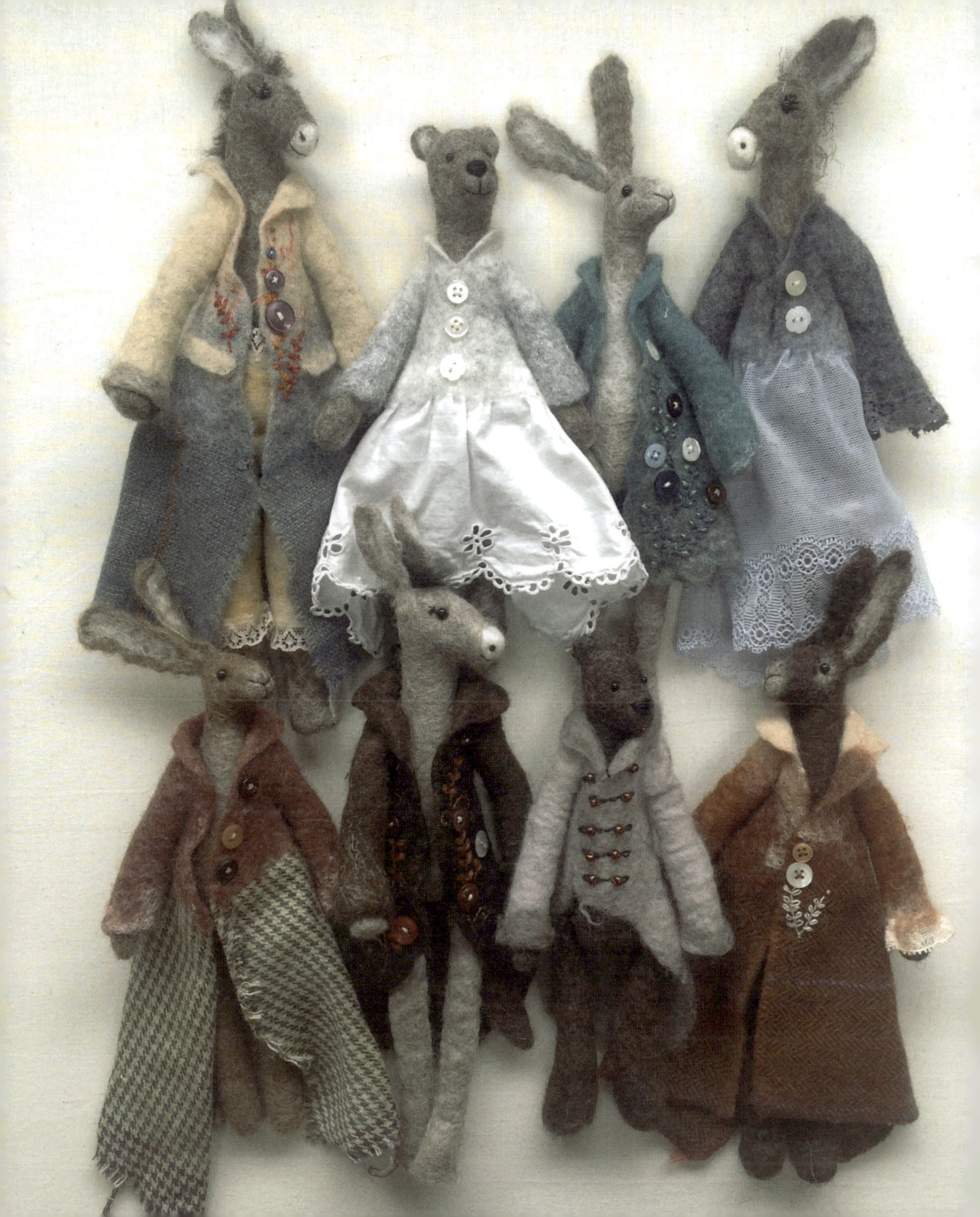

Mini wire coat hangers

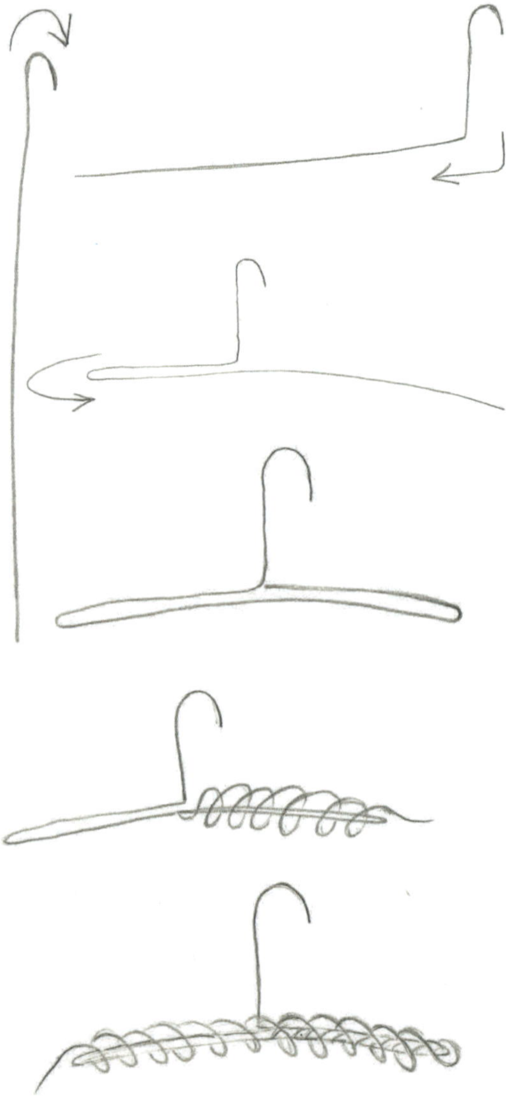

Make tiny hangers for your felt garments.
You may like to adjust the lengths and dimensions to fit your item, or make several to choose from.
It may take a couple of attempts to get the dimensions just right.
Beware of sharp edges when cutting the wire, try rubbing the ends with a metal file.

You will need jewellery pliers and wire cutters, and some lengths of wire, glue gun, and ribbon, or thread for binding.
These are made with 0.8mm or 1mm thickness, or finer wire twisted together.
Try jewellery wire, floristry or gardening wire.

Padded hanger. *(Left)*
Grip the end of the wire and bend it over to form the hook.
About 3 or 4 cms from the top, make a right-angled bend.
4cms along, bend the wire right back on itself to form one half of the hanger.
8cms from the end, bend the other end back on itself, to the centre.
Cut the wire.
Glue your chosen thread, yarn or ribbon to the centre and bind along the length of the hanger, then back as shown. Add a little glue at each end to prevent unravelling.

Twig hanger.
Cut a length of twig to your chosen length, about 7 to 9 cms.
Wrap some wire around the centre several times, and twist around to secure. Bend the wire to form the loop, and cut the end.

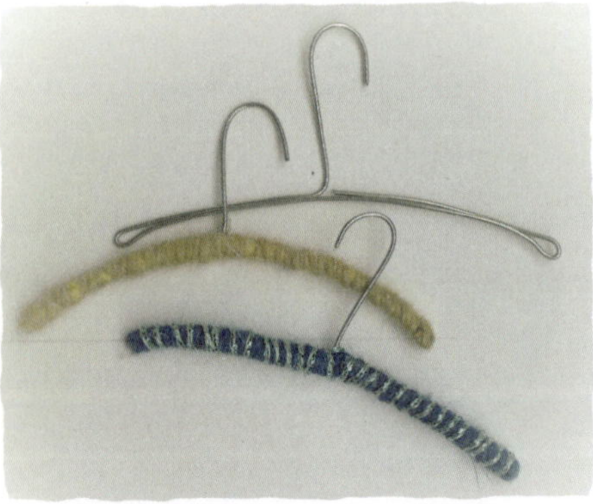

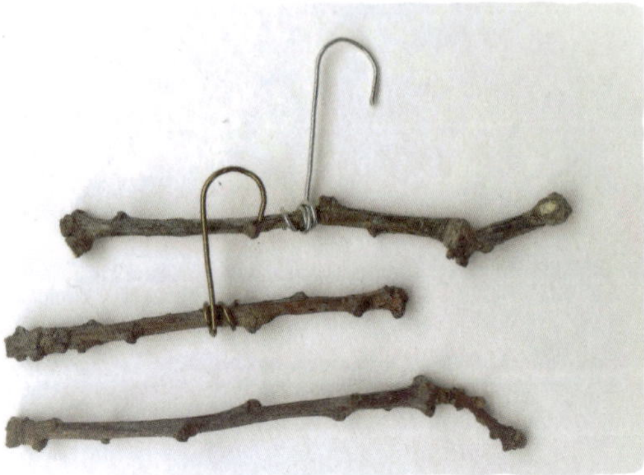

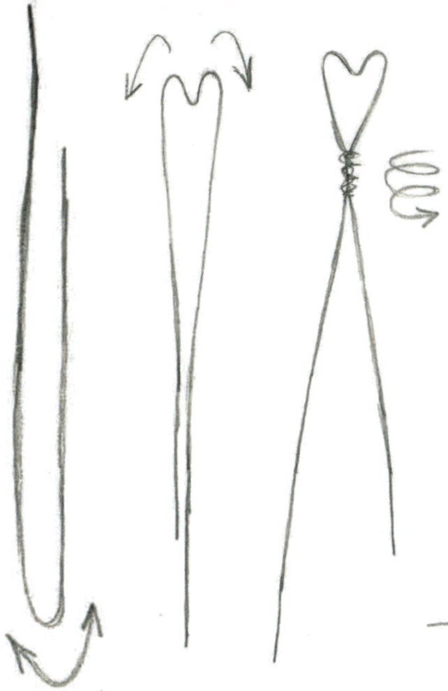

Tiny Heart hanger...

Cut a length of wire 30 cms long.
13 cms from one end, bend the wire in half.
Holding the fold in the pliers, bend each end of wire back on itself to form the top of the heart 'm' shape.
Pinch the two wires together just below the 'm' with the pliers and twist the top of the heart around twice to complete the shape.
Bend each end of wire outwards to form the base of the hanger.

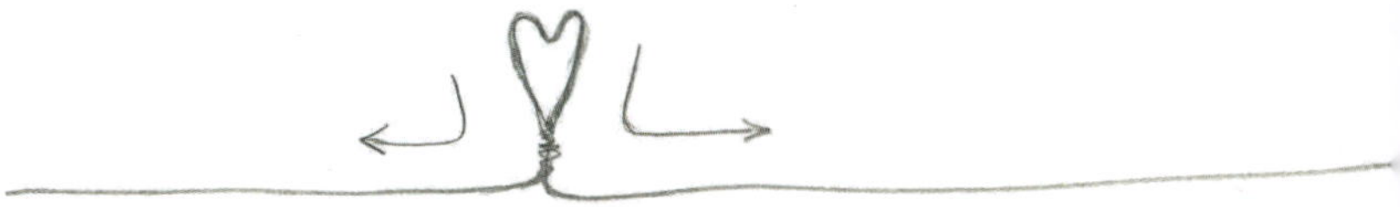

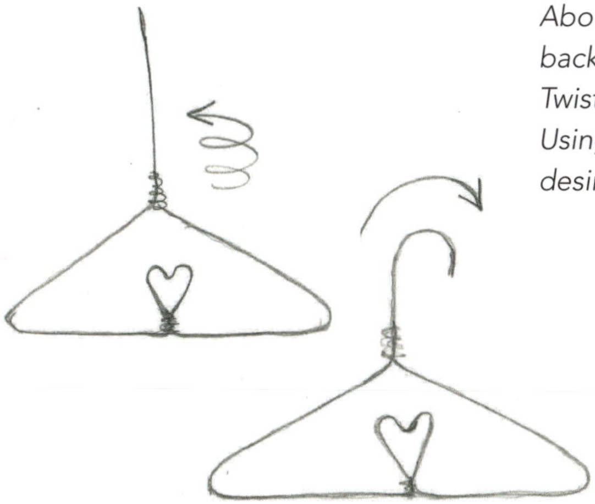

About 3.5 to 4 cms from the heart, bend each end of wire back over diagonally, until they overlap above the heart.
Twist the wires together to join them.
Using the remainder of wire, bend to form the hook at the desired length, and cut any excess wire away.

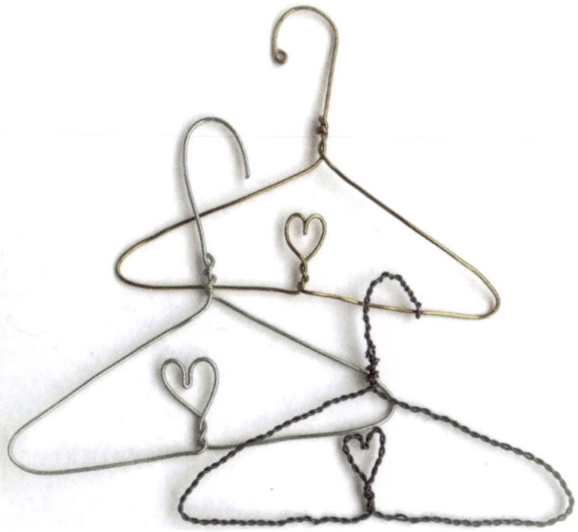

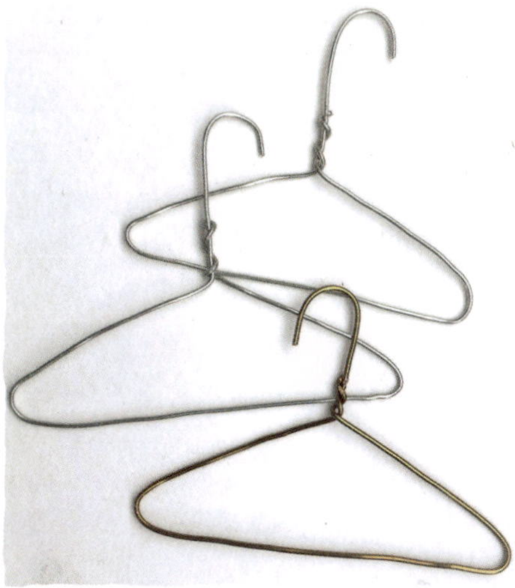

Plain coat hanger. *(Left)*

Cut a length of wire about 20 cms long.
Form the hook first, then twist the other end of wire around the base of the hook to form a big loop.
Pull the loop outwards to form the corners, bend the corners into the desired shape with pliers.

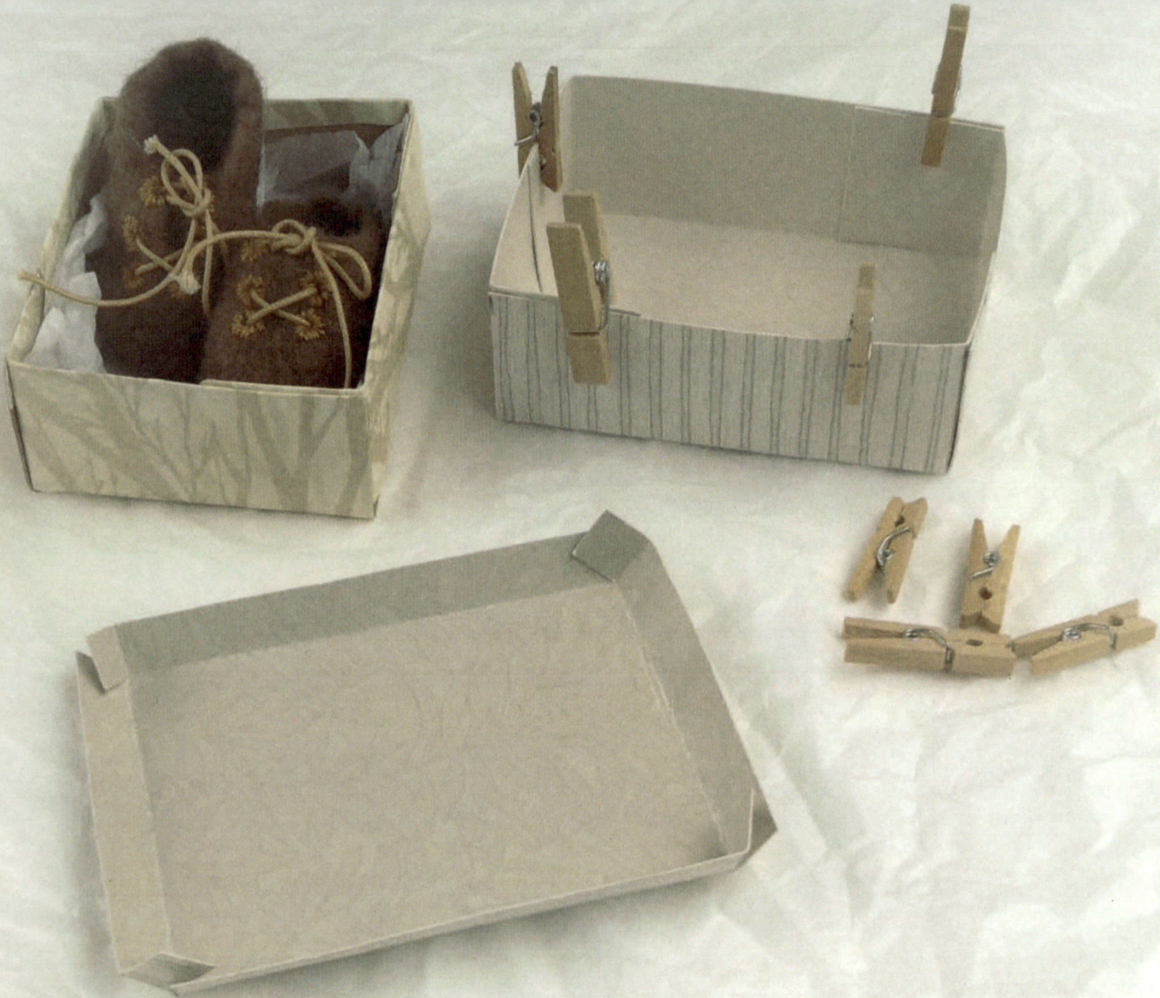

Mini shoe box

Make a made to measure gift box for your felt keepsakes.
You may like to adjust the lengths and dimensions to fit your gift.
Measure the dimensions and add a little for space around the edge.
Make a paper version first to check the fit.
This example (not to scale) makes a box that is 9 x 7 x 3cms the lid is slightly larger to fit on top, so 9.5 x 7.5 x 1cm
Try using craft card, or recycled food packaging, just glue some nice paper over the printed surface.

Draw out your chosen shape onto your card. (Including the sides all around)
Cut out and score the fold lines for a neat edge.
Cut along one side of each corner as shown.
Fold up the sides of the box, and glue the 4 tabs inside.
Use a mini peg to hold the join until it dries.
Repeat for the lid. Make the lid slightly bigger to fit your box.
Line with tissue paper.

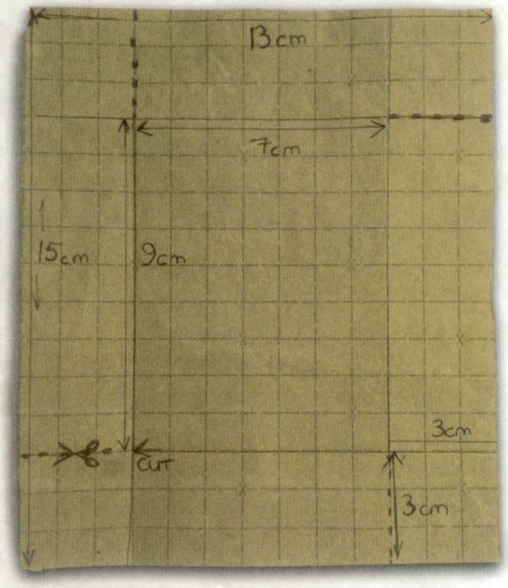

What next? Be inspired!

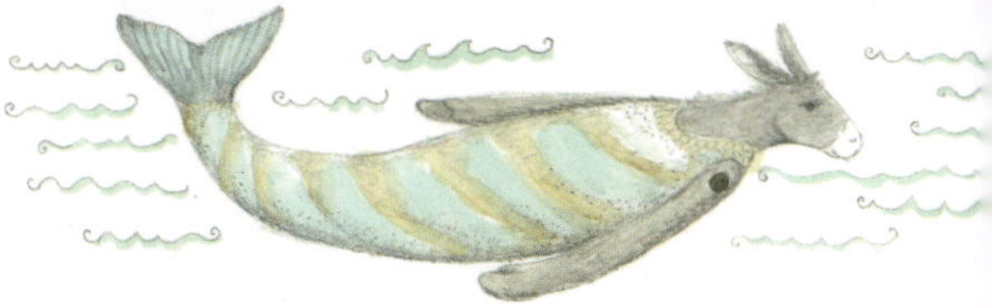

I hope you are really happy with your handmade felt creations, and have found it very rewarding to see them emerge in your own hands.
Here are a few suggestions for what to do next, find inspiration, and develop your own style of felt making. You can choose to explore more of the techniques that appeal to you most.

Enjoy your artwork.
Wear your flowers and beads and artwork as accessories, just add a brooch pin, hair clip or hat pin.
You may like to display some your little garments or gloves behind glass to protect them, box frames are perfect for this. Choose a frame deep enough, so the glass does not squash against the felt, add other items to complement your work, or simply hang inside.

Collect inspiration
If you haven't done so already, treat yourself to a nice small sketchbook, and pens you like to use. Make your own handmade felt cover for it. Keep it handy when you are making, as ideas will come to you. Jot them down, draw or doodle them, record them for future ideas, before you know it, you are designing!
Or it can simply be a list to explore later, things that interest you, or that you have seen on your travels, or something you always wanted to make or collect.

Create a painting in wool.
Work from photographs and create a portrait or scene, or invent an abstract design. Make your image using the coloured fibres as paint.

Go large....think about the scale and size you would like to create.
The garments could be made life size to wear. With a bit of planning, lots of space and more elbow grease, you can make wonderful outfits in felt. If not in one go, you can make large sheets of felt to be cut and stitched together from a pattern. Scarves, gloves, slippers, hats, waistcoat, dress, skirt, you name it, it can be made in felt!

Felt with function...
Many lovely useful things can be created and coordinated with your home ~ cushions, window blinds, table runners, place mats, drinks coasters, rugs, tea and egg cosies, oven gloves, hot water bottle covers, so many things to try.

Go to workshops, join felt making groups.
You can learn so much and share ideas with other fibre artists.
Try the International Felt makers association for more information, details on page 111.

Visit a wool festival...
There are many Fibre, textile and yarn festivals organised to celebrate the wonderful things created with wool. There are some from the uk listed on page 111. Try searching online for one near you. Maybe we'll see you there...

Problem solving...

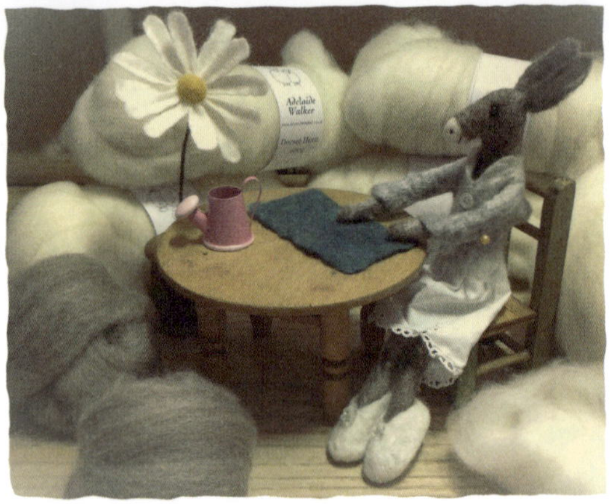

Felt is loose and fluffy... re-wet the wool with warm soap solution and continue to rub or roll the felt, it may need more fulling.

Wool shrinks more in one direction.
Try rolling more in the wider direction. When laying out fibres, make sure you place them in both directions, or randomly to cause shrinking in all directions.

Wool is slow to felt... Try warming up your felting solution. Try adding more soap by rubbing with a bar of soap. This may be a slower fibre to felt, keep going. Try the throwing method on page 20.

Too many soap bubbles... Sponge away some of the excess bubbles, then add warm water to dilute the soap content.

Not enough soap... Cover the felt with net and rub a bar of soap onto the surface to introduce more soap.

Holes in the Felt ... If you see thin areas in your work before it is fully felted, you can try to add more fibres to the hole, overlapping, and gently encourage them to join with rubbing. If it's too late, when the felt is dry you could needle felt some more fibres into the thin area. Place a piece of sponge beneath the wool to felt onto.

Felt too thick. This is difficult to resolve, you can try to stretch it out a little, but next time use less layers of wool.

Felt shrinks too much or too little... this will depend on the amount of felting, thickness of felt and the type of fibres. Enlarge or reduce your original layout. Try a sample first to see the rate of shrinkage.

Surface design lifts from the surface...if you have added surface design and it moves or lifts from the surface when felting, cover the felt with netting, then give it a gentle soapy rub, to encourage the fibres to merge.

How much to enlarge your design?
If you don't know how much your wool will shrink, try an estimate of about 33%
To enlarge your design, times the finished dimensions by 133%

If you have made a measured sample with your fibres, you can calculate the shrinkage with the simple formula on page 21... good luck.

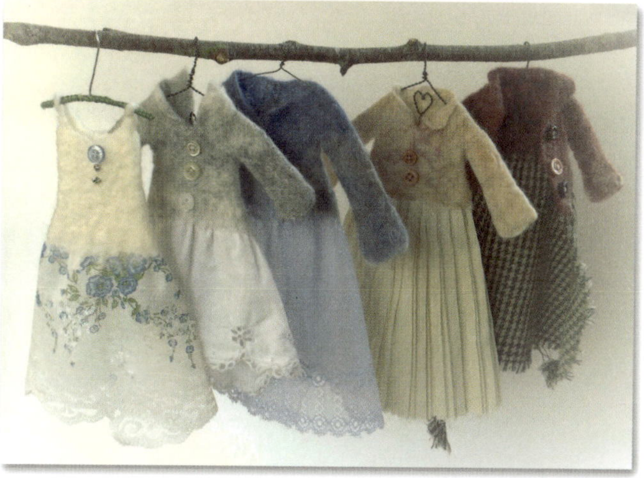

Suppliers and useful info...

Wool, fibres, hand carders, felting needles

Here are just some of the UK suppliers of wool fleece for spinning, dying and felt making. Try searching on the wonderful worldwide web for suppliers near you.

www.adelaidewalker.co.uk
www.wheeldalewoolcrafts.co.uk
www.winghamwoolwork.co.uk
www.norwegianwool.co.uk
www.worldofwool.co.uk

Wire, pliers and wire cutters, glue gun etc.

Garden centres, markets or homeware stores
Or try florist or jewellery and craft suppliers.
www.wilko.com
www.hobbycraft.co.uk

Beads

Different size beads are available from craft stores and jewellery findings suppliers.
www.abakhan.co.uk
ww.hobbycraft.co.uk

Doll kits

The ceramic and clay dolls that feature in these pages are sculpted by Jenny Barnett, and kits are available from www.jennybarnett.co.uk

Other books in this series...

Needle felting workshops with Jenny Barnett, more details overleaf...

Other useful sites

www.feltmakers.com The International Feltmakers Association
www.campaignforwool.com
www.facebook.com/nothingtodowithwool for abandoned husbands

About the author...

Before becoming a felt maker and author, I worked for many years as a clay modeller, sculpting for giftware companies like Coalport, Wedgwood, Royal Doulton, and designing collectible figurines under the name of Jenny Oliver's faeries.
From then I went on to create a range of expressive sculpture of mothers and children, combining the fired ceramic figures with handmade felt.
Needle felting then became my main activity, including animal portrait commissions, workshops and publishing my first book, to help and encourage others to learn this wonderful art form.
Now there is a growing collection of needle felted animal sculpture, handmade dolls, miniature felt garments, kits and workshops, and more books to follow, including illustration of my husband's story books. All work is created on our narrowboat studio.
New developments can be seen on the following web pages.
Please get in touch if you would like to know more.

jennyneedlefelt@gmail.com

www.jennybarnett.co.uk
www.facebook.com/jennybarnettfelt
www.jenny-barnett.blogspot.co.uk

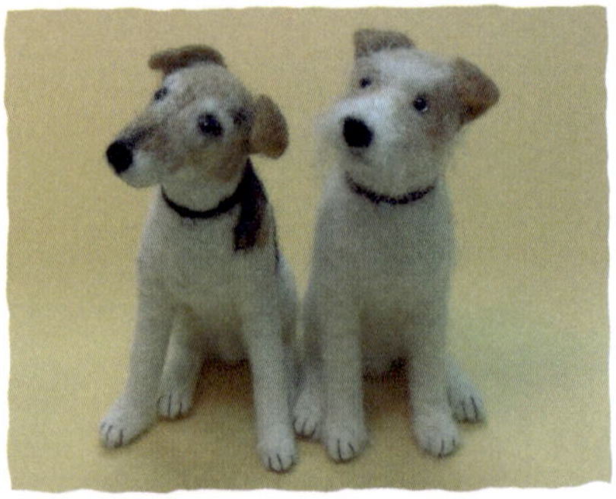

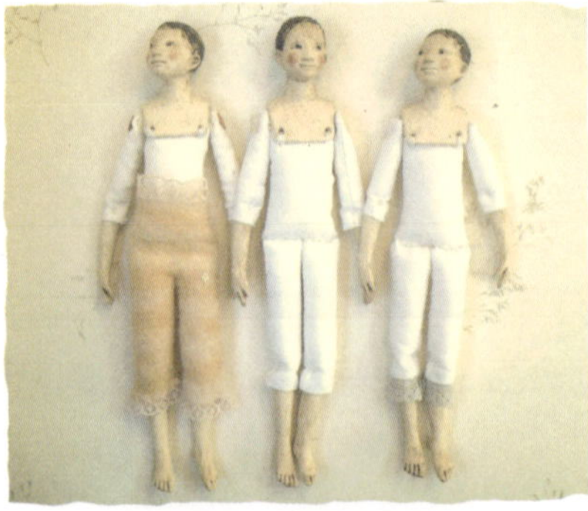

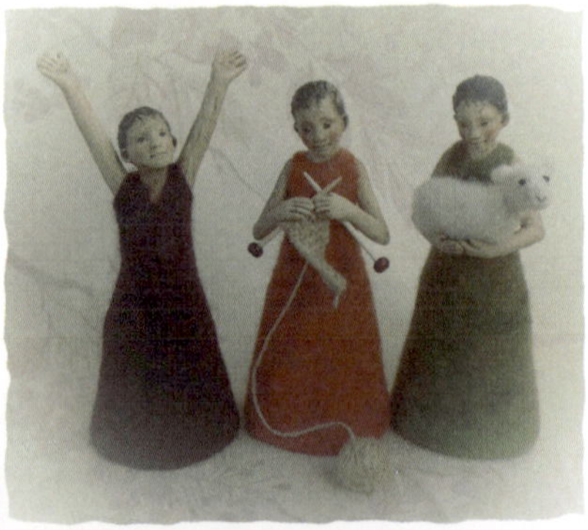

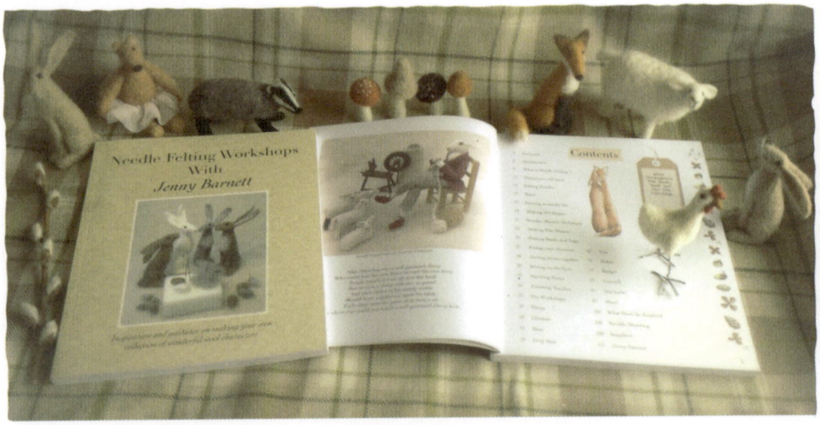

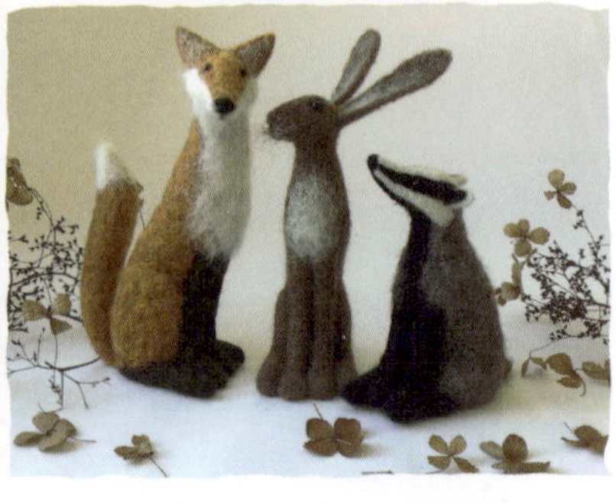

Needle Felting Workshops with Jenny Barnett
Inspiration and guidance on making your own collection of wonderful wool characters.
Learn to needle felt using wool fleece and barbed needles to sculpt the wool into a range of charming animals.
Book one published in 2014 by Jenny Barnett

Images from top to bottom~
Needle felt portraits
Ceramic and cloth doll kits
Ceramic and handmade felt figures
Animals from the needle felting book.